Phonics Plus Five gets re ave said:

"Our son has been usi*r over one year. His first-grade teachers indicate that his reading skills are well beyond his peers. He is able to work independently on reading and writing and actively seeks reading as an activity."*

—Beth B., mother of a six-year-old

"Thanks to Dr. Blank's reading system our son is at the top of his first-grade class and according to his most recent report card he is 'exceeding the expectations of the school.' Along with his new skills, he has acquired greater self-confidence and self-esteem. As an added benefit, he now loves to read."

—Michael M., father of a six-year-old

"Dr. Blank's system has not only taught my son to read, it has also taught him extremely valuable learning habits that are carrying over to other areas."

—Linda L., mother of a nine-year-old

"My son was in first grade and struggling. We started him on Dr. Blank's programs and within six weeks there was an immediate difference—not only in his ability to read, but in how he felt about himself. He felt very successful and on par with his peers. It's a remarkable system."

—Donna H., mother of a six-year-old

"With Dr. Blank's programs, my son's progress was not only fabulous, but I was always able to keep track of his growing ability to read and comprehend. With other approaches, I never felt I had a handle on how well he was doing."

—Kathy T., mother of a seven-year-old

"My son was four and one-half years old when he began Dr. Blank's programs. We had only recently come to the United States and English was new for him. We were amazed at how quickly he was able to pick it up."

—Ophira H., mother of a five-year-old

"I was just not comfortable with how my daughter was handling reading in first grade. So I started her on Dr. Blank's programs and today I've been told that she is one of the best readers in her class. She's at the top and it's due to Dr. Blank's programs."

—Stephanie H., mother of a six-year-old

"Our son has attention deficit disorder and Dr. Blank's programs made all the difference in his ability to learn to read. It also gave him a good foundation for work in school."

—George R., father of a seven-year-old

"When our daughter was nine years old, we were told that she would have to leave the prestigious private school she was in and go to a school for learning disabled children for two to three years. Miraculously, within just three months' time of starting Dr. Blank's programs, she made enough growth that she was able to stay in the school she was in—and did not need a special school."

—Wendy G., mother of a nine-year-old

"My son has had language difficulties that have limited his progress in school. Dr. Blank's programs have enabled him to organize his language and grow as a reader to a level far beyond his current grade level. He is able to decode unseen material much more successfully than my daughter who learned to read with a strict phonetic method."

—Jane F., mother of a six-year-old

"Before I started Dr. Blank's programs, I had traveled to many 'reading specialists.' Although they helped my son make some progress, he was still unable to read fluently at grade level. Dr. Blank's programs are brilliantly designed, tailor made to fit the needs of different children. It teaches them to read and enjoy without overburdening them. It has given my son a tool for life."

—Shayne F., mother of an eight-year-old

"Thanks to Dr. Blank's system, my son is now reading beautifully. It is responsible for his success in life. He is now graduating university and starting a graduate program."

—Patrick T., father whose son was ten years old when he started the programs

The
Reading
Remedy

The
Reading
Remedy

Six Essential Skills That Will Turn Your Child Into a Reader

MARION BLANK, Ph.D.

JOSSEY-BASS
A Wiley Imprint
www.josseybass.com

Published by Jossey-Bass
A Wiley Imprint
989 Market Street, San Francisco, CA 94103-1741   www.josseybass.com

Jossey-Bass books and products are available through most bookstores. To contact Jossey-Bass directly call our Customer Care Department within the U.S. at 800-956-7739, outside the U.S. at 317-572-3986, or fax 317-572-4002.

Jossey-Bass also publishes its books in a variety of electronic formats. Some content that appears in print may not be available in electronic books.

Library of Congress Cataloging-in-Publication Data

Blank, Marion.
  The Reading remedy: six essential skills that will turn your child into a reader/Marion Blank.
       p. cm.
  Includes bibliographical references and index.
  ISBN 13: 978-0-471-74204-3
  ISBN 10: 0-471-74204-X (alk. paper)
1. Reading—Remedial teaching.   I. Title.
  LB1050.5.B525   2006
  372.43—dc22   2005028349

Printed in the United States of America
FIRST EDITION
HB Printing   10 9 8 7 6 5 4 3 2 1

C O N T E N T S

To GABE and ANDREA,

who are always in my thoughts.

PREFACE

No other skill taught in school and learned by school children is more important than reading. It is the gateway to all other knowledge.

—American Federation of Teachers

Many people ask me when my interest in reading began. That question takes me back to a Sunday afternoon when I was a kindergartner about five years of age.

That afternoon, as on so many other weekend afternoons, we were visiting one of my many aunts and uncles. On this particular day a stranger came into my aunt's apartment with some papers that he asked her to sign. I was taken aback by the sight of my typically self-assured aunt becoming timid and tentative as she signed an X and then stepped aside so that my father could write his signature underneath.

At first I was confused. Later it was explained to me that my aunt could not read or write. She did not even know how to write her name. All she could do was write an X that was then certified with a real signature by someone who was literate.

I also found out that in my family she was not alone. Several of my older relatives had the same handicap. They had emigrated from a poor and war-torn Eastern Europe as young adults, and they had never had the opportunity to attend school.

The realization was shocking. No one in my family ever talked about it, but time after time the illiteracy problem would appear and have to be dealt with—usually at great personal cost to people whom I held dear.

I was determined to do something about the situation. So at six years of age, when I found that my own dream of learning to read and write was becoming a reality, I decided to teach my newfound ability to my grandmother, whom I adored. She was a phenomenal person. Like so many women of her era, she endured hardships that are unimaginable to today's generation. She arrived in this country as a teenager, alone, without knowing a word of English. She married in her early twenties and was widowed in her early thirties. She worked tirelessly to raise her six children, taking any and all jobs she could get including laundry, housecleaning, sewing, and plucking feathers off chickens in butcher shops. Nevertheless she was jolly, resilient, and totally willing to allow her little granddaughter to be her teacher. Sadly, within a short time she became seriously ill and the lessons ended. Nevertheless that experience deeply affected me. I had started on the path that I was to follow for the rest of my life.

In traveling this path I have worked with thousands of students of all ages and backgrounds. As any teacher will tell you, the students themselves are central to the teacher's own learning, and I am deeply grateful to my students for all they have done to show me the way. Throughout this book I have attempted to outline the key insights I arrived at with their help—insights that form the basis of what is now the Dr. Blank's Phonics Plus Five reading system.

There is no skill on earth that children want to acquire more than reading. As you use the techniques described in this book with your child, I am confident that you both will experience the exhilaration that reading mastery brings. I extend to you my very best wishes for your journey to success!

ACKNOWLEDGMENTS

Throughout this project I have been extraordinarily fortunate to have had the help of my family. My son Jonathan is a superb writer and thinker, and he has been amazingly generous in making his talents available to me. At every step of the way he has been instrumental in helping me craft this book so that it clearly expresses the ideas I was striving for, to help parents understand both the cause and the cure of reading difficulties. My son Ari is a computer wiz, and he has been central in helping me design the teaching materials so that they are attractive and easy to use. My husband, Martin, is a biophysicist, and although his interests are far afield from reading, he too has been actively involved at every step of the journey. He has listened patiently to my ideas and reviewed endless drafts, always guiding me with wise and thoughtful comments. For years my dream has been to empower parents to lead their children to total mastery of reading. I am forever indebted to my family for providing the skills to help me achieve these goals.

This book would also not have been possible without the children and their families who invited me into their lives and who have made the path to reading immensely interesting and rewarding. Their involvement and enthusiasm have been phenomenal. Often, years after the sessions with their children have ended, parents call to update me on what has been happening and proudly report on their children's success. Nothing is more gratifying than feeling you have made a difference. The names are far too numerous to list, but special thanks are due to the Gannaway family, whose generous personal and financial support has been central in allowing me to make this material available to you.

Among my deepest feelings of gratitude are those for the educational institutions that have made a difference in my life. When I entered college, this nation was far less wealthy than it is today. Still, educational opportunities abounded. New York City, where I was raised, was extraordinarily generous in supporting its students, and I am one of the many fortunate beneficiaries of its largesse. I had the phenomenal good fortune to attend a fabulous, tuition-free college—the City College of New York. The professors there were beacons, teaching me to analyze "accepted truths" and to seek better alternatives. I have no doubt that they played a central role in the new approach I developed for teaching reading. After college, my good fortune continued with a full fellowship from the University of Cambridge in England. That was followed by a postdoctoral grant from the National Institutes of Health, which permitted me to start my research on language. In this day and age, when I see so many students struggling to manage the expenses of higher education, I feel blessed to have grown up in an age when a farsighted society offered generous support to motivated students. I hope that the work I have done over the many decades that have followed has helped to repay the debt I owe to so many.

I am also deeply indebted to Stephanie Warner, Maria Quinlan, and Brian Zick, who did so much to bring the materials for the reading program to life. Their work, support, and effort are greatly appreciated.

The Reading Remedy

INTRODUCTION

It's Official: OUR KIDS CAN'T READ

—*New York Post*

Now Johnny Can Read If Teacher Just Keeps Doing What He's Told

—*Wall Street Journal*

Bush's Plan to Push Reading in "Head Start" Stirs Debate

—*New York Times*

U.S. Suffers from Wide Literacy Gap

—*Chicago Sun-Times*

It's no news that reading problems plague our country. The media have informed us of this over and over again. What *is* news is the extent of the problem—a rate of failure almost beyond belief.

The Startling Statistics

Most people, even those whose children are facing the horror of reading difficulties, are totally unaware of the fact that the problem is not limited to 5 percent, 10 percent, or even 20 percent of the population. The shocking fact is that approximately

40 percent of all children—perfectly healthy, normal children—experience difficulties in learning to read.

It seems impossible to believe that a skill this important could be in this much trouble. But it is. In state after state, the figures for failure hover around the same numbers. For example, in a report titled *The Nation's Report Card: Fourth-Grade Reading 2000,* the National Assessment for Educational Progress (U.S. Department of Education, 2001) found 37 to 40 percent of fourth graders to be reading "below basic levels," and only 29 percent to 32 percent to be "above proficient levels." Think about it—more children are doing badly than are doing well!

The statistics are shocking: approximately 40 percent of all children have significant difficulty in learning how to read.

Out of the four to five million children who enter first grade each year, approximately one to one and a half million children will have serious problems in this area. Because reading is the single most critical and important skill children will need to succeed in school and in life, failure in this area can be devastating—for the children, their families, and the nation.

All too often the children who struggle with reading are diagnosed as "learning disabled," placing the problem in the child and not in the system. But as a prestigious government report acknowledges, 80 percent of children with learning disabilities are in special education "simply because they haven't learned to read." They are "instructional casualties and not students with disabilities" (President's Commission on Excellence in Special Education, 2002, p. 25).

We could delve into a whole range of issues that contribute to this horrendous state of affairs. Kids watch too much TV; teachers are overburdened; books cannot compete with high-tech devices. But if you want to cut to the quick, there is a single, simple source: the current teaching of reading rests on a slim set of weak, inadequate techniques that can do nothing more than leave many, many of our children in the dust. As long as these techniques are used, failure is ordained!

Reading education in schools has limited itself to two systems: *phonics* and *whole language.* Phonics, the dominant force, focuses on having children convert the letters on a page into the sounds that become real words. The whole language approach concentrates on providing children with complete, or "whole," books that are deemed to be more "natural," "authentic," and "motivating" than traditionally used teaching materials.

Despite the fact that these inadequate systems have resulted in a 40 percent failure rate, the schools are not trying anything else. It's like hitting your head against a wall. The pain won't stop until you stop the banging! Or as Albert Einstein put it, "There is nothing that is a more certain sign of insanity than to do the same thing over and over and expect the results to be different." As long as current reading techniques are used, the frighteningly high rate of reading failure is ordained!

Schools often try to calm the many doubts that parents raise with well-intentioned messages, such as, "Children are different. Just give him time," or, "She's really beginning to make progress," or, "We are using a balanced approach and offering your child everything that will lead to reading success."

As long as current reading techniques are used, the frighteningly high rate of reading failure is ordained!

Those messages can be deadly. What you sense about the advantages of success in early reading is true. And what you sense about the dire consequences that follow from early reading difficulties is also true. The sad fact is children who do not read well by third grade almost never end up reading well, and as a child grows, reading problems only worsen—it's a snowballing handicap. Without the skills that school brings, job opportunities, job satisfaction, and high earnings often fall out of reach. The average annual income in 1998 for high school graduates was $23,594, but for those who had not graduated from high school, that figure was $16,053 (Newburger & Curry, 2000). For each year in college, the figures rise steadily, so that a college graduate on average earns $15,000 to $20,000 more per year than someone with only a high school degree.

You want to give your child every opportunity, and so you should not accept messages that will not get you to that goal. Now you no longer have to accept those messages. Through the simple tools offered in this book, you will be able to assess for yourself whether your child is indeed acquiring the skills for true success in reading.

If you want reading success for your child, you have to get a handle on what is currently being taught to your child and why it is not working. That is what the first part of this book aims to accomplish. It lets you see clearly that failure in reading is not an unfortunate consequence but rather the inevitable consequence of the dominant modes of instruction. You will also learn what reading actually demands, and you will see all the skills your child is not being taught in school. The essence of what reading demands is conveyed in the Skills of Reading diagram shown here.

The Six Skills of Reading

Physical Skills		Language Skills			
Sequencing (letter order)	Writing (letter creation)	Phonology (sounds)	Semantics (meaning)	Syntax (grammar)	Text (books)

In the first part of this book (Chapters One through Three) you will find out what these skills are and why they are the core of reading.

That is not all the book has to offer. It's frustrating to see a problem with no outlines of a solution. In the second part of this book (Chapters Four through Eight), you will get a full description of what needs to be done in order to take the phonics approach that has failed and transform it into an innovative, comprehensive system that offers a cure for students' reading woes. This solution is Dr. Blank's Phonics Plus Five—the reading system that I have developed over the past four decades.

The Design of Phonics Plus Five

Phonics Plus Five teaches all the areas of reading through a multilevel system composed of seven programs. The first level contains the two Get Set programs: Sequences in Sight and Letters to Write. These are preparatory programs that teach the physical skills of visual sequencing and handwriting. The remaining five levels—Boarding, Runway, Liftoff, Airborne, and Soaring—are reading and writing programs that teach all the language skills needed for literacy.

The five reading/writing programs are designed so that a set of words is taught, and then a book using those words is presented. This cycle repeats six times within each program. The Phonics Plus Five program chart displayed here profiles the full set of programs, which are all provided in Part Three of this book (Chapters Nine through Thirteen).

As you will discover when going through the chapters, true success in reading rests on a broad foundation of skills and hidden abilities. With completion of the final program, your child will have those skills and be prepared to maintain steady progress in the future. Among those skills are the ability to read and write with total accuracy and understanding.

The Phonics Plus Five Programs

	Physical Skills		Language Skills			
	Sequencing	Writing	Phonology	Semantics	Syntax	Text
Level 1: The Get Set Programs						
Sequences in Sight	▓					
Letters to Write		▓				
Levels 2–6: The Reading and Writing Programs						
Boarding			▓	▓	▓	▓
Runway			▓	▓	▓	▓
Liftoff			▓	▓	▓	▓
Airborne			▓	▓	▓	▓
Soaring			▓	▓	▓	▓

The value of accuracy cannot be overstated. Struggles with reading have become such an accepted part of classroom life that teachers are often unperturbed seeing a child slowly plod through a text, making many errors along the way. This type of reading is comparable to building a house on a cracked foundation. Even when a child is willing to read and reread to correct errors, the process represents an inadequate base that cannot support the reading needed at the higher grade levels. Slow, tedious, and error-laden reading understandably leads to children to hate reading and to avoid it as much as possible. Smooth, accurate reading is the prerequisite for the more complex skills that are to follow. Phonics Plus Five provides that foundation.

After reading about the material and deciding that it is right for you, you can choose to take matters into your own hands and teach your child to read and write with amazing effectiveness. The third part of this book provides you with the information you need to create all the programs for use in your home. The system is designed to be used with and complement any school-based reading instruction your child is receiving. If you don't want to prepare all the materials yourself and instead would like to purchase the complete Phonics Plus Five system as a fully prepared kit (which includes thirty full-color books, thirty-two easy-to-use workbooks, and comprehensive testing materials), you can place an order or get more information by calling 1-866-DRBLANK (372-5625) or visiting http://www.phonicsplusfive.com.

By broadening the scope of what we teach children and the way we teach children, we can give them access to powerful abilities that are inside each and every human being. It is then that the door to reading opens wide. With the right tools, children not only learn to read but do so with total mastery.

I have used this system to help literally thousands of children—strong and struggling readers alike—learn how to read. I have personally witnessed the tremendous positive changes that occur in children's lives when they learn how to read. Now you can use this system yourself.

Your child can easily learn how to read successfully! This book will show you how it's done.

PART 1

Understanding Reading

Teaching Reading

Why Isn't It Working?

Our focus in this chapter is to understand current reading practices and to see why they cause as many problems as they do. Before starting out, it's worthwhile to define some key terms.

Setting Out the Terms

We'll begin with three keys terms: *reading, writing,* and *literacy.* The first two are near-inseparable partners. Technically, the most accurate term to use to describe reading and writing ability is *literacy,* because it encompasses both processes. However, in everyday parlance, you'll usually find the single term *reading* used as a substitute for *literacy.*

Four processes are seen as central to attaining literacy: two (*decoding* and *comprehension*) are associated with reading, and two (*spelling* and *composing*) with writing. Don't be put off if these terms are unfamiliar. As you will see, their meaning is straightforward.

In order to read, you must be able to take the letters on a page (for example, *c-a-t*) and convert them into words (*cat*). The term for that process is *decoding.* Having decoded the words, you then have to figure out the message they are conveying. The term for that is *comprehension.* The two processes are independent of one another. For example, you can easily decode, or read, this string of words: *house if sleep between go red not lost,* but you cannot comprehend these words because they do not make sense within this string.

Writing offers a comparable set of terms. In order to write you must be able to take the sounds of words you speak and convert them into letters. The term for

The Key Terms of Literacy

Reading	*Decoding*—converting letters into words *Comprehending*—understanding what you have decoded
Writing	*Spelling*—producing the letters to represent words *Writing* (*composing*)—creating meaningful messages

that is *spelling*. You also have to be able to take the words you spell and combine them into meaningful messages that others can read. The term for that is *composing,* or *writing*.

In general, reading receives more time and effort in school instruction than does writing. However, poor achievement permeates both—with writing generally showing even more serious deficiencies than reading.

To let you see the problems for yourself, we will go through a brief tour of reading instruction and see what children must deal with on a regular basis.

Looking Back Before Looking Ahead

Despite all the recent attention it has been getting, the issue of reading failure is far from new. Half a century ago an "aroused parent," Rudolph Flesch (1955), wrote a book that took the country by storm, *Why Johnny Can't Read: And What You Can Do About It.* In it, Flesch railed against the teaching establishment. He made the astounding claim that there were "no remedial reading cases" in most European countries and that there "never was a problem anywhere in the world until the United States," around 1925, switched its method of teaching from the phonics instruction to the whole word method. In the *whole word* approach, children were taught through *look and say* techniques to recognize, or decode, whole words. Flesch likened this approach to reading "English as if it were Chinese," as if each word were represented by a different symbol.

Though attention getting, Flesch's claims about the previous absence of failure were unfounded. The widespread testing needed to substantiate them simply did not exist generations back and would likely have contradicted his claim if they had. Still, the book struck a chord in the many parents who then, as now, were grappling with the ordeal of children struggling with reading. More to the point, Flesch offered a clear, simple answer: go back to basics, and teach children to decode with a solid phonics approach.

Phonics is now the central method of reading education used in our nation. Its hold is so pervasive that the term is almost synonymous with the teaching of reading. Although many variants exist, at their core is the idea that reading is based on sounding out the letters in words. Flesch himself set out a three-part program that starts by teaching children that "single letters . . . stand for single sounds," for example, *t* = *tuh, b* = *buh,* and so forth. His program then moves on to more complicated issues, such as the sounds that are "spelled by two-letter or three-letter combinations" (such as *ow* as in *cow, ay* as in *say, chr* as in *Christmas*), and finally to the idea that "some of the letters do not spell one sound but two." For example, the *a* in a word like *cat* is pronounced very differently from the *a* in a word like *watch.* If you've seen your child, or some other child, at the start of reading instruction, you'll find these ideas familiar because they are largely the ones used in classrooms around the nation.

Flesch's views were strengthened and given academic respectability with the publication in 1967 of Jean Chall's *Learning to Read: The Great Debate.* In this book, Chall, a professor at Harvard, evaluated the phonics and whole word positions and, in the end, came down firmly on the side of phonics as a more effective way of teaching reading. Under these pressures, phonics instruction reassumed its long-standing role at center stage. The only problem was that the failure did not stop.

The better results obtained with phonics compared to whole word teaching did not mean that traditional phonics instruction was effective. It was just better than the limited alternative that had been offered.

No one should have expected that it would. Despite Flesch's claims, whole word teaching had not appeared out of the blue. It had emerged as an effort to stem the failures generated by phonics. Unfortunately, the solution had not worked. Whole word teaching proved to be even more ineffective than phonics. That did not mean that phonics teaching was effective. It was just better than the only available alternative.

Back to the Present

Fast forward now to the 1970s. Phonics once again holds sway, and to everyone's dismay, the failure continues. Once again there is a call for reform. This time, rushing in to fill the gap is whole language—a new movement based on a seductive argument. Abandon the tedium and dreariness of phonics. Instead, cater to children's imagination by providing complete, integrated, appealing books that represent "authentic" experiences and that make reading meaningful and rewarding.

The only problem is that like whole word teaching, whole language teaching causes reading scores to fall even further. So once again, decades later, history repeats itself as educational leaders push for a return to phonics as the remedy for the "new" reading crisis.

A key difference this time is that the great debate has morphed into the great accommodation. No longer are two techniques being pitted against one another for the purpose of declaring a winner and loser. Instead, in a spirit of reconciliation, the two methods—phonics and whole language—have been joined, on the grounds that each supplements the other. The end result is that many if not most children today, under the rubric of *a comprehensive approach* or *balanced teaching,* receive reading instruction that combines phonics and whole language.

Nevertheless, with its stronger techniques and longer history, phonics is almost always the dominant member of the partnership. It has been, and continues to be, the backbone of teaching kids their ABCs. In fact it is so widely taught that it has almost become a synonym for reading instruction. This is in part why the first thing parents typically do when trying to help their youngsters read a word is to say, "Well, let's sound it out. What sound does this letter make?" They do so because that is the way they were taught.

Why, then, are so many children still experiencing such difficulty in learning how to read? It certainly is not from a lack of attention. Seen as critical, reading dominates the school day for the first three to four years of a child's education. What is taught in this time, however, is plagued with problems. The remedies that have been tried over the years have been restricted to variants of methods that simply do not work for a large percentage of the children. No matter how they are repackaged, these techniques don't work. The current problems with reading education are not the fault of the children; they are due to the incomplete methods being used to teach them.

Seeing the World Through a Child's Eyes

A while back some distinguished researchers from Harvard University, in the course of studying children's thinking, realized how difficult it was for them to position themselves so they could understand just how children were viewing the world. In characterizing this gap between the children and themselves, the researchers said, "It is curiously difficult to recapture preconceptual innocence . . . It is as if . . . mastery . . . were able to mask the . . . memory of things now distinguished" (Bruner, Goodnow, & Austin, 1956, p. 50). This statement gives voice to a critical point: even though we were once without skills ourselves, once we have learned a skill, it is almost impossible for us to appreciate what it is like for someone who is just beginning.

This results in a serious paradox that besets all teaching, including the teaching of reading. The skill to be taught must be designed by individuals who already possess the skill. Otherwise, the content would be meaningless. But precisely because these persons *have* the skills, they cannot see what the novice really needs to get going.

Fortunately, there is a way out of this paradox. The knowledgeable person must somehow be placed in the position of the novice so that he or she can see the world through the eyes of the person who does not yet have the skills.

To that end much of what follows in this chapter is designed to place *you* in the position of a child who is starting on the path to reading. In other words, you are going to lose your advantages as an expert reader so that you can see the world through a child's eyes.

Although it may seem impossible to lose your reading abilities that quickly, it's not that difficult. All it takes is removing one language component you have long taken for granted. That component is the alphabet. Instead of the usual ABCs, you will be working with foreign symbols. In other words, the letters on a page will be as unfamiliar to you as our usual alphabet is to first-time readers.

In your newly created life as a child, you will go through a set of three exercises that emulate typical methods used in phonics and whole language teaching. The first involves a phonic lesson focused on decoding; the second, a whole language lesson focused on reading; and the third, a whole language lesson focused on writing. Each will enable you to see firsthand what it is about current reading instruction that leads to so much failure.

It's likely that you will find yourself unwilling to complete the work. Many of the colleagues I enlisted in this endeavor got so frustrated that they refused to continue. It's difficult to find yourself stripped of powers you long assumed were yours forever. If that is your experience, do not be upset. Just on its own, it will tell you a great deal about the experience children have in current reading education. So, on that cautionary note, try tackling a typical phonics lesson prepared for children in kindergarten or first grade.

Returning to Our Youth: A Phonics Lesson

This lesson, like much phonics instruction, is aimed at having you use the technique of *sounding out* to decode the words on the page. Sounding out new letters is difficult, and you would be overwhelmed if you had to deal with the entire alphabet. To ease your burden, you have to deal with a set of only nine letters.

We start with the assumption that you have already learned the eight letters that follow, all of which are symbols for consonant sounds (shown in the second row):

Letter	Δδ	Ηη	Λλ	Μμ	Νν	Σσ	Ττ	Ξξ
Sound	*duh*	*huh*	*ell*	*mm*	*nn*	*ss*	*tuh*	*ecks*

In each pair, the letter on the left is uppercase, and the one on the right is lowercase. The letter on the extreme left, for example, is a capital *dee*, the one immediately to its right is a lowercase *dee*. They make the sound *duh* (just like the *d* of our alphabet). The next set of letters contains upper- and lowercase *ayches*, and they make the sound *huh* (just like the *h* of our alphabet). And so on.

Now, in this lesson you are going to learn a new, ninth letter. It is the α and it has the sound *aah*. It also happens to be the first vowel you are going to be using. Because all words must have a vowel and α will be our only vowel in this lesson, keep in mind that this letter will appear in every word.

Now, to our lesson. As in any good phonics lesson, you "simply" have to sound out each letter and then combine it with the sounds of the other letters until you come out with the complete word. Remember, if the sounds don't end up sounding like a real word, try again. All the words are ones you know well. Go ahead and try your skill.

Δαν ηασ αν αξ.

Ηασ Δαν αν αξ?

Σαμ ηασ ηαμ.

Ηασ Σαμ ηαμ?

Δαν ηασ λανδ ανδ σανδ.

Ηασ Δαν σανδ?

Σαμ σατ.

Δαν σατ.

How did you do? How long did it take, and what was it like to sound out twenty-six ultra-short words limited to nine letters of the alphabet? For most people the experience is tedious, error laden, and difficult. Even the simplest real language has too much variation to allow traditional sounding out of letters to yield clear, user-friendly material for the beginning reader. Keep in mind that the task is not impossible. If you have tenacity, you can do it. It is just unpleasant, unrewarding, and demanding. Just as you can plow through the words if you have sufficient determination, your child can as well.

By the way, did you ever finish reading those twenty-six words? If not, here they are for you translated into a more recognizable format:

Δαν ηασ αν αξ.	Dan has an ax
Ηασ Δαν αν αξ?	Has Dan an ax?
Σαμ ηασ ηαμ.	Sam has ham.
Ηασ Σαμ ηαμ?	Has Sam ham?
Δαν ηασ λανδ ανδ σανδ.	Dan has land and sand.
Ηασ Δαν σανδ?	Has Dan sand?
Σαμ σατ.	Sam sat.
Δαν σατ.	Dan sat.

If translating those symbols was hard for you, imagine how it is for a child with no experience of reading. Some kids do learn this way. Some even learn without any instruction at all. You might be one of them. You would find that out in about three to four months. That seems to be the length of time successful children need to sort things out. For this group, after working diligently with material of the sort you just encountered, within a few months the jumble of letters begins to dissolve and to be replaced by real words. That is why many first-grade teachers are heard to remark, "By Christmas, the kids just get it. They start to read, and they zoom ahead."

For many children, though, that is not what happens. The clouds don't disperse. Things only darken further, as failure and despondency take over. Who in their right mind could possibly recommend unpleasant, unrewarding, and demanding tasks as the way to teach five- and six-year-old children? Yet this is what youngsters across the nation are asked to do every day. This fact alone can help you understand the astounding failure rate that marks the reading scene.

In addition, keep in mind that we've restricted ourselves to a range of extremely simple, mostly three-letter words where each letter can be sounded out. For example, with a word like *sat,* you can come up with a sound for each letter: *ss, aah, tuh.* These sorts of words are not at all representative of the words children actually see when they look at real books—even those designed for kindergartners and first graders.

The addition of even a single letter generally makes straightforward sounding out impossible. See, for example, what happens when you sound out each letter in four-letter words like *make, baby, seat, coin, loud,* and *bush.* The problem is perhaps best explained by pointing out that if phonics worked the way it is supposed to, the word *phonics* itself would be spelled *foniks.*

To overcome this problem, traditional phonics rapidly goes beyond sounding out and requires children to memorize hosts of complicated rules. Studies have shown that almost 600 rules are required if you are going to use explicit rules to decode basic English. And even with that astounding number, you will not be able to figure out how to pronounce "many of the most common words in English, like *one* and *have* and *of*" (Gough & Hillinger, 1980, p. 185).

You may have heard of some of the rules that children confront. Two of the most common are the silent *e* rule (where the *e* at the end of a word like *make* is silent) and the double vowel rule (where the double vowel *ea* in a word like *meat* gets a single sound). Not only are these rules tedious to learn, but they turn reading into a laborious process where each word has to be studiously analyzed before it can be deciphered.

Educators have over the years become increasingly aware of the many children who lack the skills to allow current phonics instruction to work. Instead of seeking a new approach that meets the needs of these children, they have tried to change the children to meet the needs of phonics. They have developed training in what is called *phonological awareness,* the skills deemed to be the precursors for phonics instruction. In this method children are taught various types of sound analysis. They are taught to rhyme (for example, "Say a word that rhymes with *man.*"), to dissect the sounds of words (for example, "What would *bend* sound like without the *b?*"), and to break words apart (for example, "Clap for how many syllables there are in the word *opening.*").

But after the phonological awareness training has ended, the children are still left to confront what I just asked you to do. They must decode unfamiliar symbols, carry out seemingly endless sound–symbol associations, pay attention to minute details, and blend the many different sounds they come up with in the right sequence (all of which is commonly known as *reading!*).

You already have these phonological awareness skills, but you may have noticed that they didn't help you read the passage in an unfamiliar alphabet. Similarly for many children, even when they have developed the phonological awareness skills, reading is still fraught with difficulty. Endless sounding out doesn't work for them.

Additionally, today's children, accustomed to high-impact TV and video games, are at an even greater risk of failure than their parents and grandparents. To put it bluntly, students of previous generations were used to being bored. Phonics was anything but exciting, but in that respect it did not differ from the many tedious tasks children were typically expected to carry out. For example, children routinely had to accomplish long memorization tasks. A homework assignment might have been to memorize Lincoln's Gettysburg Address and then recite it the next day before the entire class.

Such diligence-demanding skills are totally beyond the ken of many of today's kids. The occasional sounding out of words is manageable and helpful, but repeated sounding out is a difficult chore, and children often cannot stay the course. The result is kids who do not learn how to read successfully.

Returning to Our Youth: A Whole Language Reading Lesson

As I explained before, phonics is generally not the sum total of children's instruction today. They are also exposed to the techniques of whole language. Now I'm going to ask you to take a short whole language lesson, to see if that method works any better.

The whole language approach focuses on a different aspect of language. Instead of concentrating on the dissected *sounds* of words, it provides children with complete stories, or *texts*. You will hear whole language proponents maintaining that stories are more "natural," "authentic," and "motivating." If you provide children with such stories, the thinking goes, their reading will naturally blossom.

In an effort to keep the material as simple as possible, a common technique in whole language is to use *predictable reading* material, in which small sets of words and phrases are repeated, as in the following passage (Segment 1). This is a typical lesson for a beginning reader in kindergarten or first grade.

Segment 1

Black bear, black bear, what can you see?

I can see a green bird looking at me.

Green bird, green bird, what can you see?

I can see a gray duck looking at me.

This rhyming verse, consistent with the whole language philosophy, is certainly more entertaining than the "Dan's ax" and "Sam's ham" passage used for the phonics lesson. Nevertheless, it shares the phonics aim of smooth decoding, or using the right words for various groups of letters. However, rather than repeating a letter, like the α in the phonics lesson, this approach repeats words and themes (for example, "what can you see? I can see a . . . looking at me").

To see how this works in practice, read Segment 1 until you have it memorized. Then move on and read Segment 2. It contains the same words—but in our foreign alphabet. Now you'll see how easy it is to read predictable texts.

Just repeat the sentences you have memorized, making sure to match each spoken word to the appropriate written word (for example, say "black" while looking at βλαχκ, and "bear" while looking at βεαρ, and so forth).

Segment 2

Βλαχκ βεαρ, Βλαχκ βεαρ, ωηατ χαν ψου σεε?

Ι χαν σεε α γρεεν βιρδ λοοκινγ ατ με.

Γρεεν βιρδ, γρεεν βιρδ, ωηατ χαν ψου σεε?

Ι χαν σεε α γραψ δυχκ λοοκινγ ατ με.

See? You're *reading*, just as lots of children do when they start memorizing stories that are read to them on a regular basis.

But what exactly have you learned? To find out, let's use the identical fifteen words but put them in a different order. OK, give it a try. Try to read Segment 3.

Segment 3

Δυχκ! δυχκ! Χαν ψου σεε?

Με, με? Σεε ωηατ?

Χαν ψου σεε α γρεεν βιρδ?

Ι χαν σεε α βλαχκ βιρδ.

You may have found that the decoding of Segment 3 posed some difficulties. That is certainly the case for many children. The use of this predictable reading method often leads to a laborious, error-filled reading of the text. Further, in this situation you may not even have the advantage of sounding out because you may not have been taught the sounds of the individual letters. That is why whole language teaching on its own fares less well than phonics. Neither is ideal, but phonics provides more systematic tools for dealing with new material.

The problems of whole language are obvious even when a text is limited to just fifteen words. With the inevitable introduction of more material, the difficulties soar. You will hear whole language proponents maintaining that the inherent appeal of well-written stories will automatically lead children to master the reading process. As you have just seen for yourself, it doesn't work out that way.

The presentation of stories early in reading instruction means children can often prematurely face a much wider range of words than they can manage. So while traditional phonics offers children tedious rules that are difficult to apply, whole language leaves them stranded without the controls a learner needs to master a new terrain. The number of words in any meaningful text is simply too great for the majority of novice readers to handle effectively.

In case you are interested, here is the translation of Segment 3:

Segment 3 Translation

Duck! duck! Can you see?

Me, me? See what?

Can you see a green bird?

I can see a black bird.

Returning to Our Youth: A Whole Language Writing Lesson

Whole language instruction is not confined to reading. In contrast to phonics, this approach rightly places enormous value on writing. Writing is, if anything, more difficult to teach than reading, and parents and educators alike are concerned about the extent to which it has been neglected.

There are good reasons why phonics downplays writing in the early grades. Imagine a young child wanting to express a relatively simple idea such as, "My dog is sick." Imagine further that the child is totally willing to abide by the phonics rules that have been taught. In this case the writing of this single idea could legitimately end up as, "Mie dawg iz sik," or as "Mye daug iz sic," or as any number of other variations. From a phonics point of view, it would be almost impossible to explain to the child why his or her writing is "wrong."

Whole language gets phonics off this uncomfortable hook. It says that children should not be constrained to use what adults have determined is *correct* spelling. Instead, they should be allowed, indeed encouraged, to use *invented spelling*. As captured in the title of an influential book (Bissex, 1980) on this topic, *Gnys at Wrk* (meaning "genius at work"), in this technique children write words in whatever way they feel is appropriate.

Many, if not most, schools today use phonics as the basis for teaching reading, and whole language as the basis for teaching writing. So for the final exercise, I am going to ask you to try out some whole language writing techniques.

Here is a typical writing lesson from the early grades that once again employs the foreign alphabet we've been using in these exercises. The teacher starts by saying:

Let's try some writing. I'd like you to use the words we've been reading like these—

βεαρ	βιρδ	γρεεν	δυχκ	σεε	γραψ
bear	bird	green	duck	see	gray

—to express your own ideas and experiences. To help you with other words, here is the whole alphabet:

α β χ δ ε φ γ η ι φ κ λ μ ν ο π θ ρ σ τ υ ϖ ω ξ ψ ζ

Remember, all your ideas are important. Feel free to say anything you'd like. Just make sure, in the space below, to write at least three sentences using the new words you've learned—along, of course, with other words you need to make meaningful sentences. For example, if you want to write the word *fly,* you can write φλψ. But don't feel constrained. You may also use the invented spelling technique of whole language, in which you can create your own spelling and write the words in whatever way seems comfortable. [In other words, you may do just what young children do when they write *puld* for *pulled, wantid* for *wanted,* and *grl* for *growl.*]

Τηισ ισ μψ στορψ **(This is my story)**

_____

_____

_____

It's tough going, isn't it? When you have to keep creating words that you don't know, the process is slow and grinding. Schools will proudly boast how they teach children to love writing. If you speak to the children, though, you will hear a far different message. For the novice, the goal is often to do anything to get by. Children cope by writing the shortest sentences they can think of, by reusing the same types of sentences, and by spelling words in a haphazard manner. Each session works to ingrain patterns of poor writing that can haunt students for the rest of their lives.

Sorting Out the Means and the Ends

The experiences in this chapter may have been uncomfortable, but I hope you got to complete one or two of the tasks. Only through firsthand experience can you begin to sense the problems of current methods of instruction and to see why they are the source of so much failure.

These problems in no way deny the value of the goals that phonics and whole language have set for themselves; these goals remain on target. If children are to master reading, they must learn how to decode words smoothly. That's what makes phonics central to any effective method of teaching. Things go awry when we imagine that current sounding out techniques are the way to go in reaching that goal.

Similarly, if children are to master reading, they must know how to read books knowledgeably and write texts effectively. That's what makes the focus on meaning in whole language so important. Once again, however, that goal should not be equated with having to accept the complex and insufficiently structured materials that have been used in that approach. The goals of phonics and whole language approaches are correct. Their methods are failing.

The question is, What are the alternatives? The next chapter provides an answer.

The goals of phonics and whole language are correct. It is the methods that are failing.

What Reading Really Requires

The Six Essential Skills

In the last chapter we saw that the problems of phonics and whole language do not stem from their goals. Both systems aim for children to master processes that are absolutely essential to literacy. But that is not the same as saying that these goals are complete. They aren't. Literacy demands far more than both systems offer, even when they are combined. The essence of what reading demands is conveyed in the Six Skills of Reading diagram.

The Six Skills of Reading

Physical Skills		*Language Skills*			
Sequencing (letter order)	Writing (letter creation)	Phonology (sounds)	Semantics (meaning)	Syntax (grammar)	Text (books)

In this chapter you will find out what these physical and language skills are and why they are the core of reading. We will start by fitting the two major systems of reading instruction into the Six Skills of Reading diagram. Phonics focuses on placing sounds on letters so that you can convert them into real words. The processing of sounds falls under a language category known as *phonology*. (This is where the name *phonics* comes from.) Phonology is one of the six skills listed on the diagram. The whole language approach focuses on providing children with complete stories. The processing of stories falls under a language category known as *text,* which is also one of the six skills listed on the diagram.

When we apply this information to fill in the appropriate boxes on the Six Skills of Reading diagram, we see that even when phonics and whole language teaching accomplish their objectives, they are still woefully inadequate. When combined, they still cover only two of the six areas that children need to master for effective literacy.

Phonics and Whole Language and the Six Skills of Reading

	Physical Skills		Language Skills			
	Sequencing	Writing	Phonology (sounds)	Semantics	Syntax	Text (books)
Phonics			▓			
Whole language						▓

The end result is that these two reading systems leave children with huge gaps in learning. All the empty spaces in the diagram are skills that your child is currently *not* being taught.

When these abilities are left untaught, the inevitable outcome is endless error. It is no wonder so many children say they "hate reading." Incomplete and inadequate teaching leads them to experience reading as a pit of failure. As their self-esteem plummets, they do whatever it takes to avoid reading.

It doesn't have to be that way. Over the past four decades I have developed a new approach to reading. This system teaches children *all six skills* required for successful reading, and it does so in a way that promotes accuracy, avoids error, and is easy for parents, teachers, and children to follow. What these skills are, and why they are the core of reading, is what this chapter is all about.

It is no wonder so many children say they "hate reading." Incomplete and inadequate teaching leads them to experience reading as a pit of failure that should be avoided at all costs.

The Physical Skills

This section focuses on the two physical skills of reading: *sequencing* and *fine motor skills.* In learning to read, children have to transfer the language they have been speaking to the language they are seeing. In other words, reading is language. Like any language system, it requires particular physical skills. In the realm of spoken language, those skills involve our ears (so that we can listen to language) and our mouths (so that we can produce language). In the realm of written language, the comparable skills involve our eyes (so that we can read the language) and our hands (so that we can write the language).

No one would deny that literacy rests on a base of physical skills, but it is taken for granted that these skills will develop on their own. After all, kids use their eyes and hands for years before they start to read. So it has seemed reasonable to assume that they will simply carry over these skills to reading and writing. That is why you almost never see the physical aspects of literacy discussed in any book on reading instruction.

Kids use their eyes and their hands for years before they approach reading. So instructional programs have assumed that they will simply bring these skills to reading and writing, and minimal effort is made to teach the skills that form the physical base for literacy. For many children, this neglect has meant reading failure.

But even though some kids pick up these skills, many do not. Unfortunately, the consequences for those children can be reading failure.

We should not be surprised when this happens. The fact of the matter is that the ways our eyes and hands perform in reading are radically different from the ways they are used in other activities. We'll start by looking at the way we use our eyes.

Component 1: Visual Sequencing

The Skills of Reading

Physical Skills		
Sequencing	**Writing**	

From birth, human beings are enormously skilled in visual processing. Even a toddler can effortlessly recognize thousands of objects. But in all that recognition the viewer consistently dismisses one aspect of the visual world. To see what this aspect is, take a look at these pictures:

If we were asked to name any one of these pictures, we would be likely to say something like "a box of fruit," or "some fruit in a box," or "a bunch of fruit." The words we used would not reflect any awareness that from one box to the next the fruits are shown in different sequences.

This fact of everyday visual life is present from the smallest to the biggest of clusters. We can see it in a two-element cluster like this:

a three-element cluster like this:

or a multi-element cluster like this:

From the earliest days of our lives, we learn to identify clusters of objects while paying no attention whatsoever to the left-to-right sequence of the units within the clusters. In the case of the bird and her fledglings, for example, we are likely to say, "The pictures show a mother bird and her two babies." We would not dream of describing the sequence by saying, "Well, in the first picture, there is a mother bird with two babies on the left, while in the second picture, there are two baby birds with their mother to the right." Our description stays the same whether any particular bird is to the left or to the right of its family members. This approach to visual information provides a fast, efficient, and effective means of handling tasks in the everyday visual world. Imagine how awkward it would be if we always had to describe objects in terms of their relation to other objects.

A New Way of Seeing. With the introduction of reading, our habitual approach must be dramatically transformed. Suddenly, the dimension that has never mattered becomes critical. Just like objects, letters appear in clusters. But these clusters completely change their identity depending on the sequence of the units they contain. For example, consider the following words:

cars	scar	arcs
spot	pots	stop

In each row, the units contain the identical four letters (*a-c-r-s* in first set, and *o-p-s-t* in the second). Nevertheless, we know that the words in each set are different in every possible way—in the sequence of their sounds, the meaning they represent, and the ways we are expected to spell them. They are different words not because they contain different letters but because the identical letters they contain appear in different sequences.

The examples of this are endless. Here are a few more (reading downward in each pair of rows):

left	from	rats	pans
felt	form	star	span
rat	table	trains	scare
art	bleat	strain	cares
cat	plane	nest	sour
act	panel	sent	ours

Reading English is marked by an unalterable fact: it requires us to scan each and every element in a cluster of letters from left to right. Further, it is our only major activity demanding left-to-right visual sequencing. Nothing in a child's prereading life prepares him or her for these demands. Indeed, thousands of encounters up to this point have taught the child to ignore left-to-right sequencing. This means that the child not only has to learn a new skill but also has to undo a pattern that is one of the deeply embedded habits of everyday visual life. Until the child overcomes those habits, or at least abandons them in dealing with the world of print, he or she will not become an effective reader.

Reading is our only major activity demanding left-to-right visual sequencing.

As always happens, some children cue in readily to this new fact of visual life. For many other children, though, the shift can be confusing and painful. Forced to cope, they come up with a variety of mechanisms, such as learning to swap individual letters so that a word like *stop* may at times be *stop*, but equally often it may be *tops* or *spot* or some other meld of letters. In some cases children simply revert to their old pattern of ignoring left-to-right orientation, leading them to be labeled with the damning, but inaccurate, label of "reversing" what they see. That is not what they are doing. Just as you were not seeing the set of birds backward if you described the middle picture (where the babies are to the left of the mother)

as "a mother bird and her two babies," they are not seeing words backward. They are simply continuing patterns that, until now, have served them well in handling visual input.

You may be thinking that left-to-right sequencing is so obvious a prerequisite skill for reading that it must be part of the curriculum. Surprisingly, it isn't. Currently, neither the phonics nor the whole language approach systematically teaches children the way visual sequencing works in the world of words, and there is no supplementary system that provides children with this essential skill. As a result, many children have great difficulty in this area.

The Need to Teach Sequencing. I discovered the importance of visual sequencing in the 1960s, when I was studying how fourth graders with and without reading problems dealt with complex visual matching tasks (Blank, 1978). In these studies the kids would see a pattern such as this:

$$| \square \, \nabla \, \nabla \, \cup \, \wedge \, | \perp$$

They would then have to pick out its identical match from one of three patterns like the following:

$\| \square \, \nabla \, \nabla \, \cup \, \wedge \, \| \perp$	$\| \perp \square \, \cup \, \nabla \, \nabla \, \wedge \|$	$\| \perp \nabla \, \cup \, \wedge \, \nabla \, \perp \square$

Contrary to all predictions the children scored extremely well, with no differences between those who were ranked high in reading and those who were not. It was only when I asked the kids how they approached the activity that differences appeared. The differences were dramatic. The good readers, on the one hand, systematically worked in a left-to-right sequence, treating the sets of symbols just the way they treated sets of words. The kids who had reading problems, on the other hand, used a range of non-sequence-based strategies, such as noticing whether the shapes on the two ends matched the model. After four years of reading, left-to-right scanning had *still* not become the way they viewed sequenced patterns.

I then saw that for reading instruction to be effective, it must teach visual sequencing. Further, ideally, that teaching should occur before children are asked to read actual words. If real words are used when sequencing has not yet been established, the children will scan them using their established non-sequence-based patterns, thereby setting in place an inappropriate system. My subsequent research has confirmed these findings.

The Phonics Plus Five system uses a simple but highly effective method that teaches children the rules of visual sequencing in reading. This is accomplished through the Sequences in Sight program, which uses activities that are designed to expand children's visual-processing strategies. Once children have completed these activities, they have a solid foundation from which to approach reading on a visual level.

Sequences in Sight is one of two preparatory programs that teach the physical skills needed for reading. Although the figure will vary according to the number of sessions conducted in a week, most children complete the Sequences in Sight program in three to five weeks, and they are then set to deal with the real words they are going to encounter in reading. This program and its major features are described in Chapter Four.

Not all children need to go through the Sequences in Sight program. You need to implement it only if a brief skills check that you carry out shows that your child needs to develop the visual sequencing skill. As with all the components of the Phonics Plus Five system, if the skills are already in place, bypass the program. In this way the system is tailored to each child's individual needs. Children never waste time relearning skills they have already mastered.

Component 2: Motor Skills

The Skills of Reading

Physical Skills		
Sequencing	Writing	

Written language has two faces. There is the language we take in from others; that process is reading. There is also the language that we produce for others; that process is writing. The production of written language calls on the second key physical skill we will be considering. It is the area known as *fine motor skills*.

Motor Skills Develop Slowly. Behaviors such as tying shoelaces, cutting food with a knife, and writing the letters of the alphabet with their demands for small, delicate, coordinated hand movements represent the essence of fine motor skills. Every time parents urge their five- or six-year-olds on with statements such as, "Come on, you need to learn to tie your shoelaces," they're urging them to improve fine motor skills.

The fine motor system develops very slowly, with many children experiencing difficulties throughout the primary grades. In some areas, advances like Velcro for sneakers have rendered certain delays irrelevant. So far, though, there is no Velcro for handwriting. If children are to produce written messages, they have to form the letters on their own, using the traditional paper-and-pencil materials that have been with us for centuries. (Even the computer does not allow kids to bypass motor demands. If they are to get letters onto the screen, they need to use the set of fine motor skills required for manipulating the keyboard.)

Fine motor skills are absolutely essential to the creation of letters. In the realm of literacy, those motor skills are known as writing.

Motor Skills and Handwriting.   Once they enter kindergarten, children regularly face demands for writing. Teachers spend a lot of time, for example, on having children learn to write their names. These activities involve producing the letters of the alphabet, because no writing can take place without them. The slow pace of motor skill development, however, means that for many children the writing activities occur before the necessary skills are in place.

That is why children's early writing looks so immature. The letters are uneven, letter size varies in a seemingly random fashion, and the lines on the page are ignored.

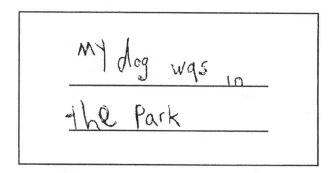

The difficulties are obvious and undeniable. Current conventional wisdom, however, views them without concern. They are seen as signs of a normal developmental progression that will be taken care of by time. Once again, an essential physical skill that underpins literacy is expected simply to emerge by itself.

The limitations of this approach are obvious. Imagine trying to become an expert at any physical activity—golf, tennis, baseball—without careful, deliberate instruction. That is precisely why so many kids have problems in this area.

When writing is not fluid and easy, it becomes a draining process that many children detest. Handwriting problems left unaddressed at the outset lead children to develop poor habits that can haunt them the rest of their lives. That is why the Phonics Plus Five system addresses motor skills at a very early stage through the Letters to Write program. Within a few weeks children develop the skills they need to form letters in a smooth, automatic manner. Once that is achieved, they can focus on what they are writing instead of on the physical act of writing itself. The Letters to Write program is described in Chapter Five.

The Language Skills

With the physical skills in place, the stage is set for the move into language itself. Using language is an extraordinarily complex behavior composed of thousands of abilities. Typically, these abilities are clustered into four areas:

1. *Phonology*—the sounds of words

2. *Semantics*—the verbal concepts, or ideas, that the words convey

3. *Syntax*—the grammar that strings words together

4. *Text*—the messages we send and receive through books, articles, notes, signs, and so on

Each of these abilities needs to be taught if a reading system is to provide children with what they need.

Component 3: Phonology

The Skills of Reading

Physical Skills		Language Skills	
Sequencing	Writing	Phonology	

We'll start with the area of *phonology.* Of all the areas of reading, this is the one that has received the most attention. Phonics, which is an offshoot of phonology, refers to the specific skill of sounding out letters to form words. Its influence, however, has been so great that the term *phonics* has almost become synonymous with reading education.

Certainly, the ability to recognize and reproduce the sounds that letters make in forming different words is an essential skill of reading. Problems arise, however, when (1) that is the only skill that is taught, and (2) that skill is taught in ways that create their own set of problems for the beginning reader.

The Limitations of Sounding Out. These problems arise from a couple of key roots. If you concentrate on short, simple words, such as *cat, bin, pot,* and *sand,* the sounding-out process is often doable, but it is slow and tedious. When there are many words, the situation becomes unsustainable. You saw that for yourself if you carried out the foreign-symbol reading exercise in the previous chapter. Sounding out is not a feasible system for use on a steady basis.

Then there is an even more serious root issue. Straightforward sounding out works only in a very limited domain. The pronunciation of English letters is too rife with irregularities to offer children a clear, simple sounding-out system they can use. For instance, how do you explain to a beginning reader that the same letters can have quite different sounds in different words? Consider these examples:

- The *o* of *oven* compared to the *o* of *opera*
- The *ea* of *head* compared to the *ea* of *great*
- The *y* of *happy* compared to the *y* of *fly*
- The *at* of *cat* compared to the *at* of *water*

And so on. The list is seemingly endless. The fact is, English is a very difficult language to sound out.

Phonics has addressed the inherent problems of sounding out by imposing hundreds of rules. They are cumbersome, demanding, and imprecise, but the system sees no other way to keep going. In the case of words with double, adjoining vowels, for example, children are taught that "when two vowels go walking, the first one does the talking." This means that, when two vowels combine, the first vowel is not short (like the *e* sound of *egg*) but long (like the *e* sound of *beat*).

In the case of words where the final letter is an *e* (such as *bate, mane,* and *fine*), the silent *e* rule is employed. This means that the *e* at the end of a word has no sound but changes the first vowel to a long vowel sound.

The Rules: A Quagmire for Learning.   One immediately obvious problem with these rules is that a vast number of exceptions exist for each one. In the case of the double-vowel rule, for example, we find many double-vowel words where the rule does not hold, including *good, head, boil, ouch, loud, lion,* and *said.* Similarly, many of the most common four-letter words ending in *e,* such as *come, give, love, done,* and *move,* do not obey the silent *e* rule. With so many exceptions, it is difficult to see how the rules themselves can be called rules.

Less apparent but equally important, these rules distort the left-to-right sequencing needed for reading. A child can apply each rule only by scanning a word—first, from left to right and then from right to left. For example, with the silent *e* rule, until you scan to the end of a word and determine whether an *e* is present, it's impossible to know whether to make the vowel short (as in *mad*) or long (as in *made*).

$$m \quad a \quad d \quad e$$
$$\rightarrow \quad \rightarrow \quad \rightarrow$$

Then, if (as in the case of *made*), a final *e* has been identified, the child must go back in a right-to-left scanning pattern to return to the beginning of the word in order to begin the final round of left-to-right scanning, where the *a* is sounded out according to the rules.

$$\rightarrow \quad \rightarrow \quad \rightarrow$$
$$m \quad a \quad d \quad e$$
$$\leftarrow \quad \leftarrow \quad \leftarrow$$

So—simply to see if the rule needs to be used—children have to mesh two methods of scanning: left-to-right scanning, which is critical in reading English; and right-to-left scanning, which is confusing and counterproductive in English. Instead of reading, children are forced to engage in a slow, laborious, error-prone task that disrupts left-to-right scanning. The vital skill of visual sequencing is sacrificed to maintain an incomplete system of teaching.

The silent *e* rule is just one of hundreds, many of which cause distortions in visual sequencing. This naturally leads to further reading problems, especially for children who were already having difficulty with sequencing.

The Phonics Plus Five reading programs have been designed to avoid the problems associated with traditional sounding-out techniques. They provide children with simplified sound-blending techniques that apply to any words they see. In addition, all words are taught without the imposition of rules that violate the left-to-right sequencing that is central to reading. These techniques,

The rules of phonics require children to intermesh left-to-right scanning (which is critical in reading English) with right-to-left scanning (which is antithetical to reading English). The vital skill of visual sequencing is sacrificed to maintain the rules prescribed by the teaching method.

outlined in Chapter Six, are present in all five reading programs of the Phonics Plus Five system: Boarding, Runway, Liftoff, Airborne, and Soaring. Although all the programs share the same techniques, the content becomes progressively more complex with each advancing level. Measuring your child's skill at the outset will tell you which of the reading programs represents the right starting point for him or her.

Component 4: Semantics

The Skills of Reading

Physical Skills		Language Skills		
Sequencing	Writing	Phonology	Semantics	

Semantics refers to the concepts, or ideas, that words convey. In entering this domain we are moving from sounds (which lie at the core of phonology) to meaning (which lies at the core of semantics).

The Words of Speaking Versus the Words of Reading. Well before they start reading, kids have vocabularies consisting of thousands of words. By kindergarten age they can easily express and understand complex words like *penguins, vacation, exercise, delicious, special, jaguars, restaurant, dangerous,* and *suppose.* But the decoding, or reading, of these long, multisyllable words is clearly beyond these children's reading capabilities. It is rightly taken for granted that the words children see in books have to be simpler than the words they speak.

The problem is that this restriction has been extended to the point that it works against effective learning. To see how, let's consider some of the issues children face.

The Long Wait for Words. In traditional phonics not only do the words have to be simple, they have to be *decodable.* That is, a child should previously have been taught the sound of any letter in a word that he or she sees. However, because the learning of letter sounds is difficult, only one is taught at a time. To do more would bring on failure. (You may recall how difficult the foreign symbol exercise was when you had to deal with nine new letters at one time.) This pacing means that children wait weeks, often months, before seeing the letters in meaningful words.

To picture the situation, imagine that the first four letters a child has learned are *a, c, g,* and *o.* Limited to these letters, you can't do much in the way of words. Among the few possibilities are *cog* and *gag,* which are not even likely to be part of children's vocabularies. In short, semantics, or the reading of meaningful words, is practically nonexistent in the early months of instruction.

It isn't until the children have completed about nine letters that a small corps of words begins to form. Let's assume, for example, that *t, e, i, s,* and *f* have been added to the *a, c, g,* and *o* the children have learned. These new letters open up a range of words such as *fat, sat, cat, sit, fit,* and *tag.* (Other possibilities exist, such as *coat, ice,* and *cage,* but they cannot be included because they involve the still-to-be-taught vowel rules.) It's hard to convey much of a message when your choices are limited to this set of words. The closest you can come to an actual sentence with the nine letters we now have is *fat cat sat* or *fat cat sit.*

Only when children have completed the sounds for about half the alphabet, a process that can take from three to six months, does anything resembling real sentences appear. In one reading program, for example, after having been taught the thirteen letters *a, c, d, e, f, g, h, i, l, o, s, t, u,* children are asked to read the following sentences, focused on the new (fourteenth) letter, *b.*

Bill has a soft bed.

Bob bit the hot dog.

Bob has a big belt.

Bud has a cut leg.

Bill fell off the sled.

Bud tugs the big bag.

—*Rowland, 1995, workbook 14*

As you can see, these sentences do offer words like *big, bag,* and *bed,* but most of the *b* words are children's names (*Bill, Bob, Bud*), and each is used more than once. This is done because the available letters still do not yield enough real *b* words, leaving first names as the only option for increasing their number. For this reason, early readers are replete with children's names composed of three letters (like *Pam, Sam,* and *Dan*).

This practice, however, violates the way children use words in their everyday lives. When unfamiliar people appear on the scene, children do not refer to them by their first names. Instead, they identify them through phrases they have been using from the time they were toddlers, phrases such as *the boy, a kid,* and *those girls.* But those natural terms don't fit the sounding-out rules the kids are being taught, so they are avoided in reading instruction.

This is but one example of the many ways in which reading materials distort the semantics that children are accustomed to. After waiting weeks and months to see meaningful words, the sentences children see have only passing similarity to the language they actually use.

Some children can deal with the problematic semantics that confronts them in early reading materials. Others have a much harder time of it. These difficulties can be remedied if semantics is not relegated to the shadows but is made a key skill in learning

Early reading material is notable for its weak semantics. Having been kept from meaningful words for weeks and months, children finally see sets of sentences that present a language with only passing similarity to the language they actually use.

how to read. Because they are not restricted to oversimplified sound patterns, the Phonics Plus Five reading programs open up the range of words children see, and allow words to be combined in ways that fit the natural language patterns children use. From the very first sets of stories, children see much broader—and more meaningful—combinations of words than are usually found in instructional programs for young readers. In Chapter Six, you will see how semantics, or the meaning of words, is dealt with in the five reading programs of the Phonics Plus Five system.

Component 5: Syntax

The Skills of Reading

Physical Skills		Language Skills			
Sequencing	Writing	Phonology	Semantics	Syntax	

The fifth key skill is *syntax,* or the grammar that allows us to link words together to form meaningful sentences. Like so many of the other skills, syntax has been given short shrift in children's reading education.

The Two Groups of Words. To understand why syntax has received little attention, we need to understand an important distinction that exists between words. Although we don't think about it much, the words of our language fall into two major groups. The first group, called *content words,* refers to words such as *girl, turn, made, happy, beat, fast, cloud,* and so on. They are nouns, verbs, adjectives, and adverbs, and they are the central units in semantics. They represent an enormous group, because there are hundreds of thousands of content words (estimates range from 500,000 to 1,000,000). New entries are also steadily appearing—100 years ago, no one would have been using such words as *astronaut, radar, television, Internet,* and *Google.*

The second group, the *noncontent words,* consists of all the words outside the noun, verb, adverb, and adjective groupings. It includes articles, prepositions, and pronouns, such as *the, is, was, but, there, for, to, what, he, it,* and *they.* (The verbs in this group, such as *is* and *was,* do not convey specific concepts that are found in verbs such as *run, eat,* and *fly.*) The noncontent group also contains the *part words* that we add to content words, such as the *-s* added to plurals (as in *rocks* and *dogs*), the *-ing* added to verbs (as in *going* and *sitting*), and the *-ed* used for creating past tense (as in *played* and *wished*). Although these difficult-to-define words abound in everything we say and read, their total number is tiny—there are only about 200 in all, and of these, only 100 or so are commonly used. (Most of us can get along quite well without words like *thence, whence,* and *heretofore.*)

The noncontent words play a key role in syntax, because it is almost impossible to create a sentence without them. Even the title of that quintessential phonics-based book *The Cat in the Hat* (Dr. Seuss, 1976) draws three of its five words from the noncontent category.

The Content of Noncontent Words. Despite their label, noncontent words are far from lacking in content. Consider, for instance, the way in which the presence or absence of a single noncontent word transforms the meaning of the following sets of sentences:

The man looked **at** the painting.

The man looked **for** the painting.

The kids walked the dog.

The kids walked **to** the dog.

That is **the** principle for us to follow.

That is **no** principle for us to follow.

Although noncontent words play a critical role in language, their elusive meanings have made them seem difficult to teach. That is one reason for their neglect. Another reason is that from a traditional phonics viewpoint, these words are highly problematic. They present major exceptions to the sounding-out method on which the system relies. For instance, if these words played by the rules, *was* would be spelled as *wuz, who* as *hoo, he* as *hee, they as thay, of* as *uv,* and so on. In the face of these rule violations the only recourse in traditional phonics is to teach children to regard such words as "exceptions." The feelings against them are so strong that some instructional programs teach children to label them with terms that suggest intentional wrongdoing, such as *outlaw words* and *renegades.*

Children are taught to regard the noncontent words as "exceptions." If these words played by the rules, was *would be spelled as* wuz, who *as* hoo, he *as* hee, they *as* thay, of *as* uv, *and so on. The feelings against these words are so strong that they are labeled with terms that suggest intentional wrongdoing, such as* outlaw words *and* renegades.

Thus relegated to the background, noncontent words are given almost no teaching time—with the result that children steadily encounter difficulties in decoding them. One teacher humorously expressed her frustration in teaching these words by writing a paper for her colleagues that she titled "Teaching Were, With, What and Other 'Four-Letter Words'" (Cunningham, 1980).

The treatment that noncontent words receive runs counter to the role they play in reading. Amazingly enough, the 100 or so most common noncontent words occupy the majority of any page of print you will ever see in the English language—whether the book is for a first-grader or a college student. Here are two sample texts: one from an early primary-grade reader and another from a college textbook. In each case I have placed the noncontent words in bold type.

A Reading Passage: First- or Second-Grade Level

The baby wolf **is** eight week**s** old **now. She no** long**er** drink**s her** mother**'s** milk. **She** sniff**s and** lick**s at the** mouth **of an** adult wolf. **This is how she** ask**s for** food. **The** adult spit**s up some** food **for the** little wolf. **This may not** sound good **to you. But it is** perfect food **for a** grow**ing** baby pup.

—*Batten, 1998, p. 20*

Total words: 60

Total noncontent words: 32

Percentage noncontent words: 53%

A Reading Passage: College Level

In consign**ing this** manuscript **to a** desk drawer, **I am** comfort**ed by the** behavior **of** baseball player**s. There are no** pitcher**s who do not** give **up** home run**s, there are no** batter**s who do not** strike **out. There are no** major league pitcher**s or** batter**s who have not somehow** learned **to** survive giv**ing up** home run**s and** striking **out.**

—*Brownstein, Weiner, & Green, 1994, p. 41*

Total words: 59

Total noncontent words: 35

Percentage noncontent words: 59%

The noncontent words invariably occupy 50 percent or more of every page. This rule holds true no matter what book, newspaper, magazine, or other form of text you look at.

The relevance of this truth to the teaching of reading is apparent. Noncontent words represent a huge core of what children have to read from the moment they start reading. Think about it: 100 words make up 50 percent or more of every page you will ever read in your life. To put it another way, if we teach children these 100 words, they will be able to decode half of the words they see!

That of course is not the message children currently receive. Paradoxically, they are told that the majority of words on any page of text that they will ever read in their entire lifetimes are exceptions. Needless to say, that doesn't make much sense. Its primary effect is to create a major obstacle that stands in the way of children's developing the language awareness needed for accurate decoding.

Telling children that a majority of the words they see on a page are "exceptions" doesn't make much sense. Its primary effect is to create a major obstacle that stands in the way of their developing the abilities needed for accurate decoding.

Noncontent words attracted my interest about thirty years ago when I became aware of the different roles these words played in spoken and written language. In written language it was common knowledge—later supported by scientific studies (Tunmer & Hoover, 1992)—that many children had inordinate difficulty with these "little words." The source of the difficulty was rarely if ever tied to the neglect that marked the way in which they were taught. Instead the difficulties were taken as proof that the words were, indeed, troublesome exceptions to the system that were bound to plague both children and teachers. They were, and continue to be, an accepted and expected barrier in early reading instruction.

In spoken language, however, things were quite different. A landmark study had been carried out at Harvard University documenting the stages toddlers go through in learning to speak (Brown, 1973). After spending the first stage expressing simple relationships through content words, such as *big dog* and *Mommy fix,* they move into a stage where they do something quite amazing. While still tiny tots, they spend months figuring out how to insert into their simple two- and three-word utterances the noncontent words and part words such as *the, a, -ing* (as in *sitting*), *-ed* (as in *looked*), *in, on, -s* (as in *cookies*), *my,* and *that.* Though no one has, or could have, told them about it, the toddlers sense something that evades the consciousness of even very sophisticated adults: they recognize that for speaking and understanding language the noncontent words are essential, and so they devote considerable amounts of time and effort to the mastery of these words.

The contrast between spoken language and written language was striking. School-age children on the one hand were being directed to spend almost no time on the noncontent realm, and their reading was suffering. Two-years-olds on the other hand were spending a lot of time on that very same area of language, and their spoken language was blossoming. I was convinced that if reading instruction could emulate the time and effort toddlers put into the noncontent realm, the payoff could be enormous.

Giving Noncontent Words a Place in Reading Instruction. The role of noncontent words is not limited to dominating every page of text—although that fact alone makes them worthy of our attention. These words are also critical to understanding and using the grammar, or syntax, of our language. Reading instruction must be designed to move the powerful class of noncontent words out of the shadows to which they have been relegated and into the foreground, where they can illuminate the whole process of reading. That's why Phonics Plus Five makes them a key part of the instruction. It is the only reading system that does this. As you will see, all five of its reading programs are designed to devote as much time and attention to the noncontent words as to the content words. However, to convey their unique properties, they are taught by different methods.

Noncontent words occupy 50 percent or more of every page of text a person will ever read in a lifetime. They are also critical to the processes of syntax. That's why Phonics Plus Five makes them a key part of the instruction. It is the only reading system that does this.

Chapter Seven describes the complete set of training activities used to teach the words in the noncontent domain.

Component 6: Text

The Skills of Reading

Physical Skills		Language Skills			
Sequencing	Writing	Phonology	Semantics	Syntax	Text

The final component we will consider in this chapter is *text*, the way words and sentences are combined to create complete, meaningful messages (Halliday & Hasan, 1980). You are probably most familiar with the term through the word *textbook*, but *text* includes a wide range of books and other language materials. In terms of reading, the texts children experience fall into two groups:

1. *Books designed to be read to children.* These books play an important and highly pleasurable role in kids' lives. Most children love to have stories read to them, and even though these books are not often part of formal reading instruction, the listening experience leaves children eager to learn to read.

2. *Books designed for children to read on their own.* These books, which are part of children's reading instruction, ideally should allow children to accomplish their dream of independent reading. Unfortunately, they often have fundamental flaws that lead to the opposite result. The children face repeated failure that causes their motivation to vanish into thin air—to be replaced by dark clouds of fear, tension, and misery. Children who start out loving books can begin to avoid them like the plague.

ONE PARENT'S ACCOUNT OF HER CHILD'S DOWNWARD SPIRAL

Before Michael got into kindergarten, he was one of the most cheerful children I had ever seen. He had so many interests, but books were among his greatest love. He adored being read to and he relished retelling the stories that were read to him. In first grade, all that changed. He began to avoid books. The teachers registered some surprise at his "lack of interest in the ABCs." Still, they assured me that all children were different, and with a child as bright as Michael, things would definitely "begin to click."

My concerns were somewhat different. I saw a striking personality change overtake my son. His formerly alert and cheerful manner was being replaced by a shy, moody, insecure presence. He became less and less willing to engage in any of the literacy-based activities of the class, and his independence declined. By the middle of first grade, the teachers were no longer so sure that things would eventually click. They advised me to put Michael in a *pull-out* program where he, and several of his classmates, would receive special attention in reading.

We did it. It didn't help. My husband kept accusing Michael of "not trying," and Michael got gloomier and gloomier. When the word *reading* came up, his face would darken and he would blurt out what became his mantra, "Don't talk about it. I *hate* reading."

Although it may seem that books should be a central element of reading instruction, both phonics and whole language, albeit for different reasons, pay scant attention to the books they offer children. Phonics adherents see the decoding of words as essential, so almost all the training is on individual words. It is taken for granted that once children can decode the individual words they will automatically transfer these skills to the books they see—so long as the words are decodable (that is, so long as the children have been taught all the sounds contained in the words).

The Quantum Leap to Books.   There is, however, an enormous difference between what children see on the pages when they are learning to decode words and what they see on the pages when they are reading books. Most decoding training takes place via worksheets, where, to make things as clear as possible, a few words are widely spaced across a page. A typical exercise might appear as follows:

Directions: *Read the words and then in the space next to each one, write a word that rhymes.*

hot   _____

pin   _____

can   _____

lid   _____

mad   _____

rag   _____

This sort of task places limited demands on children. Even for kids who don't recognize a single word and who have to resort to sounding out each one, the situation is manageable. They can take as long as they want to figure out a word. No matter how much time it requires, it still has no effect on the word that follows. So even very slow sounding out does not hold up the rest of the work.

The introduction of books represents a quantum change, for even the simplest texts pose far more complexity than words in isolation. For a start, *easy readers* have what amounts to a lot of words for a child. Books for the earliest levels of reading will often proudly advertise that they contain "only thirty words!" To experienced readers that seems like a very small number. To a child at the start of the process that many words can be overwhelming.

Should you have any doubts about how thirty or so words can seem like an avalanche to a novice, just recall your experience with this twenty-six-word foreign-letter passage in Chapter One:

Δαν ηασ αν αξ.

Ηασ Δαν αν αξ?

Σαμ ηασ ηαμ.

Ηασ Σαμ ηαμ?

Δαν ηασ λανδ ανδ σανδ.

Ηασ Δαν σανδ?

Σαμ σατ.

Δαν σατ.

Remember that for children who have not yet learned to read, the letters that appear on a page can be as foreign as the ones in this passage are to you. Even if a child recognizes 80 percent of the words in a book instantly, 20 percent still have to be sounded out, resulting in decoding that is repeatedly marked by long pauses. During those pauses the child is likely to forget the words that came before. This pausing, plodding process has a relatively minor effect on worksheets, with their sparse number of words, but it has a devastating effect on texts. When the child perceives many of the words as unconnected units, the flow of the message is blocked. This experience is precisely the opposite of the way a text should be read and comprehended.

Further, although worksheets are almost bereft of noncontent words, texts are not. For example, in a story focused on the letter *h*, the child may see the following text:

Ted has a hat.

Tig gets Ted's hat.

Tig hid the hat.

Ed has Ted's hat.

Did the hat fit Ed?

Ed slid. Ted's hat fell.

Doll slid.

Doll hit the hat.

Ted's hat is flat.

At last, Ted has his hat.

Ted's hat is odd.

Ted is sad.

Ted left his hat.

Ted has the flag.

Ted is glad.

—Rowland, 1995, workbook 12

Though every attempt has been made to minimize the noncontent words, eighteen of the sixty words, or 30 percent, are still from that group, and an additional five words have noncontent part words, like -'s (indicating possession), for a total of 38 percent. When, as in a story, you have a message to transmit, those words cannot be avoided. Because their word training has downplayed noncontent words, children lack the skills to deal with them effectively when they appear in real text.

Equally important is the peculiarity of the text children are often given. Just read the previous example aloud, and you will see how weird the language sounds. People in real life simply do not express ideas in the way that text does. So after having finally reached the realm of text, children see stilted writing that is fundamentally lacking in meaning.

The large total number of words, the large number of noncontent words, and the stilted meaning are but three of the many factors in traditional phonics training that leave children unprepared to deal with even the simplest phonics-based texts they are given to read. Words are arranged in books in ways that do not mirror the training the children receive, causing books to trigger high rates of failure.

Phonics-based texts present children with language that does not mirror the training they have received. There are too many words, too many noncontent words, and too stilted a language, and children cannot decode these texts with the ease that is needed for competent reading.

The Reliance on Questionable Assumptions. Despite its emphasis on books, the other major system of reading instruction—whole language—also fails to provide the texts that children need. Adherents of this approach view children as already possessing, in their spoken language abilities, a rich inner base for effective reading. All the children need is the opportunity to experience appealing, authentic books, and their natural talents will take them the rest of the way.

That is why books used with whole language instruction are not specially designed for teaching. Indeed, it is a tenet of whole language that books should not be artificially created to teach particular patterns. Rather, they must be "authentic" and must contain the natural language that can arouse children's interest and imagination.

Those books are often wonderful to read *to* children. However, they are not wonderful for children to use in their learning. Authentic books are both longer and more complex than phonics-based texts, and they invariably engender even higher rates of error. Whole language supporters are generally not perturbed by these errors. They view them as part of the learning process. Children, though, do not view them in the same light. Like Michael, they rightly see them as irrefutable signs that they do not know how to read, and their only defense is to avoid the pain by avoiding reading.

As with the other reading skills, reading instruction must be reconfigured so that text plays a major and appropriate role. Children should see meaningful, connected language, and they should be taught the skills that allow them to read that language easily and effortlessly. The thirty books of the Phonics Plus Five system accomplish this goal through a number of features, including

1. Tightly controlling the initial books so that the number of words they contain is far fewer than in other systems.

2. Teaching, to high levels of mastery, all the words that will appear in a book, so that children never see words they do not know.

3. Systematically introducing the language structures found in authentic books, so that children will be fully prepared to deal with those books in the shortest possible time.

Chapter Eight describes the way these books are structured to achieve these goals, and Chapter Twelve shows you how to create these books.

Answers to Frequently Asked Questions

To get a fuller sense of how the system works, here are answers to the questions that parents most frequently ask about Phonics Plus Five.

1. Who is the program for?

Phonics Plus Five is aimed at children in the general school population or those who will be going into the general school population. The program is designed primarily for three groups:

- Young children who are four and one-half years of age and up whose parents want them to get into reading in a smooth, problem-free way and have a leg up in school. If your child has been attending preschool or kindergarten, then the program is likely to suit him or her well.

- Children in the early primary grades of school whose parents want them to attain the highest possible level of skill in reading, writing, and comprehension so that they shine in all aspects of literacy.

- Children in the primary grades who are, often inexplicably, experiencing difficulty in learning to read.

2. At what age can I start the program with my child?

I recommend starting the program when your child is about four and one-half to five years old. If you do, smooth patterns of reading are established at the outset and school performance is greatly improved. The basic requirement is that your child should, without strain, be able to work on tasks for fifteen to twenty minutes at a time.

3. Until what age can the program be used?

Phonics Plus Five can be used with children of any age who have been experiencing problems with traditional teaching. However, it is best if the program is used up through about fourth grade.

4. How long does the program take each day?

Each day's lesson takes only fifteen to thirty minutes, depending on which lesson you are doing and your child's proficiency with that particular task.

5. How many sessions should there be in a week?

The more frequent the sessions, the faster the progress. Children who are not yet in first grade should use the program at least four times per week. Children in first grade and up should use the program at least five times per week, and, if possible, they should use it every day.

6. Where does my child start in the system?

One of the major advantages of Phonics Plus Five is that your child works only on the skills he or she has not yet mastered. In other words, the system is designed to start a child off at exactly the right level and go at a pace that fits his or her needs. As a rule, children who have no reading skills, or very limited reading skills, start with the Get Set preparation programs. Children who have some reading proficiency start with one of the language and reading programs that best fits his or her level of skill. The actual determination is made more precisely using the guide in Section Three of this book.

7. How long does it take for my child to complete the program?

The length of time your child will need to complete the Phonics Plus Five system varies depending on your child's skills. To complete the entire set of programs takes about fifteen months, assuming your child is completing approximately five sessions a week. Some children can take a little longer (up to one and a half years). Many children, who already have some reading skills, can often complete the programs they work on in as few as three to six months.

8. What level of reading will my child achieve?

With completion of the final program, your child will be reading at about third-grade level. Of even greater importance, he or she will have a broad set of skills that will improve learning in all other areas. Among these are the ability to read with total accuracy, to attain fluent decoding, to develop accurate writing, and to achieve full understanding. These skills not only supply reading mastery, but of equal importance, they also supply the sense of confidence that effective reading requires.

9. Can the program be individualized for my child?

Absolutely. That is another great feature of Phonics Plus Five. Once you have started the programs, there are regular Progress Checks that tell you exactly what lessons your child needs to carry out. In the Get Set programs, once your child learns the skills he or she needs, you are shown how to move up to the next level. In the Boarding, Runway, Liftoff, Airborne, and Soaring programs, before each word is taught, your child is asked to complete a mini skills check by writing the word that is coming up. If he or she writes it correctly, the program moves on to the next word. So all your child's time is focused on learning material not known and not on what has already been learned.

10. *How do I know if my child is making progress?*

You will notice obvious progress almost immediately. You will see your child easily completing and remembering many reading and writing tasks. Further, the programs are designed to have you carry out Progress Checks on a regular basis. They are accompanied by guidelines that tell you how to move on, based on the results you have obtained.

11. *How does Phonics Plus Five fit with the program my child is using in school?*

Phonics Plus Five works extremely well with any other program your child may be using. As your child masters the hidden abilities of reading, all his or her learning skills improve, and so classroom performance and grades are naturally improved as well.

12. *My child has a learning disability. Can he or she use the program?*

Although Phonics Plus Five has been designed for children with typical abilities, children with learning disabilities can definitely benefit from it.

13. *I am worried about my child's progress with learning how to read, but my child's teacher tells me not to be concerned. She says "children are different," and she assures me that I should be patient. Should I be?*

Should you be patient while your child has difficulty with the single most important skill he or she needs for learning in life? No, obviously not! Although the common, well-intended advice is to be patient, it is not wise to follow it. Even if your child's skills were to even out in a couple of years, during that lag, your child is steadily comparing himself or herself to peers and is coming up short. The damage to morale and self-esteem cannot be overestimated. Additionally, as schools track students' progress, they are often categorized in ways that can have lasting negative consequences on their education. Why not offer your child every opportunity for success? There is no advantage in waiting for things to clear up and every advantage in helping your child succeed right now.

chapter 3

The Hidden Abilities in Reading

In addition to the six skills outlined in Chapter Two, effective reading rests on a powerful, but often overlooked system. It is best introduced through an example created by George Bernard Shaw, the renowned Irish playwright. As a passionate champion for literacy, he long fought for spelling reform. He was troubled by the many irregularities that exist in the English language. As evidence he took the word

fish

and justified spelling it this way:

ghoti

He explained that he was employing *gh* as it is used in the word *enough* for the sound of *f, o* as in *women* for the sound of the *i,* and *ti* as in *nation* for the sound of *sh.*

Shaw's proposed spelling makes a funny point—but for our purposes it also conveys another message. As clever as Shaw's example is, readers intuitively know that it could never exist in reality. We would simply never find a person who would ever pronounce *ghoti* as *fish.* At the same time, almost no one can explain precisely why *ghoti* can't be *fish;* people "just know" that it can't.

What they cannot verbalize are the implicit rules of English spelling, which preclude pronouncing *ghoti* as *fish* because

The *gh* pair can have an *f* sound but not when it starts a word—then it has a hard *g* sound, as in *ghost.*

The *o* can have the *i* sound but not in a one-syllable word.

The *ti* can have the *sh* sound but not without an adjoining *on.*

Our Amazing Hidden Abilities

Even though readers can't verbalize these and other rules, they can sense them and use them. In other words, hidden from their awareness but always working for them is a set of abilities that enables them to read and write in an easy and effortless manner. I call these skills *hidden abilities.*

We can find hidden abilities in all aspects of reading. For example, consider the following sentences:

We ought to **record** that he broke the **record.**

A large farm was used to **produce** the **produce.**

The dump was so full that it had to **refuse** the **refuse.**

I had to **subject** the **subject** to a series of tests.

The soldier decided to **desert** in the **desert.**

This is not the time to **present** the **present.**

Each sentence contains *homographs*—identically spelled words—that you decided, without hesitation, to pronounce differently. The key to these different pronunciations lies in the noncontent words that we discussed in the previous chapter, and knowing that key is one of our many hidden abilities.

Always working for successful readers is a set of hidden abilities that makes reading smooth, easy, and automatic.

One of the identically spelled words in each sentence was preceded by the word *the.* This cued you to expect the next word to be a noun—because *the* regularly precedes nouns. That led you to give the word the pronunciation it has when it is a noun. The other, identically spelled, word was preceded by *to.* This cued you to expect the next word to be a verb—because *to* regularly precedes verbs. That, in turn, led you to give the word the pronunciation it has when it is a verb.

Knowing How, Without Knowing Why

What exactly are these hidden abilities? Although they resist definition, the examples we just went through illustrate their essence. They are the skills that allow us to create amazingly intricate constructions with language without ever being aware of the reasons responsible for what we are doing.

They are also skills we have never been explicitly taught. No matter how much phonics instruction you received, for example, no one ever told you to use non-content words to help you determine the pronunciation of homographs when you see them in sentences. Instead, in the course of your learning to become a skilled reader, totally outside your awareness, you developed these hidden abilities and have been using them for years. They are extraordinarily powerful because they enable you to know exactly how you should proceed through the channels that reading demands without ever knowing why you are doing what you are doing.

Hidden abilities are the backbone of effective reading. They even enable us to overcome the many rules of traditional phonics that would hobble us if we actually applied what we have been taught. For example, if you ask a typical reader what sound the letters *ph* make, you will invariably be told that they make the sound *f.* The hours of traditional phonics training show their power. No other answer ever comes to our minds. Nevertheless, if we are skilled readers, when we come upon words like *uphill* or *shepherd,* we do not pause for even a second to wonder if we should consider saying *ufill* or *sheferd.*

Similarly, despite months of instruction in first grade, when we were taught that *at* is pronounced like the *at* of *cat,* we would not for a moment think of using that pronunciation in other words containing that letter combination, such as *great, attend, patrol, water, fatigue, station, watch, data, matrix,* and so forth. (If you're drawn to statistics, you might find it of interest that in over 70 percent of words with the letters *at,* those letters are not pronounced the way our first-grade teachers told us they were.)

Furthermore, we are not the least bit bothered by having broken the rules we so assiduously memorized in the primary grades. Our hidden abilities let us sense that these rules represent a miniscule, imprecise sampling of the skills that actually have to be applied if we are going to read effectively.

In language research it's long been recognized that hidden abilities are central to the remarkable skill young children show in learning to speak. Starting with a dozen or so words at about one year of age, youngsters at age five have a vocabulary consisting of thousands of words that they combine in complicated sentences. They do all this without the benefit of anyone teaching them the rules for saying what they learn to say. Their progress comes from steadily using their hidden abilities to crack the complex code that swirls about them.

Although this is an accepted fact of spoken language, it has never been an accepted fact of written language. Indeed, it is assumed that in this respect the two systems are dramatically different. As noted by David Elkind (1987), a leading developmental psychologist, "If learning to read was as easy as learning to talk . . . many more children would learn to read on their own. The fact that they do not, despite being surrounded by print, suggests that learning to read is not a spontaneous and simple skill" (p. 32).

But the fact is that learning how to speak properly is not as easy as we might assume. For instance, children do not do well if the language they have to depend on for learning to speak fluently comes out of a television. They need a parent or teacher who steadily adjusts his or her language so that it matches the child's level of understanding. Each and every day children observe many models and receive vast amounts of feedback that convey the patterns underlying all components of spoken language. This astonishingly elaborate and comprehensive system provides the basis for the hidden abilities of speaking.

Nothing comparable has ever been offered to children in the teaching of reading. When it is provided, as it is in Phonics Plus Five, the hidden abilities develop, just as they do in spoken language, and children then have the basis for truly effective reading.

How Some Kids Do It on Their Own

At this point you may be asking how the 60 percent of children who succeed in reading on their own do it without having this type of support. Although no firm answer can be offered to that question, research in reading has provided us with some clues.

Some individuals have remarkable skill in linking words with things they see. In the literature this is referred to as *naming ability*. They are the ones who rarely if ever have to face the annoying tip-of-the-tongue phenomenon. That's the unpleasant experience of wanting to name something but being unable to come up with the word. It seems to be stuck on the tip of your tongue.

Individuals with good naming ability are born with this skill, and in the first few years of their lives they use it for learning words easily and using those words to identify the things and people they see. When reading appears on the scene, this skill gives them an enormous advantage. Just as they can easily come up with the names for objects they see, they can easily come up with the names represented by the words they see. This lets their reading move at a fast pace and with high levels of accuracy. That's an enormous benefit. They simply bypass the slow, plodding reading that so many other kids have to endure.

Other individuals have great skill in visual memory. After looking at something once, they know it for life. The advantage this gives them in reading is phenomenal. It doesn't matter how they initially link the words they see with the words they hear. If they are receiving whole language teaching, someone might tell them the words; if they are learning phonics, they might sound out the words on their own; if they are watching TV, they might see the words in a commercial. Regardless of the source, they have to do this only once or twice. Having seen a word and then having been told what it "says," they do not have to analyze it or ponder it again. They see words clearly in their heads and can spell them with great ease. Repeated experiences of drearily sounding out the same word over and over again never become a part of their lives.

Still other individuals have the ability to do what has been termed "going beyond the information given." With minimal input they see the patterns that others develop only after many more experiences. When they apply these skills to reading, they are way ahead there too. Whereas others may be confused by all the "exceptions" they see on a page, these children are not in the least bit disturbed. They are not the ones who ask the teacher, "But why isn't *great* pronounced as *greet?* You told us the double-vowel rule, and so it should be *greet.*" These children are immune to the weaknesses and distortions of the rules they have been forced to memorize. None of their strength with words is conscious. In much the same way that children with other hidden abilities operate, they are adept at taking the experiences they have with a few exception words, such as *sure, come, love,* and *bread,* and coming up with groupings in their heads that reflect real language as opposed to the rules they have been taught.

Each of these abilities puts a child ahead in reading. For those few fortunate individuals who have more than one hidden ability, their reading will benefit even more. They are among the ones who never require formal instruction at all. When teachers talk about children like this, they often say such things as, "He'd have learned to read if he'd been raised in a closet." That's not quite true, of course. All kids need some input. However, relative to other children, the help that children with these abilities need is minimal.

In this respect reading is no different from any other skill. All abilities, from tennis to math to art, come more easily to some children than to others. That's why some kids on the baseball field are called *naturals*. What is important is that all children can get to a high and competent level of performance—if they are given the tools they need.

With programmed reading instruction that fosters their hidden abilities, children easily learn how to read and achieve their full potential.

That is what Phonics Plus Five does. It fosters the hidden abilities that are the backbone of truly effective reading. The system combines all the techniques and insights I have developed in forty years of working with children from every background and walk of life. Time and again, I have seen how, given the right tools, children can easily learn how to read and can achieve their full potential. By using this system, children gain the foundation needed for masterful reading. The door to reading opens wide!

PART 2

Teaching Reading

Teaching Sequencing

The Skills of Reading

Sequencing	Writing	Phonology	Semantics	Syntax	Text

The heart of the Phonics Plus Five system is its teaching programs. In this chapter you will find out how the physical skill of sequencing is developed.

Let's start with a simple fact of reading: if you are going to read English, you have to scan left to right. That's what you just did in reading this sentence. If we didn't adhere to this left-to-right rule, we could read right to left, or part left to right and part right to left or in any number of other combinations. This could result in your reading, for example, the word *right* in the first sentence in this paragraph as *right, ghirt, rhtig, thgir,* or *ghitr,* and you might start reading the complete sentence as *reading you fact simple Let's with have to English start,* or even, *fi uoy Let's thiw a edaring inggo ouy.* You get the idea. Without the left-to-right rule there are countless possibilities. With the left-to-right rule there is only one.

Left-to-right scanning is such an accepted fact of reading life that it may seem pointless to raise it. But even though you take it for granted, it is a skill you had to learn at some point when you were a child. In other languages words may be read from right to left or top to bottom. Children in countries using these other patterns must learn to sequence their reading and writing differently.

Reading: A Unique Way of Seeing the World

Although it is obvious that left-to-right sequencing is required for reading, far less obvious is the fact that reading (and here I include the reading of mathematical symbols) is the only visual activity requiring this skill. Everything else we perceive with our eyes can be scanned in a variety of directions without altering its meaning.

As we saw in Chapter Two, in looking at objects in the real world, people for the most part ignore the left-to-right sequence as it relates to identifying what they see. So just imagine being a child who has spent the first four to five years of his or her life learning to overlook the left-to-right sequence of objects and who then enters school and suddenly confronts a new world in which the sequence of objects (letters) forms the very basis of understanding. Once children begin learning how to read, even minute changes in the left-to-right sequence become critical. This awareness of sequencing is how a child can tell the difference between

b	d
p	q
pot	top
tea	eat

The issue of sequencing became prominent in the 1920s through the pioneering work of a physician, Samuel Orton (1928). Creating the term *strephosymbolia,* meaning "twisted symbols," he maintained that difficulties in sequencing were central to reading problems. This led to the view that *reversals* (such as seeing *b* for *d,* or *saw* for *was*) were a sign of neurological dysfunction and dyslexia.

Over the years this idea was discounted, as many children, not simply those with dyslexia, showed signs of reversing words and letters in early reading. So the notion of reversals as a telltale symptom was abandoned, to be replaced by the idea that failures in sequencing were a normal part of development. Currently, the dominant view of sequencing in reading education is that children will "pick it up." So even though it is a critical skill required for reading, it is never taught in a systematic manner. As happens with many skills, some kids do pick it

Despite the fact that left-to-right sequencing is a critical skill required for reading, it is never taught in a systematic manner.

up without instruction. But with no effort made to assist those who are having difficulty, many children are also left behind.

The Results of Not Seeing Sequence

Sequencing issues extend into realms generally not thought about even though they have profound consequences for reading. Seeing the letters of a word in the correct sequence is only a first step. If the sequence is to be useful, it must stay in the child's mind once the word has disappeared from view. If that fails to happen, the child has no means of recognizing the word when it reappears.

Imagine, for example, a child who does scan left to right and sounds out each letter in a word like *spot*. For that activity to pay off, the sequence now has to be retained in his or her mind. Should that not happen, when this sequence of letters appears again the child has no means of determining what the word is. All he or she can do is to repeat the tedious sounding-out process to determine, once again, the word in view.

These problems are a direct consequence of current instruction. Having failed to recognize the importance of retaining visual sequences, it has created no place for this skill in the curriculum. As a result, failures in word recognition have become the accepted norm in reading.

Worried parents often bring up this issue with teachers because they are, rightly, troubled to see their children not recognizing words they have seen over and over again. Typically, the parents are assured that over time the laborious sounding out will automatically be converted into the instant word recognition that true reading demands. For far too many children this does not happen.

The retention of letter sequences may be so poor that children fail to recognize words they have just sounded out. That's why you may see them sounding out a word even when they completed sounding out the same word just seconds before in the line above. This is comparable to having to relearn the names of simple, basic objects such as *cookie, chair, bed,* and *dog* every time you see them. Without a solid memory for visual sequences, reading is a grinding chore.

Because children are not taught how to remember the sequences of letters in words, they do not recognize words they have seen before. Failures in word recognition make reading unbearable. But the pattern is so widespread that, instead of being viewed as a problem, failures in word recognition have become the accepted norm in reading.

How Is Your Child Doing?

This section offers you a way to see if your child has developed the visual sequencing needed for reading. If your child is consistently and accurately reading and writing at least twenty-five words, you might want to skip this section, because he or she has probably developed the necessary skills. But if your child has not started reading or is at the very beginning of the process, you might want to try the following set of activities.

Step 1. Prepare some small blank cards on which you and your child can write letters. As in a Scrabble-like game, set out two rows of these small cards, one above the other, on which your child sees something like the following activity for the word *plant:*

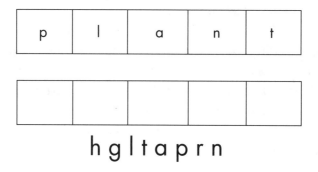

Each of the cards in the top row contains a letter of the word, with the letters combining to form the complete word. Under the bottom row, there is a larger set of letters that includes all the letters in the word *plant* and also some letters that are not in that word.

Step 2. Using the bottom letters, your child has to copy the word *plant.* Do not name the word or the letters. Simply say, "Start here [*pointing to the first blank card on your child's left*], and use the letters to make this word." Now watch what your child does and record it by writing down the order in which your child enters the letters. Make sure not to offer any corrections.

Step 3. Repeat this activity with the words *robot, jump, start, walk,* and *candy.* For each word, write down what your child does.

Step 4. If, on three or more of the words, your child enters the letters in any order other than the left-to-right sequence, it is likely that his or her left-to-right sequencing is problematic. This is so even if the final product is spelled correctly. For example, in copying the word *plant,* your child might enter an *a* in the middle position, then a *t* in the end position, and so on, but even though the letters are in the right boxes, they have not been entered in left-to-right sequence.

When that is the case, you can stop the activity because you have the information you need. Your child will benefit from the sequencing training offered in the Sequences in Sight program. However, if your child does show perfect left-to-right entry of the letters (that is, with the word *plant,* the *p* is entered before the *l,* the *l* before the *a,* and so on), move on to steps 5 through 8, which involve hiding the model from view.

Step 5. Ask your child to look at another word, such as *truck:*

t	r	u	c	k

Step 6. Using a blank sheet of paper, cover the word *truck* so that it is hidden from view. Then, show the blank cards with letters underneath, as illustrated here:

k r l t a u r c

Point to the first blank card on your child's left and say, "Start here, and use the letters to make the word you just saw." Again, offer no guidance and avoid naming the word or the letters. You want to see what your child does independently.

Step 7. Repeat this activity with the words *plane, trip, house, talk,* and *going.*

Step 8. If your child, on at least four of the hidden words, consistently starts at the left and proceeds to the right, entering all the letters correctly, then you have strong evidence that he or she has the sequencing skills needed for reading. If, however, that is not what has happened, you have still acquired important information. Even though your child saw the word only seconds before, once it is out of sight, he or she has no solid memory of it. There is no need to view this as a source of concern. What you have done is to spot one of the key skills your child needs for reading success. You can then move on to provide the necessary training, which is simple to carry out.

What Children Need to Learn

In trying to teach any skill, we always face the temptation to try to resolve the problem by simply telling the child what to do. In the case of teaching sequencing, we might want to say to the child, "Start paying attention to left-to-right direction."

That is not the way to go. Sequencing skills, like the other hidden abilities of reading, do not develop through learning explicit rules. Children may easily spout the rules, but they will have little or no effect on what they do. The necessary abilities emerge only through repeated, carefully constructed exercises that establish smooth, automatic scanning patterns. Further, if possible, the training should take place prior to the teaching of actual words. Unless it does, children will of necessity apply their available but inappropriate scanning skills to the words that they first read and write, thereby setting in place methods that do not work. To develop the necessary skills, carefully constructed exercises are provided at the very start of reading via Sequences in Sight—the program in the Phonics Plus Five system that teaches visual sequencing.

Before learning more about the Sequences in Sight activities, it is useful to understand what children will not be doing in this program. At no point in the program will they be working with familiar letters. This may seem strange, because the end goal is for them to recognize the sequence of the letters in actual words. There is, however, a good reason for avoiding familiar letters. Familiarity actually works against the development of effective sequencing.

Parents who have watched their children studying for spelling tests have probably unknowingly experienced this phenomenon. The students dutifully memorize lists of words by repeatedly saying a word and then naming the letters it contains. The students might sound like this:

help	aych ee el pee
help	aych ee el pee
help	aych ee el pee
start	ess tee ay ar tee
start	ess tee ay ar tee
start	ess tee ay ar tee
join	jay oh ie en
join	jay oh ie en
join	jay oh ie en

This effort seems to yield some short-term benefits. On a test given during the week of their studying, children may even achieve a 100 percent correct score. But if they are asked two or three weeks later to write or spell the same words, they have often completely forgotten how.

This result is not surprising. For the vast majority of people, memory of sets of disconnected items rapidly disappears. For example, recall the times you have looked up a number in a telephone directory and diligently held it in mind—until you dialed it. Once that was done, you forgot the number. We simply do not hold that sort of information in mind. That's why naming of letters has no long-term payoff for word recognition.

How then do we teach children to use and retain sequences of letters? Odd as it may seem, it is best to start by avoiding letters that can be easily named. When children have to retain sequences of letters for which they have no names, they are drawn to visualization—which is precisely what we wish to achieve.

Still, from as young as two years of age, children practice letter naming. It's probably the most common educational activity. So where are we to find unnamable letters?

The answer is to be found in the foreign symbols we used in the earlier chapters. They show us that there are many letters in the world that are unfamiliar to us, letters whose names we've never heard. When the goal is visualization, these foreign symbols are perfect. They have all the properties of real letters because they are real letters. At the same time, because they are foreign, we do not have names for them.

Key Features of the Program

The use of unnamable foreign symbols is one key component in teaching visual sequencing. It is combined with several other features that enable children to develop the hidden abilities responsible for effective sequencing. These features involve using materials that mirror key aspects of reading without requiring actual reading. In particular these materials

- Introduce short left-to-right sequenced patterns that smooth children's introduction to this feature of print. Sequencing is so novel that even sequences of just two elements can be problematic. Therefore the initial training starts with short patterns, which will be easiest for your child.

- Involve sequences that must be held in memory, so that the child retains a visual image of the sequence. It is only through activities that demand memory that children begin to retain the unique sequences needed for reading.

• Present sequences that increase in length until they involve at least four symbols. Most words contain at least this many symbols so any training patterns should as well. Unless children can scan sequences of this length, they will not be able to retain the words they will regularly confront.

To see these guidelines translated into operation, it is useful to look at the sorts of activities your child will be dealing with when the program is put into action, as described in Part Three of this book.

Level 1

At the outset your child sees two rows of symbols, with the top row presenting a short, two- or three-symbol sequence. In the example that follows, the sequence in the top row contains two symbols ($\delta \phi$). The bottom row contains the same two symbols along with additional ones.

$$\delta \ \phi$$

$$\gamma \ \delta \ \phi \ \lambda$$

You point to the top row and say, "Look at these." Then you point to the first symbol on the left in the bottom row and say, "Find the ones down here that are the same as the ones at the top." Your child needs to point, in the correct left-to-right order, to the same two symbols in the bottom row that appear in the top row.

This type of activity is repeated, over several sessions, until your child displays a high level of skill. At that point your child has become familiar with the first of the hidden abilities outlined in this chapter. He or she is scanning, in left-to-right order, short sequences with elements that are difficult to label.

Level 2

At level 2 of the Sequences in Sight program, memory is introduced. You can see how this is accomplished by completing the following activity example yourself. First, look at the sequence of symbols. Once you feel you know what the sequence is, cover the symbols so you can no longer see them.

$$\psi \ \pi \ \sigma$$

Now, without looking back, move on to the example that follows this sentence, and select, in left-to-right order, the symbols you just saw in the previous example:

$$\psi \ \gamma \ \pi \ \sigma \ \lambda$$

At this point you are working from memory. When you can't see the original model, the only way you can make the correct selection is by retaining an image of the original pattern. It is not an easy task, but with a bit of effort kids can do it. What is more, they see it as a challenging game that they are motivated to conquer. With its mastery, the base for remembering sequences of visual elements is in place—ready to be used with real words.

Level 3

Once your child has become accustomed to using memory for sequences involving two and three symbols, the patterns increase to four symbols. Although four is just one more than three, it represents a quantum leap in difficulty. So when the longer patterns are introduced, the teaching reverts to direct matching with no demands for memory. In other words, both lines of symbols appear simultaneously (as they did in level 1). A four-symbol task might appear as follows:

δ φ δ θ

δ θ φ λ δ θ

Level 4

In the final level of the program, your child returns to using memory—this time for all the sequences, whether they consist of two, three, or four elements. At the conclusion of this step your child has achieved the sequencing skill necessary for effective reading of actual words.

Depending on your child's rate of progress, the sequencing skills program generally takes from three to five weeks to complete. Keep in mind that all children do not go through the program. It is implemented only if a skills check, like the one described earlier in this chapter, indicates that your child needs to develop these skills. As with all Phonics Plus Five programs, when your child already has the skills taught in a program, you can bypass that program. The key throughout is to meet your child's individual needs. Children never go through the tedium of relearning skills they have already mastered. However, if they do need a set of skills, the programs offer them the full range of teaching that allows their abilities to blossom. You can find precise instructions for constructing the Sequences in Sight program in Chapter Nine.

We now move on to Chapter Five and an examination of the teaching of hand-writing—the second set of physical skills that prepares your child for reading.

Teaching Handwriting

The Skills of Reading

Sequencing	Writing	Phonology	Semantics	Syntax	Text

O ver the years I have seen hundreds of children who are bright but still struggling to produce their ABCs. Their problems are rarely caused by their lack of familiarity with the alphabet. Like most American kids, they have had endless experience with letters, and they know them well. Instead, their troubles arise when they have to create, or write, the actual letters when they are asked to do so.

All sorts of problems emerge. Big letters, like *k* and *h,* may be made small, and small letters, like *i* and *c,* may be made big; letters that should stay on the line, like *s* and *a,* may float up in space, and letters that should cross the line, like *g* and *p,* may rest on it.

In addition, inconsistency seems to be the rule rather than the exception. Children regularly produce the same letters in different ways and at times end up with identical letters having almost no resemblance to each other across the lines.

This goes against everything that handwriting should be. Like any motor skill, if it is to be useful, it has to be executed with smooth, automatic, efficient, and consistent movements. Imagine what would happen if every time you drove your car, you changed the way you did things. It would not only be annoying and confusing but in the end your driving would be disastrous. That essentially is what many children experience when they write, and it has profound effects on their progress in literacy.

Parents often spot the problems their children are having, but the conventional wisdom advises them to "stop worrying, because children will develop the skill over time." The reality, however, is that poor habits, once established, are unlikely to change. In fact, it takes more effort to unlearn a bad habit than to learn the behavior correctly in the first place.

Nevertheless, the resistance to setting up effective handwriting training runs deep. Ironically, the resistance stems from practices that were put in place in the hope of making kids like writing more, rather than less.

When Good Intentions Go Awry

When public education began, during the nineteenth century, training in handwriting was emphasized, generally not under the most pleasant of circumstances. The schools, dominated by the strict Victorian values of the time, were poorly equipped, joyless places, where children were typically required to perform dreary, repetitive tasks. Endless penmanship drill fit neatly into the system—not because it was in the children's interests but because it was one of the easiest and cheapest activities to carry out.

Around the turn of the twentieth century more child-friendly attitudes were advanced, championed by leaders such as the noted American philosopher and educator John Dewey. Over the next few decades progressive education began to take hold, and with its ascendancy came a strong reaction against the harsh practices that had dominated classroom instruction. A guiding motto became "drill is kill," conveying the message that learning was harmed rather than helped by relentless, boring repetition. Handwriting, as a prime representative of boring activity, was greatly affected. Essentially, sustained penmanship practice was halted. Since then, teaching of handwriting has largely been light, unsystematic, and optional.

We are witnessing the results of this change today. Generally, the amount of time given to handwriting training and the sequencing of that training are left totally to the teacher's discretion. This has resulted in a steady and marked decline in the teaching of this skill, to the point that penmanship instruction time for children in the first three years of school averages a scant five to ten minutes a week. This is scarcely sufficient to develop the smooth, fluid movements that effective handwriting requires.

There is little to suggest, moreover, that things will improve in the foreseeable future, because teachers are receiving the message that the area is not significant. Kate Gladstone, a champion of handwriting reform and National Director for the Annual American Handwriting Competition, states that over 95 percent of the top education colleges do not offer any training in handwriting (personal communication, July 24, 2005).

Writing Demands Increase

Ironically, as handwriting has been downplayed, writing itself has been emphasized, owing to the whole language movement. A key goal in this approach is to have children write about their experiences as early as possible—even in the years prior to first grade. The idea is that interest in writing is far more productive than drill in handwriting and that children will produce effective letters if they have an "authentic" reason to send a message. So handwriting is embedded in "real" writing; that is, writing that has meaning. Children can write any way they choose—the smooth, effective production of letters is inconsequential. The aim is to have them produce messages they want to convey. The belief—which is totally without foundation and in violation of everything we see—is that with practice, handwriting will steadily improve. The reality is that children left to their own devices produce handwriting that is endlessly variable and phenomenally inefficient.

This outcome is unavoidable, because the current situation forces children to grapple simultaneously with two skills: handwriting, a physical skill, and composing, a language skill. Each is challenging to a new student, making it difficult to get both of them correct. Typically, the kids concentrate very hard on what they want to say and attention to the construction of the letters themselves falls by the wayside. Required to carry out extended writing activities before they have mastered handwriting, the children can respond in no other way than by resorting to immature skills. With repeated practice these immature approaches become ingrained and increasingly hard to overcome.

As the teaching of handwriting has declined, demands for writing have increased—even at the kindergarten level. The end result is that children are left to their own devices, producing handwriting that is endlessly variable and highly inefficient.

As children encounter repeated frustration in trying to produce readable writing, their enthusiasm evaporates. The end result is a near epidemic of poor handwriting. Even worse, many young pupils begin to talk about "hating" to write, and to devise ways to avoid it. The misery that begins to surround this activity is reflected in one handwriting program's title—*Handwriting Without Tears,* by Jan Olsen.

It doesn't have to be this way. What children need are solid techniques that simplify the process of letter recognition and construction. This chapter introduces those techniques. The fact is that the key skills of letter recognition and construction can be learned easily with the right methods.

How Is Your Child Doing?

At this point you may already be certain that your child would benefit from training in handwriting. You've watched him or her write often enough to know that help is needed. If that is the case you can bypass the remainder of this section because you have the information you need. However, if you are wondering how to judge your child's writing efforts, you might want to try the following short set of activities to help you make a determination.

Step 1. Start by taking a blank sheet of $8\frac{1}{2}$-by-11-inch paper and placing two rows of lines on it. Then, as shown here, on the top row of lines, print the letters *c j o u p s*.

Step 2. Once you have the paper prepared, sit with your child and provide him or her with a thin marker or pencil. Point to the *c* and, without naming it, say, "Here is a letter." Then point to the blank line under the *c*, and say, "Now make one just like it down here." Do not offer any guidance or corrections. Continue in this way until your child has reproduced all six letters. As your child creates a letter, note whether he or she starts the letter at its top or starts it from the line and then goes up.

Step 3. When your child has finished, score each letter on the following points:

Point A: starting point. The letter has been produced by starting at the top.

Point B: placement. The letter is placed correctly relative to the line (the letters *c, s, u,* and *o* must touch the line; the letters *j* and *p* must "break" the line and go below it).

Point C: size. The size of the letter is similar to the size of the model letter you produced (it is neither significantly bigger nor significantly smaller).

Point D: shape. The letter has the correct shape (*c* is rounded; *j* has a straight line ending in a curve; *o* is circular; *u* has an open, cup shape; *p* has a straight line with a circular shape in the appropriate place; and *s* has two curves in correct orientation to each other).

Use a form like the Chart for Scoring the Letters for evaluating each letter on the four points. Enter a score of 1 when the letter meets a point; leave the box empty when the letter does not meet that point. There is obviously a level of subjectivity in the scoring. The goal is to try to be as objective as possible but don't be overly concerned. Just let your first impression guide you, because it usually is right.

Chart for Scoring the Letters

	Letter					
	c	**j**	**o**	**u**	**p**	**s**
Point A						
Point B						
Point C						
Point D						

If your child achieves a score of 20 or more points, it is likely that his or her handwriting skills are up to the mark for effective handwriting. However, if your child's score is below 20, it is likely that he or she will benefit from the handwriting training offered in Letters to Write—the program in the Phonics Plus Five system that teaches handwriting.

What Children Need to Learn

As you learn about the Letters to Write program, you may find yourself surprised at not seeing components that you have come to expect as part and parcel of handwriting activities. There is a good reason for their omission. Despite their prevalence, they work against children's progress. It's useful to understand what these commonplace components are.

The Capital Game: Rethinking the ABCs

The first component is a familiar one in initial letter training. You can see it at work in the example shown here, which was created by a highly motivated four-year-old.

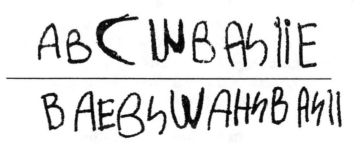

If you're familiar with young children's writing, this writing sample seems perfectly fine. You are probably neither surprised nor disturbed to see that all the letters are capital letters (they are *uppercase*). As in the following additional writing samples, this is what you have come to expect young children's writing to look like.

But think for a moment about the material children read. That material—just like the vast majority of the material adults read—is almost entirely in small letters (*lowercase*). It's a simple fact of reading: only a tiny percentage of the letters that appear on any page are in uppercase. The following segment from a story for beginning readers illustrates the point.

Bears are curious.

They are almost always

hungry, too.

<u>T</u>his mother bear

and her cubs

are looking for

something good to eat.

<u>T</u>he mother bear

sniffs the air.

<u>H</u>er nose tells her

that bees are living

in the hollow tree.

—Milton, 1998, pp. 4–5

Of the 170 letters in these segments, only 5 are capitals. All the rest are lowercase. As a general rule, fewer than 10 percent of the words on a page appear with even one capital letter, and far fewer than 1 percent of all the letters appear as capitals.

Children's training, though, is set up as though the exact opposite were true. Almost all the alphabet material they are given shows capital letters dominating. Even when lowercase letters are included in the early activities, they often play second fiddle to the uppercase letters. On a typical worksheet, for example, the child first sees a letter in uppercase and, to its right, its lowercase version. The child's task is to make several copies of the letter.

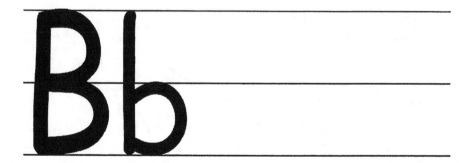

With its prominent position (first in the left-to-right sequence) and its large size, the capital letter clearly conveys the message that *it* is the more important member of the pair. As the following writing sample shows, children get the message. Although the writer started off maintaining the uppercase and lowercase distinction for the first few letters, by the end of the first line, that distinction is lost. All the letters, big and small, have the uppercase shape.

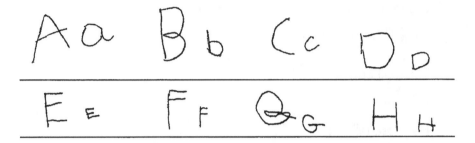

It is reasonable to teach children that letters have both an uppercase and lowercase format, and that the uppercase format plays a unique role in marking the start of certain letter sequences, such as the first letter in sentences and names. However, when the teaching emphasizes letters that occur only a tiny percentage of the time, children learn to focus on the wrong component and to develop poor habits. The uppercase emphasis is responsible for the erratic patterns many children show in their writing. Instead of confining capital letters to the starting word of a sentence and a few names, children sprinkle capitals liberally throughout their words and sentences. They're showing that they know both formats exist but that they haven't been taught how those formats operate.

The current approach to teaching the alphabet has the huge disadvantage of creating a chasm between the process of reading and the process of writing. Essentially, the children's training in reading has them using the lowercase forms of letters, while their training in writing emphasizes the uppercase forms of letters. Instead of the two processes supporting

A high school student consulted me for help in his essay writing. He showed me samples of his work, with every letter in uppercase. When he was asked about this, he flashed a winning smile as he said, "In the early grades I never could figure out where and when to use capital letters, and I kept getting back my papers with red marks because of all the mistakes. Then in the fourth grade I was able to convince my teacher to let me do all my writing in uppercase. After that the other teachers went along with it, and I have been writing that way ever since."

one another, they are presented as two different systems—with the children left to figure the differences on their own.

For effective mastery the initial teaching should be modified to highlight the similarities between reading and writing, not the differences. This goal is best achieved by downplaying the uppercase and emphasizing the lowercase alphabet. This approach is a key feature of the Letters to Write program. It achieves two major aims: (1) children end up with a

In traditional education the early teaching of writing emphasizes uppercase letters, even though fewer than 1 percent of the letters on the pages children read appear in uppercase. This leads to a conflict between their children's reading system and their writing system.

unified system for reading and writing, and (2) children are helped to get past barriers that if not overcome will hamper their handwriting for years to come.

The Order of Teaching: Why C-L-I-O Is Better Than A-B-C

The order in which letters are taught is another key dimension in writing. Which letters should be taught first, and which ones should follow?

Almost always the answer has been to rely on the order of the alphabet itself, just as we and our children hear it in the "The Alphabet Song":

A B C D E F G

H I J K L M N O P

Q R S and T U V

W X and Y and Z.

Now I know my ABCs.

Next time won't you sing with me?

It seems so natural to start with A and end with Z. Practically all handwriting books for children are set up in this manner. Because we are so used to it, it seems to make perfect sense. After all, it is alphabetical order!

To an early reader, though, it doesn't make any sense at all. The key to whether or not a child will produce an accurate letter rests, not with alphabetical sequence, but with the complexity of the letter's shape. Some letters have simple shapes, such as the circle of an *o*, whereas others have far more complex shapes, such as the intersecting diagonals of an *x*.

It just so happens that the first letter in the alphabet, whether uppercase *A* or lowercase *a*, is in the complex category:

- The uppercase *A* requires two diagonal strokes—a type of line that young children typically find hard to master before seven or eight years of age.

- The lowercase *a* requires two strokes (a circular *c* shape on the left and a straight line on the right) that must be carefully aligned. If they aren't aligned, they won't form an *a*. The tight alignment of parts is another feature young children often find difficult.

It simply makes no sense to start letter production with one of the hardest letters for children to write, even if it is the first letter in the alphabet. It's like trying to teach children to walk before they can crawl. The teaching of any skill should build systematically from the simple to the more complex.

The letter *b* is also complex and difficult for children to produce. The letter *c*, in contrast, is fairly simple. Not only is it made with a single line (rather than two different lines), but that single line takes a circular shape. Circles are the first shapes children draw, largely because they are the easiest to make.

The letter a is one of the most complex of all letters. Its position as the first letter of the alphabet is no basis for making it the first letter children should be taught to write.

So the letter *c* is among the first set of letters that is taught. In that set as well are all the other letters that are composed of single, unbroken strokes—the simplest type of stroke for a child to produce. These letters are *l*, *i*, *o*, and *j*.

Further, in contrast to the typical setup in writing practice, in this program a page is never devoted to a single letter that the child is to repeat over and over again. Instead, across any page the letters steadily change. After producing a *c*, for example, the child might be asked to make a *j*, and the letter after that might be an *o*.

This interweaving mirrors a key aspect of real words—the letters constantly change. A child never sees a word like *aaaa* or *bbbbb*. Even the simplest three-letter words contain varied letters (such as *c-a-t*, *d-o-g*, *k-i-d*, *r-u-n*, and so on). By having to deal with this feature from the outset, children are better prepared for the writing of real words.

At the next level, letters with more complex shapes are added. These are letters such as *f*, *t*, and *e*, which involve two or more shapes that have to intersect with one another.

Following that, letters like *a, b, h,* and *m* are added. These are among the most complex letters to produce, because they require retracing, or repeating, part or all of a line that has already been made. For example, in constructing an *h,* after making the long vertical line, the child has to go up part of that same line to complete the ∩ shape that has to be added.

All of this means that in the Phonics Plus Five handwriting program, the teaching is organized not by the alphabet but by the complexity of the letter shapes. The end result is learner-friendly material that makes the writing process easier, faster, and smoother.

The Naming Game: Rethinking the *Ayes,* the *Bees,* and the *Cees*

Another traditional given in teaching children the alphabet is the naming of letters. Letter naming occupies vast amounts of time in the preschool and kindergarten curriculum. In some programs children are not even permitted to move on to handwriting until they have demonstrated the ability to name every letter.

Ironically, learning the names of the letters is totally unnecessary for a child who is learning how to read! In reading, children have to recognize the letters. They do not have to name them. Recognition is independent of naming. For example, we all can recognize people we see on a regular basis, such as cashiers in supermarkets, without ever knowing their names. Similarly, a child can learn how to read perfectly well without ever learning the names of letters. A child needs to learn to recognize the letters and to know the sounds they make.

Despite the emphasis it receives, learning the names of letters has nothing to do with learning how to read. A child can learn to read perfectly well without ever learning the names of letters.

There is nothing wrong with children learning the names of letters, if they want to do it and it comes easily to them. From the point of view of teaching, however, there is no need to require children to learn, or use, the names of letters. So this program has been designed to have the child learn to write effectively, without imposing the unnecessary requirement of learning the names of the letters.

Being There

Generally, when children are asked to write, they are given pages containing models of the letters, and they are asked to copy or trace these letters. Again, this is such an accepted practice that it seems unassailable.

Like many other accepted practices we've been considering in this book, however, it doesn't work. The fine motor skills of writing are intricate, and children need steady and immediate feedback on the work they are producing. A young child does not benefit from incorrectly producing a whole page of letters and then being told that the work needs to be changed.

You will find it far more effective to sit with your child and, for each letter, to provide the information he or she needs to produce it. This is best accomplished by modeling, by creating the letter while your child is watching. In this way your child can see the precise manner in which the letter is produced and then follow that pattern in creating the letter independently.

Even with the simplest letters this process is invaluable, because it helps children with the many decisions they must make. Should the line of a letter start at the bottom and go up, or should it start at the top and go down? Should the circular motion for a letter like *o* start with the left side or the right side? Should a letter like *p*, which crosses the line, be made in a continuous stroke or not? Because modeling—without a word—readily answers questions like this, it is one of the most productive means of encouraging effective learning.

Supporting the Hand

The next point we are going to consider may come as something of a surprise, because, in my experience, it is almost never used in teaching handwriting. Specifically, you might find it extremely useful to support your child's wrist when he or she is writing.

As I pointed out in Chapter Two, the act of writing calls on a range of intricate motor skills that without the proper techniques can be hard to master. Children, particularly those under six years of age, can have trouble maintaining the necessary physical stability without giving up on something else. That something else is usually the smooth execution of the letters. With the wrist supported, stability is ensured, and the child is free to focus on the central issues—namely, shape and movement. (Incidentally, if your child makes a lot of tongue and mouth movements when writing, it's a strong sign that hand support will be useful.)

As shown in the accompanying illustration, the support is provided by lightly placing your palm under your child's wrist, with your index finger under his or her thumb. If your child is right-handed, sit to your child's right and use your left hand to provide the support. If your child is left-handed, sit to your child's left and use your right hand to provide the support. As your child's wrists and hands become stronger with age, he or she will no longer require the support.

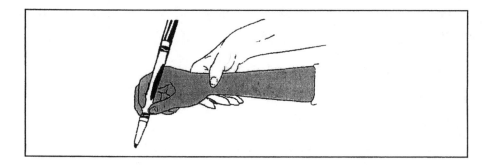

Although the benefits can be impressive, some parents resist the suggestion for wrist support. Typically, their first reaction is, "But he can do it on his own!" That's true. However, much better letters are produced when the wrist is supported. In addition, the support pays off in the long run because the child will have more effective handwriting when he or she starts to write independently.

Key Features of the Program

The many inefficient practices associated with handwriting instruction have given the task of writing a less than desirable reputation. All of this can be changed through simple, systematic teaching. I have seen, over and over again, parents who are amazed and delighted at how easy it can be to get their children to write effectively and who in the process also see their children take great pride in their writing accomplishments.

The systematic instruction is not, and should not be, boring. Effectively organized and presented, the lessons can be limited—in terms of both the daily time required and the total length of time needed to complete the process. In Phonics Plus Five the daily letter-construction sessions generally run under ten minutes, and the total handwriting program process is completed in about four to six weeks.

The key program features that allow effective handwriting to be achieved include

- Emphasizing lowercase, not uppercase, letters
- Sequencing letters from simple to complex shapes, and not in alphabetical order
- Avoiding naming of the letters
- Developing consistent patterns for producing the letters
- Supporting your child's hand

All the work is carried out on an $8\frac{1}{2}$-by-11-inch worksheet with two rows of lines, as shown in the following example. For each letter the adult models the letter on the top row, and the child immediately reproduces the letter on the bottom row.

Worksheet for Writing Letters

_____	_____	_____	_____	_____	_____
_____	_____	_____	_____	_____	_____

The Phonics Plus Five handwriting program contains five levels.

Level 1

In the first level the child learns the letters *c, i, j, l,* and *o,* that is, letters that are restricted to single strokes and simple shapes.

Level 2

At the second level the double-shape letters *e, f, k, s,* and *t* are introduced. All the letters from level 1 are maintained as well. Each of the new letters is drawn in two separate steps, so that the child has the chance to focus on the way each of the strokes is constructed.

Level 3

The letters used in level 2 continue, but in level 3 all are now produced in a single step.

Level 4

In level 4 all the remaining letters—*a, b, d, g, h, m, n, p, q, r, u, v, w, x, y,* and *z*—are introduced. Many require retracing, which means going over part or all of an already drawn line. As in level 2, these letters are constructed in two steps. All the letters from the previous levels continue to be produced as well.

Level 5

Your child is now constructing all the letters of the alphabet in a single step. He or she is ready to use these skills in writing real words and sentences.

Precise instructions for constructing the Letters to Write program are available in Chapter Ten.

chapter 6

Teaching Content Words

The Skills of Reading

Sequencing	Writing	Phonology	Semantics	Syntax	Text

O nce the physical skills are in place, your child is ready to move on to reading and writing words. Words, or more accurately one group of words, have long been at the center of reading instruction. These are the content words—the ones we're used to thinking about as *words*. They are primarily the nouns, verbs, adjectives, and adverbs of our language, such as *cat, run, big,* and *really.* In this chapter we'll cover the way in which content words are taught in the five Phonics Plus Five reading programs: Boarding, Runway, Liftoff, Airborne, and Soaring.

Figuring Out the Words

When a child is just starting to read, a page of print looks like little more than an array of meaningless squiggles. For reading to happen, the child has to transform that jumble into meaningful words. Most of the teaching time in the primary years is aimed at having children master this aspect of reading.

Invariably, the route to success is deemed to rest with sounding out. It's such an accepted method that virtually everyone, from parents to teachers, when confronted with a child who is stumped by a word, will encourage him or her by saying, "Just sound it out."

As with so many of the accepted practices in reading, advice that seems simple and obvious often doesn't work. The troubles generally do not appear at the outset, when the teaching is focused on having children link single letters to particular sounds (learning, for example, that the letter *b* is the sound *buh,* the letter *c* is the sound *cuh,* and so on).

If you are familiar with the worksheets children are given, you are likely to have seen the type of task illustrated in the following example, where the goal is to have the child identify the beginning sound of each picture and then enter the letter representing that beginning sound.

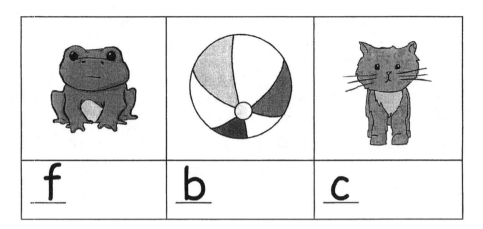

Moving from One to Three

Once single sounds are learned, the teaching moves on to blending sounds so as to form complete words. That's where the trouble begins. Logically, the step up from one sound is two. That would mean taking two letters, such as *a* and *t,* and seeing the way they combine. Logical as it may seem, this rarely occurs. Why? Because in the traditional sounding-out approach, the two-letter words of our language are fraught with problems. In a high percentage of cases, as you can see by looking at words such as *go, do, be, to, of, by, no,* and *he,* the words do not follow the "rules." If they behaved as they should, *go* would be spelled *goe,* *be* would be spelled *bee,* and so on.

So invariably, the step after sounding out one letter is to sound out three letters—or at least particular sets of three letters. Because children have been taught to work with the principle that "every letter should be sounded out," many three-letter words have to be avoided. Many common words—like *say, buy, ate,* and *egg*—are in this excluded category. If each letter were sounded out, none of these words would end up sounding the way it is supposed to. Instead, words are carefully selected to represent what have been termed *consonant-vowel-consonant words.* These are words that start and end with a consonant, and have a vowel as the middle letter. Some common examples are *cat, fan, hop, fat, sit, pan,* and *bed.* For the sake of brevity, they are often referred to as *c-v-c words.*

Blending: No Easy Matter

Even with all these controls the jump from one to three letters is huge. Generally, when isolated consonants are sounded out, a vowel sound appears with the consonant sound. That's why a *c* comes out as *cuh,* a *d* as *duh,* a *g* as *guh,* and so on. Each letter essentially has two sounds: the sound of the consonant itself (for example, *c*) and the sound of the vowel that follows (for example, *uh*).

So in sounding out a three-letter word like *cat,* a child actually ends up with five sounds (*c-uh aa t-uh*). No matter how many times those sounds are said, and no matter how quickly they are said, they do not combine to say *cat.* Two of the vowels (the *uh* of *cuh* and the *uh* of *tuh*) have to disappear before the letters can be blended to form an actual word. The child has to somehow extract *cat* from this array of relevant and irrelevant sounds.

Comparable problems hold for many of even the simplest words, such as

> *puh ii guh* for *pig*
>
> *duh aw guh* for *dog*
>
> *tuh ah puh* for *top*

In all these cases children can get to the actual words only by viewing the sets of sounds as rough approximations—as a collage in which the actual words are embedded. The process is complex and demanding, and it promotes errors. For example, here is the way a reporter studying children's reading problems described one child's effort to decode the word *under:* "First-grader Sarah Strandmark studies the word in her illustrated reading book. The letters u and n are familiar. She's stumped by the d-e-r. Slowly, she strings the letters like pearls on a strand. 'U-u-n-n-n . . . under,' she says, smiling as the jumble of letters reveals itself as a word" (Moore, 2003, p. A1).

With a single word the process is slow and tedious—even when a child knows most of the letters and has to figure out just one or two of them. Still, diligent, motivated children like Sarah can make the effort when only a few words are involved. When there are lots of words, however, as there are in even the simplest page of text, the situation becomes unsustainable. You saw that for yourself if you carried out the foreign-symbol reading exercise presented earlier. The typically used methods of sounding out are simply too cumbersome to be useful.

When adherents of traditional phonics are challenged on this score, they typically react by saying that sounding out is only a means to an end, with the end being the real goal of decoding—namely, instant word recognition.

The phrase *instant word recognition* refers to the quintessential skill of effective reading. Good readers—even those who are no more than six or seven years of age—almost never sound out the words on a page. Instead, they look at words, including words they've never seen with letter patterns they've never been taught, and instantly recognize the words that the letters represent. That is what instant word recognition is all about. When this wonderful, essential, and miraculous skill emerges, it is a clear sign that a child has developed the hidden abilities required for decoding words in print.

Adherents of traditional phonics assure us that instant word recognition is bound to follow after sufficient practice in sounding out has taken place. This is simply not the case! If it were, we would not be witnessing the astounding error rates that currently prevail. From kindergarten on, the vast majority of schools in our nation teach children to sound out, and for far too many children this is simply a path to failure.

How Is Your Child Doing?

You may have seen the telltale evidence of sounding-out failures for yourself. If your child has already experienced several months of reading instruction and is still laboriously sounding out, the likelihood is that he or she is in danger of developing reading problems. To help you determine whether this is the case, you might like to carry out the following set of activities with your child. (Remember, this mini skills test is only for children who are already doing some reading. Do not give it to your child if reading instruction has not yet started.)

Step 1. In this step you are going to be looking for one key ability: whether your child decodes a word correctly via instant word recognition or via sounding out. Start by creating two identical sheets with the following group of set 1 words.

Words for Your Child to Read: Set 1

mat	pin	sit	fan
bug	nap	pet	cut
pot	den	hip	leg

Show one of the sheets of paper to your child; point to each word in turn, saying, "Try reading this word to me." Though you may be tempted, do not offer any help, guidance, or correction. Your goal is to see what your child is doing on his or her own in decoding. However, if your child is stymied by a word, then supply the word by saying, "This is _____ [*name the word*]. Try the next word."

Step 2. As your child reads a word, place a checkmark (✓) next to that word on your sheet if he or she instantly identifies it correctly (that is, if without sounding out, your child immediately says the word). If your child offers any other type of response, do not place a checkmark next to the word. These other responses might include sounding out the word, taking a long time to identify the word, coming up with the wrong word, or simply offering no response.

Step 3. Total the number of words with checkmarks. If your child is reading reasonably well at this level, he or she should have achieved at least ten ✓s. Anything less shows that your child is still struggling with the earliest level of decoding.

Months of work go into c-v-c words of the type you just used in step 1. Many children can begin to do these words easily, but then they get stuck on decoding more complex words. If you want to see whether your child is extending the earliest decoding skills to other words, try step 4.

Step 4. Here, you are again going to be looking to see whether your child decodes via instant word recognition or via some other method. Although still representing words from primer-level books, the words used in this step are ones that go well beyond the c-v-c pattern. Start by again creating two identical sheets, this time with the following group of set 2 words.

Words for Your Child to Read: Set 2

fly	rest	swim	doll
rock	plant	help	make
clean	truck	think	mice
happy	robot	puppy	tongue
animal	hungry	daisy	penny
funny	rainbow	people	open

Then follow the same procedure as in step 1 above.

Step 5. Once again, on your sheet place a checkmark (✓) next to each word that your child instantly recognizes and reads correctly.

Step 6. Total the number of words with checkmarks. In evaluating the results, use the following guidelines:

- If your child has completed at least half of first grade, he or she should have at least eight ✓s.

- If your child has completed almost all of first grade or is in the beginning of second grade, he or she should have at least sixteen ✓s.

- If your child is well along into second grade or beyond, he or she should have at least twenty-two ✓s.

   If your child fails to meet these criteria, do not be discouraged. All these words are in Phonics Plus Five programs that you can easily teach to bring your child to high levels of skill.

   At the same time, do not be misled by well-intentioned professionals who will tell you that it is unrealistic to expect your child to have the level of proficiency I have outlined. People have become so accustomed to poor levels of reading that they have come to see them as normal and acceptable. They are not! It is well known that children who start out with problems of this sort have a high expectancy for reading failure throughout their lives. There is no need for your child to be among those tragic statistics.

Decoding Words: Finding Another Way

To enable you to see how Phonics Plus Five fosters skilled, automatic decoding, we'll go over two of the techniques that are used in the system.

Simplifying Sounding Out: Bit Blends

As we discussed above, many children are stymied when the activities shift from sounding out single letters to blending three letters. Fortunately, there is no need to make children jump that big a divide. Far simpler solutions are possible through using *bit blends*—a technique unique to the Phonics Plus Five system. In place of having your child sound out the full word, you supply the initial blend. That leaves your child with the more manageable task of attaching the single sound of the final letter.

If your child is already reading, you can get a sense of how bit blends works by creating some simple materials. Let's assume your target word, the word you want your child to decode, is *girl*. Create a sheet that on one side has this cluster of letters:

gir

and on the other side has this set of words:

gird   girl

Showing the side with *gir* to your child, say, "This says *gir*." Then turn the sheet over and say, "Now find *girl*." Then give your child additional practice training by repeating the task, each time using a different set of the following words:

gill   girl

gift   girl

give   girl   gig

gird   giddy   girl

You can try this approach with words your child has never seen, including more complex words. For example, consider the word *start*. After you show your child the word *star* and say that "this says *star*," your child then has to find *start* in the following sets:

stare	start	
start	stash	
stay	start	state
start	stamp	strait

You may have noted that all the words in all the sets start with letters identical to those that start the target word. This helps children overcome a major obstacle that defeats accurate decoding. Because traditional sounding-out techniques can be so onerous, children develop the strategy of bypassing them; instead, they guess at words based on the first one or two letters they see. It's easy to understand why a child will resort to this practice, but it ultimately destroys any hope of effective decoding.

By starting the words in each set with the same letters, the bit blends technique overcomes this major obstacle. After working on a few words, children realize that scanning only one or two initial letters is useless and that they must scan further into each word to get at the letters that matter. As correct scanning patterns get established, the misleading first-letter guessing strategy drops away.

The bit blends technique eliminates many of the problems raised by traditional sounding-out techniques. It enables children to experience steady success in combining sounds to form words and at the same time leads them to overcome strategies that interfere with reading success.

Instant Word Recognition

As we discussed earlier, the ultimate goal in reading is instant word recognition. That's what you are doing in reading this page. You are not sounding out each and every word. If you were, just as you had to with the foreign symbol exercise, you would drop the book in a flash.

Of course, on occasion, when we meet unusually challenging words we do resort to sounding out. For example, when we have to deal with a word like *synecdoche* (which is on a reading test precisely because almost no one knows it), we would be bound to sound it out. There seems to be no other way to go. Unfortunately, as so often happens, the sounding-out approach fails, because *synecdoche* is pronounced *sih-neck-doe-key*—another one of the many exceptions that permeate our language. [In case you're wondering, *synecdoche* is defined by *The American Heritage Dictionary of the English Language,* Fourth Edition as "a figure of speech in which a part is used for the whole (as *hand* for *sailor*), the whole for a part (as *the law* for *police officer*), the specific for the general (as *cutthroat* for *assassin*), the general for the specific (as *thief* for *pickpocket*), or the material for the thing made from it (as *steel* for *sword*)" (2000, p. 1755).]

But the *synecdoche* experience is rare. Even with words we've never seen, we do not resort to sounding out in the vast majority of cases. This probably contradicts what you have been led to believe, but it is nevertheless the case. To get an insight into what most of us actually do in decoding new words, it's useful to try a word you've never seen before to see what you do with it.

For example, take the nonsense word *thop.* If you're like most English speakers, in reading this new word you instantly and unquestioningly came up with a pronunciation that rhymes with *hop* and starts with the soft *th* sound (like the *th* in *thin* and *thank*). It seems so obvious. What you probably did not consider at all is that English has two *th* sounds—the soft, or unvoiced, *th* that you chose and the heavier, or voiced, *th* heard in words like *the, this, there, although,* and *then.* (If you're having difficulty differentiating these two sounds, put your hand in front of your mouth and say *thin* and then say *there.* With *thin* you should feel a flow of breath across your hand; with *there* you should not.)

Now, if you are really sounding out new words, why did you not give a moment's consideration to the other *th* sound, which you have encountered far more times than the *th* sound that you actually chose? Pick up any book, for example, and it won't take you more than a sentence or two to find a voiced *th* word, such as *the* or *this.* However, you're likely to search long and hard before finding a page with an unvoiced *th* word, such as *thin* or *thumb.*

The frequencies of various words in print have been calculated, and the differences are astounding. For example, considering some common voiced *th* words, we find that out of approximately five million words of text, *the* appears 373,123 times, *this* 23,301 times, and *there* 15,194 times. In contrast, considering some common unvoiced *th* words, we find the comparable numbers for *think* to be 4,746, for *things* 1,828, and for *thin* 611 (Carroll, Davies, & Richman, 1971). If the voiced *th* so far outnumbers the unvoiced *th,* why did you not even consider using it for *thop*? Surely this seems counterintuitive.

The answer rests not with the sounding-out skills you've been taught but rather with the hidden abilities that are really behind your effective reading. Years of experience have taught your unconscious mind that the voiced *th* is associated with noncontent words—words like *the, this,* and *there,* whereas the unvoiced *th* is associated with content words, words like *thin, thank,* and *thimble.* These hidden abilities have also led you to recognize that new content words (such as *astronaut, dot-com,* and *cell phone*) are steadily being created, whereas noncontent words are not. The latter form a fixed, or "closed," class, with no new entries. So, totally out of your awareness but with perfect accuracy, you classified the new word *thop* as a content word and assigned it the pronunciation that goes with those words.

An old proverb holds that "the fish is the last one to discover water." It captures the idea that we can be unaware of some of the most powerful forces around us. This is certainly the case with phonics. Phonics is a vital factor in decoding words, but it is our hidden phonic abilities that provide an effective framework for decoding. They allow readers to innately understand the key clusters in English and the sounds that those clusters represent. That's why, after looking at a word once, experienced readers have "got it." For some children these skills come easier than for others. But given the right tools every child can figure them out. Bit blends is one of those tools. Repeated encounters is another.

Repeated Encounters

Repeated encounters means exactly what it says. The teaching material is designed so that a word appears again and again and again. At the same time, in a departure from typical reading education, your child learns only one new word in a session. Through a series of varied activities, that word is taught approximately thirty to forty times. These various repeated encounters give your child the familiarity he or she needs to attain instant recognition of a word.

For example, in one activity—*Spot 'n Sort*—children see sets of words one line at a time, and in each line the new word may appear more than once, once, or not at all. The number of correct choices is intentionally varied to lead your child to process the information as fully as possible. (In contrast, in situations where there is a single correct response, children stop looking as soon as they think they have found the right choice.) This activity is set up so that your child has to cross out all the words that are *not* the target word. In learning the word *eat,* for instance, your child might see the following matrix:

ape	eat	sit	bus
fly	ate	eat	eat
each	early	put	ear
tea	even	eat	seat
soon	boy	eat	eat
eat	meat	girl	ear

Your child does not need to know the other words. Nevertheless, he or she does have to scan carefully in order to distinguish the target word from the other words. For example, *ear* has the same two starting letters as *eat,* *tea* has the same letters but in the wrong order, and *seat* also has the same three letters and in the right order but with an additional letter at the start. All the activities are arranged so that you provide your child with immediate feedback to correct any errors he or she makes.

The nontarget words have been chosen to help children overcome the systematic error patterns that they fall into in learning to read. For example, when children accept *tea* or *ate* as the equivalent of *eat,* they are working on the assumption that clusters with the same letters can be viewed as representing the same word.

You might be wondering where these systematic error patterns come from. After all, no one ever instructed children to use them. Proponents of direct phonics instruction view these spontaneous strategies as "one of the mysteries of written language acquisition" (Templeton & Bear, 1992, p. 13). In reality, it would be more of a mystery if children did not come up with these strategies. We human beings have an unending need to make sense of the input we face. So when children first confront words, they apply patterns that seem reasonable. Given their experiences with objects in their prereading life, it's only natural for them to think that if one set of letters is nearly the same as another, the sets are likely to be equivalent. A plant, for example, can drop one or more leaves and still be the same plant. When a word drops or exchanges even a single letter, however, it is not the same word. Unlike most other visual material children have learned to deal with, words require minute attention to sequence and detail.

The material in Phonics Plus Five has been crafted to overcome the error patterns that interfere with successful reading. If you find that your child displays some of these patterns, don't get nervous. It is not a weakness in your child; it is a weakness in the instruction he or she has received. Once you adopt appropriate teaching materials and techniques, you will see that these patterns quickly fade away.

Immediate feedback combined with tightly controlled materials is central to the Phonics Plus Five programs. It is a key factor in enabling children to figure out the rules that underlie the hidden abilities of reading.

Spelling Words

Up to this point we have been considering ways to help your child read, or decode, the words on a page. An equally important skill is the ability to write, or spell, those words.

Spelling represents an area that has long aroused strong feelings. A century ago inaccuracy in spelling was seen as nearly sinful, and errors were a clear sign of poor breeding. Back in the nineteenth century, for example, Thomas Jefferson wrote to his daughter: "Take care that you never spell a word wrong. Always before you write a word, consider how it is spelled, and, if you do not remember, turn to a dictionary. It produces great praise to a lady to spell well." Imagine talking to some teachers from that era and telling them that in a few generations accuracy will be seen as not only unnecessary but undesirable. They would probably think you were insane.

When Wrong Is Right

That was then, and this is now. With the appearance of the whole language movement, demands for rigor came to be seen as impediments to learning. That left accurate spelling by the wayside. If you are familiar with current school practices, you've seen the effects in the "invented spelling" phenomenon, which encourages children to write with any spelling they choose. The goal is to avoid doing anything that might inhibit their getting their ideas onto the page as easily as possible. Because accurate spelling is one of the big inhibitions, it has to be abandoned.

The victim in this approach is not just spelling but also reading. For example, "only" a single letter is responsible for the difference in meaning between the sentences in each of the following sets:

He charged the battery.	He changed the battery.
She saw the word.	She saw the world.
We found the tool.	We found the toll.
They liked the team.	They licked the team.

Accustomed to seeing the patterns of their invented words, children are unprepared to see accurately the patterns in the words others write. Accurate spelling is the handmaiden to accurate reading. When it is not there, reading suffers mightily.

Because phonics adherents place so much stress on accuracy in reading, you might expect them to be uncomfortable with inaccuracy in spelling. Surprisingly, they are not. They justify their position by claiming that the mistakes are simply signs that spelling has developmental stages and that as children go through these stages the errors will eventually resolve (Ehri, 1992).

If you have observed the spelling skills of real children in the real world, you know that this does not happen. For huge numbers of children, even those who can read fairly well, spelling is a disaster zone. This is not a fault of the children. It is a reflection of the complexities of English and the inadequacy of sounding-out rules for dealing with these complexities.

On one occasion a parent consulted me about some concerns her daughter's first-grade teacher raised. Amy's reading and writing skills were excellent, but the teacher was bothered because the little girl wanted her writing to be accurate. So she would at times ask how to spell correctly any word she was unsure of. When told to put down whatever "seems right," she kept insisting on knowing the correct spelling. At that point the teacher called in the parent because she felt that the child's creative spirit was being blocked by a concern with being correct.

Aside from a very small group of words, almost any English word can, from a sounding-out point of view, be spelled in a variety of ways. Consider a four-letter word such as *tall*. Applying just a few of the sounding-out rules, it could be spelled *taul, tawl,* or *taull.* For a child who does not have a solid visual image of this word, there is no way to distinguish between correct and incorrect spellings.

As words increase in length the complexities mount and the possibilities continue to multiply. To get a sense of what a child beginning to read has to face, consider the following lists of five-letter words and two-syllable words, drawn from a book designed for children in the first and second grades (Bokoske & Davidson, 1993).

Five-Letter Words	Two-Syllable Words
tease	turtle
shark	dolphin
close	tiny
throw	picture
drown	angry
fight	gentle
learn	million
built	circle
raise	letter

Following the phonic rules, each word could be spelled in a wide array of possibilities. For example, *tease* could be *teas, teese, teaz, teez,* or *teiz; turtle* could be *tirtel, turtel, tertel, tertil,* and so on.

The complexities of English spelling are indeed considerable. They will never be resolved, though, by permitting children to write with error. Allowing errors to go uncorrected leads only to further errors.

How can accurate spelling be achieved? The answer rests with structuring the teaching so that it deals systematically with two components: the number of letters in words and the role of memory in writing words.

Bigger Is Better: Going Beyond Three Letters

In mathematics there is an interesting distinction between the numbers we recognize immediately and those we know only through deliberate counting (Dehaene, 1999). For example, children under one year old can distinguish between small quantities even though they are not able to count: given a choice between two candies and three candies, they'll choose the three. But when the same children have to choose between six candies and seven, they cannot distinguish between these two larger quantities. In general, young children can discern, without counting, differences in quantities up to four. After that, if they are going to identify a difference, they have to count.

A similar principle operates in the domain of words—except that (in my experience) the critical number is three. With words of two and three letters, children can spell without much effort because they seem to be able to easily grasp that number of letters. The spelling of those words, however, does little to foster the spelling of longer words. It is only when children have to produce words with four or more letters that they develop the skills that foster hidden abilities.

The hold that traditional phonics has on reading education means that those longer words have consistently been avoided because they do not fit the simple sound-letter correspondences children are taught. So in the early months of instruction, although *bit* is fine, *bite* is not; although *bed* is fine, *bead* is not; and although *pin* is fine, *pint* is not. All those four-letter words lend themselves to a *range* of possible spellings.

That is why, even after months of instruction, in traditional phonics activities such as the sample spelling task that follows, the words are systematically limited to those with three letters:

A Sample Early Spelling Activity

wig	pig
pan	man
bed	led
bug	rug

—Rowland, 1995, workbook 24

The months of early instruction are critical. They set the basic patterns for literacy that your child will have forever. By restricting initial spelling tasks to short, three-letter words, the teaching almost guarantees spelling failure for the words that follow.

Among its effects, this approach leads children to feel intimidated when they finally meet the longer words. One time I was working with a first-grader who, like his peers, had spent months on three-letter words. When he happened to see the word *helping* on a piece of paper, his eyes opened wide, and he then proceeded to count the letters—"one, two, three, four, five, six, seven." When asked if he could read the word, he quickly said, "No, that's seven letters." Caught up in a fear of length, he could not even begin to conceive of the possibility that he could manage the word. There is no reason, other than limited teaching, for conveying the message that longer words are unconquerable. Patterns like these can easily be prevented from ever taking hold by structuring the material to introduce longer words right from the outset.

This philosophy is reflected throughout the Phonics Plus Five reading and writing programs. Because the system requires no explicit rules, kids are free from the outset to learn words that are longer than three letters. Even in the level 1 reading program, the children learn four- and five-letter words like *girl, bird, rest, swim, talk, plane,* and *robot.* Over the course of the five programs, increasingly complex words are added so that the child becomes comfortable with a wide range of relatively long single-syllable and multisyllable words.

The activities are set up so in a variety of ways to ensure the accurate visual analysis needed for correct spelling. In one activity—*Find 'n Fill*—for example, children go through a series of steps where they have to (1) find the incomplete words that can become the target word, and (2) in left to right order, add the missing letters so that the spelling of each instance of the target word is complete and accurate. In the following material, for example, the child's goal is to find and fill in the word *rocket,* as often as it appears.

p l __ n __	r __ __ k e t	m __ __	r __ c k s
f l __	b __ s	r __ __ d	r o __ k __ __
r __ o t s	r __ c __ e __	w __ l __	p __ __ t s
r o __ __ e t	p l __ n e	r o __ __	h __ __ s e
s o __ __ e t	r __ __ k e t	b o __ k	r e __ d

In addition to getting children past the three-letter barrier that has for so long held up early reading instruction, longer words offer other advantages. Words like *rocket* introduce your child from the outset to phonic features that permeate words, without the need for your child to memorize confusing and difficult rules. In the case of *rocket,* for example, the child is exposed to the fact that the single *k* sound may be represented by a letter combination (*ck*) rather than by a single letter. With other words the combinations might be different (for example, the *ch* of *such,* the *ou* of *ground,* the *ea* of *head*), but the principle is the same. The controlled, steady presentation of these sorts of features is central in enabling your child to develop the hidden abilities of accurate decoding and spelling.

Using Memory to Attain Accuracy

Accurate spelling is best achieved when children can picture in their minds all the letters in a word. When activities are confined to ones where the words are always in view, this internal picture need never develop. For example, imagine having to write a long word like *elephant.* With the word in view, for each letter a child can just keep looking back to the model till the word is complete. The source of the information is the model rather than an internal picture in the child's head.

In the work I have done over several decades, I have found that techniques that emphasize memory are the most effective way to get children to visualize words in the way effective spelling demands. Also, the program activities are set up so that your child has to work with sentences in which the new words are integrated with words already learned. In one activity—*Symbol Search*—for the target word *cold,* your child might see

That ____⊇____ is ____•____ very ____⊗____ .

⊗ = cold   ⊇ = food   • = still

In this activity your child first finds the word that each symbol represents (for example, ⊇ means that *food* is the word to be inserted). Then the word is covered, and from memory, your child enters it in the sentence. Once the fill-ins are completed, your child reads the sentence. Then the words of the entire sentence are covered, and using memory again, your child writes the sentence from dictation.

If there are any errors, you briefly pause the writing and show the original sentence again. Then, starting from the first word, your child resumes writing until the entire sentence is written correctly—in the absence of the model. In other words, high levels of performance are required, but your child gets all the time and information needed to attain that high performance.

Comprehending Words

Along with decoding and spelling, a third major component is required in teaching words. It concerns comprehending, or understanding, the meaning of the words. Oddly enough, this critical area has largely been taken for granted in early reading instruction.

For decades the conventional wisdom has been that children, through their years of speaking, come to school knowing the meaning of the words they will encounter. The only thing they are seen as lacking is the "character recognition device" (that is, knowing the letters) and the ability to convert the characters into a "systematic phoneme representation" (that is, to sound the letters out) (Gough, 1972, p. 346). In other words, in this view there is never a need to worry about whether the words will be comprehended. In contrast there is no such confidence about decoding, because children do not know how to sound out the letters. That is why sound analysis, rather than meaning, is considered the important skill to teach.

Unfortunately, the concentration on sounds has led to creating pages of words that contain a distorted language, unlike anything the children know. To see this, we need only return to the passage about Dan and Sam introduced in Chapter One:

Dan has an ax.

Has Dan an ax?

Sam has ham.

Has Sam ham?

Dan has land and sand.

Has Dan sand?

Sam sat.

Dan sat.

This passage, like any well-constructed phonics passage, is governed by the principle that all words must be decodable. In other words, every word that the child sees should be one he or she is able to figure out by applying the letter-sound combinations taught up till then. At the point where a child sees this passage, he or she will have learned nine letters—*a, d, h, l, m, n, s, t,* and *x*—and indeed, every one of the words stays within the constraints of this set of letters.

Words by Themselves Versus Words in Text

The problem is not with the individual words. Each one of them is understandable. Children will have no trouble knowing the meaning of *land* or *sand* or *sat*. The problems stem not from the meanings of the individual words but from the meaning of the total passage. Like so many other passages in early phonic readers, the total passage is meaningless.

Just try saying the passage aloud, and you will see what I mean. If you hear that someone has an *ax,* you would never expect the next idea to be that someone else has *ham.* And after hearing that someone has *land* and *sand,* you would never expect that the next idea to be that the person *sat.* In real-life speaking and writing, ideas are not put together in this way. Sentences are supposed to connect and link to form a coherent message. This linking is completely absent from the passage about Dan and Sam.

We will discuss the concept of connected ideas at greater length in Chapter Eight—the chapter on text. The key point here is to recognize the problems that phonics instruction has caused owing to its limited view of comprehension. In restricting comprehension to the comprehension of individual words, phonics has forced children to deal with endless passages that are essentially incomprehensible. As a system of instruction, it dooms children to failure in the vital area of comprehension.

Selecting Words to Suit the Story

Freed from the straitjacket of having to use ultrashort words restricted to particular sets of letters, Phonics Plus Five is able to combine words in the ways that meaningful messages require. The messages of greatest interest to children are stories. Those stories determine the sets of words that will be taught. For example, in a story about a baby bear wanting some food, it is reasonable for certain words to appear, words like *baby, sad, food, berries, find,* and *saw.* These words are needed to create such sentences as, "The baby bear was so sad. He wanted some food, but he could not find any. Then he saw some berries. He ran to them . . . ." Any meaningful story demands that the sets of words connect in ways that fit our natural use of language.

The strategy in Phonics Plus Five, therefore, is to use words that permit meaningful texts to be constructed. All the content words in the programs have been selected on this basis. Once selected they are then individually taught through the techniques outlined earlier (such as bit blends, repeated encounters, and so on).

In this way children learn how to read effectively, to write accurately, and to comprehend the words they will be reading in the stories they will shortly be given.

A book is presented after each set of approximately ten words (both content and noncontent) has been taught. Each book contains all the new words in addition to relevant words previously learned. With texts structured in this way, children are easily and naturally familiarized with every word they encounter.

Using a Range of Categories

Meaningful stories naturally call on content words from the major grammatical categories of nouns, verbs, adjectives, and adverbs, and all these types of words appear in the five levels of the reading system. Nouns are needed for the characters, objects, and events in each story (for example, *boy, house, water, rain, moon, rocket, computer*); verbs are needed for the actions that the nouns carry out or experience (for example, *run, fall, cry, try, talk, rest*); adjectives are needed for the characteristics of the nouns (for example, *sad, happy, cold, nice, salty, true*); and adverbs are needed for modifying the actions (verbs) and characteristics (adjectives) (for example, *really, very, much, such*).

The story-word process enhances both the skills and motivation underlying reading. Freed from the usual word restrictions, the stories in Phonics Plus Five are more interesting than the texts children typically see at the start of reading. At the same time, they are simple enough that a child can experience total success. Additionally, the wide-ranging words prepare children for the variability that is inherent in "real" books.

Key Features of the Programs

The following list summarizes the key features of the programs that teach the content words:

- Blending of sounds is consistently required, but in order to enhance success, it is simplified through the technique of bit blends.

- Each word is taught through repeated encounters that convey all its components, including decoding, spelling, and comprehension.

- Accurate spelling is required from the outset. To avoid the limitations that over-reliance on three-letter words creates, many of the words are longer and more complex than those in other early reading programs.

- Words are selected not on the basis of conceptual simplicity alone but also on their potential to combine to form meaningful ideas.

Chapter Eleven provides the directions for creating the teaching materials for the content words.

Answering Two Common Questions

Parents and educators often raise two questions:

1. Given the focus on words, does the Phonics Plus Five approach to teaching mean that children have to be taught each and every word they are learning?
2. Does it matter which words are selected?

The answer to both questions is no. The content of the teaching is based on individual words, but the techniques of the teaching are aimed at having the children develop the hidden abilities that are the basis for truly effective reading. As long as the words take into account issues such as length, meaning, and grammatical category, the particular words do not matter.

The key is to orchestrate the presentation of the words so that children become versed in the key letter patterns of English. Once that happens, independent decoding and spelling of new words automatically starts to emerge. Indeed, many parents report that within a few months of starting this system, their children are reading and writing words they've never been taught. What these parents are witnessing is the emergence of the hidden abilities that are the basis for truly effective reading.

Teaching Noncontent Words

chapter 7

The Skills of Reading

Sequencing	Writing	Phonology	Semantics	Syntax	Text

Noncontent words—the words we will be focusing on here—are all the *little words* of our language that do not appear to have any direct meaning unto themselves. How do you show someone the meaning of words like *the, but,* and *if?* They seem to be from another world compared to the content words, which are easy to demonstrate, like *puppy, run, soft,* and *quickly.*

What We Know About These Words

Although they may be difficult to define, the noncontent words are the glue that binds the content words together. They are critical to the syntax, or grammar, of our language. To start, let's take a look at what we know about them.

- Currently, there is considerable disagreement in educational circles about precisely which words to include in the noncontent category, and there is even disagreement over what to call them. At times you might hear them referred to as *functors* and at other times as the *little words.* In general, they can be viewed as the words that are left over after you have taken away all the nouns, main verbs, adjectives, and adverbs of our language.

- Some noncontent words are not complete words but rather word particles that are attached to the content words. Such units, often referred to as *morphemes*, include endings like *-ing* and *-ed*, which allow us to change verbs like *go* to *going* and *jump* to *jumped;* the plural ending *-s,* which allows us to change nouns like *kid* to *kids;* and the *-er* that allows us to take verbs like *teach* and transform them into nouns like *teacher.* So, on any page, many words are combinations of content words and noncontent word particles. Most plurals, such as *boys, houses, cats,* and *pens,* represent that combination. (A few plurals, such as *men, children, sheep,* and *fish,* are exceptions because they do not take the plural *-s*).

- All the noncontent words together—whether whole words and part words—represent a tiny fraction of the half million to one million words estimated to be in our language. There are under 200 noncontent words in all, and many of them, such as *whence, thence,* and *heretofore,* are rarely used. Consequently, there are only about 100 noncontent words that we hear and see on a regular basis.

- Although some of the noncontent words are little used, others are used constantly. Imagine what it would be like to try to use English in the absence of words like *the, is, he, was, they, but, or, and,* and *then.* The fact is that these words make up 50 percent or more of every page of text we read throughout our lives.

- Noncontent words are a wonderful bonus for reading instruction. After learning only 100 common words, children are able to read the majority of words on any page of print they will see for the rest of their lives. No other single element that can be leveraged in the teaching of reading comes close to the effectiveness of noncontent words in assisting children to "crack the code" and become good readers.

- Another major bonus is that once children learn the role of the noncontent words, they gain a better intuitive understanding of the syntax, or grammar, of English. Such understanding is an essential part of the foundation of a reader's hidden abilities.

Despite their potential in the teaching of reading, noncontent words have been shunted aside by existing systems. The theoretical positions these systems have taken do not allow them to do otherwise.

For whole language proponents, whose chief goal is to have children experience meaningful stories, concentrating effort on the abstract, noncontent words seems a distraction.

For phonics proponents the noncontent words are among the much-decried *exceptions*. According to the rules of phonics, a word like *was* should be spelled *wuz, of* should be spelled *uv, he* should be spelled *hee,* and so on. The end result is that these words receive minimal teaching time, which leaves children with two major disadvantages. They fail to acquire the necessary solid base of noncontent words, and the lack of attention conveys the message that these words are unimportant.

How Is Your Child Doing?

If your child is past kindergarten and experiencing steady instruction in reading, it is worthwhile for you to see how well he or she is doing with this vital group of words. You can do this by carrying out the following activity, which requires reading a set of the most common noncontent words.

Step 1. Start by creating two identical sheets with the following set of sentences:

Can	she	do	some	of	this?
They	are	not	here	now.	
Who	is	there	for	us?	
Some	others	also	like	that.	
But	he	does	want	more!	

You will be folding the paper so that your child sees only one sentence at a time. So make sure to leave enough space between the sentences.

Step 2. Arrange the paper so that your child sees only the first sentence, and say, "Try reading this to me." Do not offer any help, guidance, or correction, because your goal is to see what your child is doing in independently decoding noncontent words. If your child fails to read a word, do not supply it. Simply point to the next word and say, "Try this one."

Step 3. As your child reads the words, on your sheet place a checkmark (✓) next to every word that he or she recognizes correctly and immediately. This means that there should be no noticeable delay in identifying the word. The words we are considering here should be instantly decoded; when they are not, it is a sign that your child needs support.

Step 4. When you have completed the first sentence, move on to the second sentence. Once again, arrange the paper so that your child sees only one sentence at a time. As in step 3, place a checkmark next to the words read correctly and immediately. Continue in this manner until all the sentences have been completed.

Step 5. Total the number of checkmarks. These words are some of the most basic noncontent words, and their mastery is essential for successful reading, even at the earliest stages. In evaluating your child's results, use the following guidelines:

- If your child has had four to six months of reading instruction, he or she should have achieved at least fifteen ✓s on the set of twenty-six words.
- If your child has completed almost a year or more of reading instruction, he or she should have achieved at least twenty-two ✓s on the set of twenty-six words.

If your child fails to meet these criteria, he or she can benefit significantly from the teaching offered in the Phonics Plus Five system. All the words in the five sentences used here are from the first two reading programs, the Boarding and Runway programs. Additional noncontent words are taught in the three higher-level programs: Liftoff, Airborne, and Soaring. At the end of all five levels, your child will have mastery of the full complement of the most commonly used noncontent words, including such words as *were, would, when, because,* and *which.*

Phonics Plus Five takes a unique approach to the small, but vital, group of noncontent words. It makes them a central focus of the teaching, equal in time and effort to the focus on content words. As you will see when you work with your child, the payoff for taking this approach is enormous.

As in teaching content words, three critical processes—decoding, spelling, and comprehension—must be taught.

The Path to Decoding

It has long been accepted that noncontent words cannot be decoded by following traditional phonic rules. For example, with a word like *have,* which ends in *e,* the rule to use would be the silent *e* rule, where the *e* has no sound but "makes" the first vowel *long* (as occurs, for example, with the sound of the vowel *a* in a word like *lake*). Were you to apply this rule to *have,* you would end up with the wrong word.

With the traditional rules not working, the decoding must take place without the usual phonological supports. The typical solution is to use what is termed *sight word,* or *whole word,* teaching, where the child learns the word by recognizing it as a whole, rather than by dissecting it down to its elements. This is similar to the logo recognition even very young children use when they see the big yellow arches and shout out, "Hamburger!" The sign has an obvious meaning to them, but it is not based on sound-symbol correspondences. Rather, there is a visual association. Any symbol that McDonald's might have chosen would still elicit the "hamburger" response. The sound, or spoken word, has nothing to do with the image seen— there is no way to sound out a logo.

Sight word, or whole word, teaching relies on techniques such as flash cards, where the teacher employs a cluster of cards, with each card containing one word, such as the ones you see here:

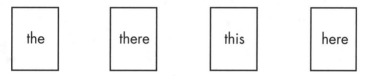

As each card is held up the children are asked to decode, or read, the word it displays. The aim is to have them recognize each one as a whole word, without making any effort to break it down according to phonic rules.

This approach, which provides children with no specific guidance, is notoriously weak. Too many of the words look alike, and for all but the best readers, inefficiency and errors plague the decoding of what educators have come to accept as "confusable high frequency words" (Krieger, 1981).

Although the sounding-out route is closed off, we can use techniques far more effective than flash cards to teach children how to decode the noncontent words.

Placing the Words in Context

One of the reasons noncontent words have the name they do is that they seem so meaningless. Some speed-reading programs even instruct their students to bypass these words entirely.

After all, what is a *but* or a *the* or an *an?* The idea that they lack of meaning, however, really holds only when the words are read in isolation. As soon as they are combined with other words, meaning comes into play. The sentences displayed earlier (such as, "Can she do some of this?") are good examples of what amalgamation accomplishes. Every one of those words is a noncontent word, yet in combination they have a definite meaning.

That's why the presentation of isolated words, as occurs with flash cards, is so ineffective. It is only by seeing the words in relation to other words that the child can easily recognize that a noncontent word is present.

Phonics Plus Five takes advantage of this fact by having children identify each noncontent word to be learned in the context of sentences. One activity—*Detect 'n Select*—uses a search paradigm, asking your child to find a particular noncontent word. In the Detect 'n Select example that follows, the target word your child searches for is *you.*

You can stay here. You do not have to leave. We have room for you and some of the other people. Will you stay? We hope you will.	What are you doing here? I thought that you were going to the game. Why are you here? If you want, you can still get to the game.	Which one of you has a car? If you have a car, please tell us. You could help us a lot with your car. So I will ask again: Do any of you have a car?

In keeping with the principle of repeated encounters, these segments of text provide the numerous repetitions that are vital to fast, accurate recognition. The range of sentences also provides a child with the chance to notice other features associated with the word being taught. In the case of *you,* these sentences show that like other pronouns, *you* is commonly associated with the *helping* verbs, such as *can, do, have,* and *are.* Children do not have to be able to read any of the words in the text except the target word to notice this feature of *you.* They only have to home in on that target word. Still, once they begin to realize that they do know large numbers of the words, invariably their hidden phonic abilities lead them to recognize the words that link with other words.

Capital Matters

When sentences are used, another feature of noncontent words is revealed. In real text, over 80 percent of sentences start with a noncontent word. You can see this pattern in the three selections from books that follow: the first is aimed at children in the early primary grades, the second at children in the mid-primary grades, and the third at adults.

A Selection from a Book for the Early Primary Grades

Once there was a town named Pompeii. **Near** the town was a mountain named Vesuvius. **The** people of Pompeii liked living by the mountain. **It** was a good place to grow grapes. **It** was a good place to raise sheep. **And** it looked so peaceful. **But** the mountain was really a dangerous volcano. **It** was like a sleeping giant. **If** the giant woke up, it could destroy the town. **Did** the people know about the danger? [Kunhardt, 1987, pp. 4–5.]

Ten of ten sentences start with noncontent words = 100 percent.

A Selection from a Book for the Mid-Primary Grades

After the Revolutionary War most people in America were glad that they were no longer British. **Still,** they were not ready to call themselves Americans. **The** last thing they wanted was to become a nation. **They** were citizens of their own separate states, just as they had always been: each state different, each state proud of its own character, each state quick to poke fun at other states. **To** Southerners, New Englanders might be "no-account Yankees." **To** New Englanders, Pennsylvanians might be "lousy Buckskins."

   But to everyone the states themselves were all important. "Sovereign states," they called them. **They** loved the sound of "sovereign" because it meant that they were their own bosses [Fritz, 1987, p. 7].

Eight of nine sentences start with noncontent words = 88 percent.

A Selection from a Book for Adults

Until 1932 he did no more than think. **He** had other work and nuclear physics was not sufficiently interesting to him. **It** became compelling in 1932. **A** discovery in physics opened the field to new possibilities . . . . **On** February 27, 1932, in a letter to the British Journal *Nature*, physicist James Chadwick . . . announced the possible existence of a neutron. (**He** confirmed the neutron's existence in a longer paper . . . four months later . . . .) **The** neutron . . . had no electric charge, which meant it could pass through . . . and enter the nucleus. **The** neutron would open the atomic nucleus to examination. **It** might even be a way to force the nucleus to give up some of its enormous energy [Rhodes, 1986, pp. 23–24].

Nine of nine sentences start with noncontent words = 100 percent

When tasks are structured to help children realize this unique role that noncontent words play in sentences, they also structure children's hidden abilities, abilities that then lead children to decode noncontent words, rather than content words, as the start of most sentences.

The starting words of sentences present another interesting feature. They always begin with a capital letter. Content words, in contrast, rarely appear with capital letters, with the obvious exception of proper nouns. By structuring the material to foster awareness of this feature, Phonics Plus Five provides children with another distinguishing feature to use in decoding and identifying noncontent words.

The content of the Detect 'n Select activity described earlier has been designed to illustrate this feature of noncontent words. As you can see in the search for the word *you,* the first letter of this target word appears in both its uppercase and lowercase forms.

At the same time, the activity is arranged so that your child is never asked to name, or identify, the surrounding words. The goal is for him or her to be able to identify and name, with ease, the single target word (in this case, *you*) in the kinds of contexts found in everyday materials. Because your child may not yet know the other words, it would be counterproductive to ask him or her to decode them. When these sorts of features are carefully controlled, error is kept to a minimum and the base for rapid and accurate decoding is established.

This activity also suits the teaching of part words, such as *-ing, -s,* and *-ed.* In learning to decode these part words your child needs to use particularly careful discrimination, because the part words are embedded within other words. These other words are of necessity content words, and the result is that your child begins to grasp the interplay between content and noncontent words. You can see this in the following Detect 'n Select activity, aimed at teaching the *-ed* ending. In each segment your child has to identify and name the words having that ending (in the first segment the word is *looked,* in the second, *jumped,* and in the third, *walked*).

The man looked into the car for a tool. Then he looked into the truck. He looked and looked but he could not find the tool.	Some boys jumped onto the truck. They jumped on it because it was so high. Some of the girls also jumped on it. It was not good that they did that.	The dog walked behind some rocks. The kids walked there too. All of them walked in that place when they could. It was such a nice place.

The Role of Spelling

For the noncontent words, just as for the content words, spelling is the most demanding of the word analysis skills children have to learn. Content words are difficult to spell because, in terms of the rules, there are just too many possibilities. Noncontent words can be equally hard because it is virtually impossible to sound out most of them. Words like *he, she, they, why, of, want,* and *was* simply do not look the way they sound.

At their core, however, the two groups of words are more alike than different when it comes to spelling. Neither lends itself to the sounding-out rules that children are taught. Children can retain the correct spelling only by forming a clear, stable mental representation of the word. Without that representation, we see endless error. It particularly haunts homonyms (words that have the same sounds but different meanings), such as *where* and *wear; some* and *sum; there* and *their; here* and *hear; by* and *buy; for* and *four; your* and *you're; to, too,* and *two;* and so on.

The two major techniques described for teaching the spelling of content words fit with noncontent words as well. They involve the number of letters in words and the role of memory in writing words.

Using Longer Words

As we discussed in teaching content words, traditional approaches have consistently tried to limit the initial words children learn to three letters and particularly to the *c-v-c words* (which start and end with a consonant and have a vowel in the middle, such as *man, run, pin,* and *cat*). Although this restriction actually works against learning to spell, it is a hard one to knock down. It has been used for a long time, and it seems like a reasonable way to keep things simple for children.

Once noncontent words enter the picture, this barrier naturally disappears. Many of the most commonly used noncontent words, such as *this, also, what, that, these, there, where,* and *which,* require four or five letters. When the ever-present *-ing* is added to any verb, the resulting word cannot avoid having at least five letters and often more (for example, *going, running,* and *sitting*).

So if you are going to teach noncontent words, there is no possibility of limiting the teaching to those with three letters. Fortunately, the techniques of Phonics Plus Five are well suited for teaching longer words. In one activity—*Letter In*—the material is designed to help children master spelling by inserting the letters that will complete a word. For the target word *where,* for example, your child sees a matrix such as the following:

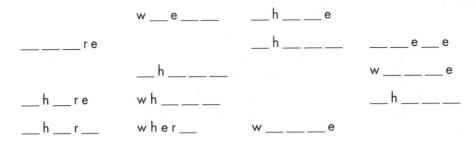

This arrangement is different from the typically used spelling tasks in which children have to repeatedly write the same word in exactly the same way. Identical repetition often lowers attention and lessens learning. In contrast, in the Letter In activity, because the missing letters vary from one word to the next, each experience your child has with the word is different from the one before. This variability increases the level of attention while also leading your child to attend carefully to each of the individual letters in a word.

Calling on Memory

Spelling becomes truly successful only when a word is placed into memory. Several Phonics Plus Five activities are set up to help your child internalize the letter patterns in words. One activity—*Cipher Wiz*—presents a number code that when converted into words forms a meaningful sentence. As in all Phonics Plus Five activities, the messages contain both the target word and words already mastered, so that there is a steady review of material worked on previously.

The following sentence, designed for the target word *still,* illustrates the format used for the Cipher Wiz activity. The sentence your child will be creating is, "That kid was very sad, but still she did not cry at all." The material your child sees at the outset appears as follows:

4   5   6   1   3   2   7

_____

_____

1 = but still	2 = cry at all	3 = she did not
4 = That kid	5 = was very sad	6 = ,

7 = .

In this activity your child starts by looking beneath the writing lines and finding the phrase that corresponds to the first number—the 4—above the writing lines. In this case, the phrase corresponding to 4 is *That kid*. After your child finds the phrase and reads it, you cover the words. Then, without seeing the model, your child writes the phrase on the line. This process is repeated, phrase by phrase, until the sentence is complete.

You may have noticed that punctuation is a part of this activity, just as it is a part of many of the Phonics Plus Five activities. Sentences are critical in teaching noncontent words, and sentences demand punctuation. This stands in striking contrast to most current programs, where punctuation is rarely introduced in the earliest stages of reading. The delay in this aspect of instruction contributes to the notorious difficulties that children have with producing accurate punctuation. Most of them know that sentences need some periods and some capitals, and they toss them around, hoping that they have gotten at least some of them in the right places. The early, systematic introduction of punctuation prevents many of these difficulties from arising.

The Role of Comprehension

We now turn to the issue that has been so central to the neglect of the noncontent words—the consistently held view that these words are meaningless. Given that view, it seems impossible to raise the issue of comprehension. How can you ask a child to understand the meaning of something that is seen as having no meaning?

The Content of Noncontent Words

The answer rests with abandoning the misleading idea that the words are meaningless. Once we free ourselves from that dogma, it is clear that these words *do have* meaning. Consider the following sentences to see how a single change in a noncontent word transforms the message that the sentence is conveying:

> The people **that** are leaving are sad.

> The people **they** are leaving are sad.

The key problem is not meaning but awareness. For the most part we use noncontent words without awareness. When we speak, content words are the focus of our attention, and in the flow of natural speech the noncontent words seem simply to meld into the content ones. Children are no different from us in this. In fact, if they have not yet learned to read, their lack of consciousness about these words is even greater than ours (because reading brings noncontent words somewhat more to a person's attention than speaking does).

You might get a glimpse into the process if your child is not yet able to read. What you can do is to say a number of sentences, such as

> A girl ate the cookies.

> The bear jumped in the water.

> The little baby was crying.

At the end of each sentence, ask your child to tell you the number of words in the sentence. Most young children will exclude some or all of the noncontent words in their count, so that a five-word sentence (such as, "A girl ate the cookies") will be heard as having three words (*girl, ate, cookies*).

This lack of awareness is the source of some major problems when reading starts, because print presents the noncontent words to us in ways that are very different from the ways we perceive spoken language.

- First, there are noticeable spaces between words, separating the noncontent words from their partners. Instead of hearing a smooth flow where one word glides into the next, the child sees, for example:

> The   bird   was   flying.

Each word stands by itself, disconnected from the others. It must be read, and understood, without the flow of spoken language that ties words together.

• Second, at the outset decoding is slow, resulting in delays between decoding one word and then decoding the next word. Suddenly a *this* or a *then* is read all alone, and in that isolated state these words do not mean very much. Disconnected from their partners, the words seem anomalous and confusing. Their meanings are revealed only when they are linked with other words.

So it is not surprising that children who are just starting to read make more mistakes on noncontent than on content words. They also take longer to read noncontent words. Because this difference is measured in milliseconds, it is not readily apparent. However, using sophisticated equipment, researchers, including myself, have clearly measured the effect. It is a sign that children have mentally placed content words and noncontent words into separate categories (Blank & Bruskin, 1982).

Within a few months of starting to read, the timing and error differences vanish for children whose hidden abilities emerge quickly. For children who are having difficulties, this does not happen. For them the teaching must be structured to convey the implicit principles that allow effective decoding.

The Right Connections

Several program components can help children see the connections that make noncontent words meaningful. One involves the systematic patterns in which these words appear. For example, some words, such as *the, this, an, these,* and *that,* link to nouns, forming combinations like *the kid, this book, an apple, these plants,* and *that toy.* Others, such as *was, have, were, is,* and *are,* link to verbs, forming combinations such as *was going, have seen,* and *were swimming.*

Linguists term these links the *distributional properties* of the words. This term is meant to describe how the words do not appear at random but rather distribute themselves, or position themselves, next to other words in definite ways.

One of the clearest examples of a distributional property can be seen with the most common word in our language—*the.* Its unequaled frequency results from its ability to pair with any noun—singular or plural, masculine, feminine, or neuter. No other *noun connector* has this property. For example, the somewhat similar word *a* attaches only to singular nouns, and it also changes to *an* when the noun starts with a vowel (*a boy,* but *an eagle,* for example). It is worth noting that our unconscious skill in using these words appropriately (such as intuitively saying *an* rather than *a*) is part of our hidden phonic abilities.

When we are teaching *the,* its attachment abilities can be conveyed by showing it with nouns that vary in a number of ways; they can be single objects or multiple objects, animate figures or inanimate objects, and male figures or female figures, as the accompanying graphic example shows.

With these pairings, children are reading phrases like *the dog, the birds, the truck, the kids,* and so on. As you can see, by placing *the* next to a variety of pictures, this teaching can take place even when a child cannot read a single word other than *the.* Similar techniques can be used to teach words like *some, more, a,* and *this.*

As children's word base increases, the linkages among words become richer and easier to create. For instance, once children know some verbs such as *walk, run,* and *go,* these content words can easily be linked with noncontent words such as *can, likes to,* and *wants to* (as in *can walk, likes to run, wants to go*). Across the five levels—Boarding, Runway, Liftoff, Airborne, and Soaring—your child sees the wide range of combinations that fosters mastery in this area.

Pairing with Pictures

In the examples for teaching *the,* you saw the role pictures can play in allowing a young child to "read" simple phrases even when he or she knows only a few words. Pictures have an even more important role to play in teaching the noncontent words. They are invaluable in imparting the meaning of many noncontent words.

This may seem incongruous—how can pictures be used to reflect words that seem to refer to nothing in particular? But that's a problem only if you keep the words in isolation. Consider, for example, having to teach the word *was,* which as part of its meaning conveys the idea of *past* or *no longer present.* Any attempt to talk about this idea with your child would be boring and potentially confusing to him or her. The situation is transformed, however, when in place of long explanations the child sees a picture of a cat relaxing, accompanied by carefully constructed sentences.

This cat was jumping.
Now he is resting.

This is an example of the truth of the old saying, "A picture is worth a thousand words." Interestingly, graphics are even more important in teaching noncontent words than they are in teaching content ones. Words like *bus, coat, happy,* and *boat* may be more fun when accompanied by pictures. However, the pictures are not essential to understanding the meaning of such words because they are simple words that children have used for years. In contrast, pictures are essential in helping children to understand the relatively abstract meanings of noncontent words.

In these situations the graphics are not serving as substitutes for the words. With the cat who is resting after jumping earlier, for example, a child cannot look at the picture and guess the eight-word text that accompanies it. The pictures do not replace reading. Rather, they are tools for transmitting the subtle meanings of noncontent words.

This use of pictures is very different from their common use in early reading instruction. When children are having trouble in decoding, they are often encouraged to "look at the picture" and guess at the meaning. Ultimately, this seemingly reasonable strategy does not pay off, because most words cannot be pictured. For example, in many sentences that a child might see in early readers (such as, "'I feel sick,' Lewis said."), there is not a single word that can be decoded by "looking at the picture." These limitations apply to a vast range of the content words that children read, including *come, day, like, live, make, play, people,* and *see.*

The use of this well-intentioned strategy leads children to develop one more of the hidden interfering patterns. Guided by misleading instruction, they do look at the pictures and end up reading with high rates of error.

The graphics in Phonics Plus Five are structured to enable children to get past this bias as soon as possible. For example, the text for the resting cat shown earlier is arranged so that the past tense, non-pictured concept *was jumping* is the first verb the child reads, not the verb *resting.*

Children should not be encouraged to guess at words by "looking at the picture." Because few of the words they read can be pictured, the strategy does not apply to the vast majority of words they see. The advice, though well intentioned, sets them up for failure.

Children who have the strategy of seeking meaning via pictures will often evidence surprise when they come to a word like *jumping,* and they may even ask, "Why does it say 'jumping' when the cat is not jumping? " Within the course of a few words, though, they realize that their strategy of relying on pictures does not work and they abandon it. They then replace matching words and pictures with reading for meaning. So, along with their visual appeal, graphics are useful for transmitting hard-to-convey meanings.

Putting It All Together

The components we have been discussing are integrated into activities such as *Write In to Read*—which contain sentences where the target word is missing and has to be written in. After your child enters the word, he or she reads the entire resulting sentence, so that spelling and reading are combined in sentences that have been carefully structured to convey the meaning of the word. For example, the sentences in the Write In to Read activity shown here are designed to teach the word *but,* and they do so by focusing on the meaning that word has in denying or negating some aspect of a situation.

Target word: but

 Write In to Read

What to do: (1) Point to target word. Say, "This is *but*." (2) Cover word. (3) Point to first line in left-hand box below. Say, "Write *but* here." (4) "Read the whole thing." Immediately correct any error. Repeat for each box. (5) Cover boxes. Say, "Now you'll do some more writing." Provide lined paper and dictate words in first box, 1 word at a time. If there are any errors (including capitals and punctuation), stop, show words, cover them, provide fresh paper, and have child redo writing from first word.

Here is a toy, _____ the toy is not a plane.	**Kids can swim, _____ the kid is not swimming. Kids can jump, _____ the kid is not jumping.**
The cat can rest, _____ the cat cannot rest here.	

This activity has several major features:

• In terms of meaning, *but* has to be able to deny, or limit, something that has been asserted. So other words are needed to create the assertion in order for the meaning of *but* to come across. Words like *is, here,* and *can* are excellent for this purpose because they can refer to simple, present tense conditions that children readily comprehend. For example, in the sentence about the cat, the initial part asserts what the cat is capable of doing (*the cat can rest*). Then the remaining part starts with *but* and moves on to limit what the cat is permitted to do (*but the cat cannot rest here*).

• In terms of graphics, we see the way pictures convey meaning without substituting for words. For example, in the statement *Here is a toy, but the toy is not a plane,* the object being discussed (the robot) is identified first as a member of the general class of toys. The text then moves on to limit the identity of the robot by asserting what it is not (*the toy is not a plane*). The robot itself is never specifically mentioned. It doesn't need to be. Our goal is teaching the meaning of the word *but*. The object best serves that purpose by not being named.

• In terms of mastery, as is always the case, every word in the various sentences has already been taught. By steadily interweaving the known noncontent words with the new, unfamiliar word, the meaning of all the noncontent words is enhanced. For example, words like *here* and *are*, which assert a presence or quality, gain deeper meaning when they link with words that deny a presence or quality.

When the teaching is structured in this way, the rules governing each of the words are steadily conveyed to your child. This is central to helping him or her create the base of hidden abilities responsible for effective reading.

At the same time, your child never has to go through the wasteful and dreary procedure of analyzing and memorizing the rules that control the operation of these words. Indeed, there is every reason to avoid going that route. Traditional phonics is hard for so many children precisely because it requires memorization of all sorts of rules that despite numbering in the hundreds are still only partial reflections of hidden abilities. Phonics Plus Five has built these factors into the system, so that every child attains the feeling of effortlessness that is the hallmark of using language in a skilled manner.

Key Features of the Program

To summarize, Phonics Plus Five offers these key features in its teaching of noncontent words:

- Decoding is taught by highlighting the words in contexts that mirror real texts and that reveal the key properties of the words.
- Accurate spelling is required from the outset, and the techniques are designed to enable children to retain the words in memory.
- Comprehension is emphasized through a series of techniques that include consistently embedding the words in meaningful sentences that reveal the words' essence and using graphics to support meaning.

Chapter Eleven provides directions for creating the teaching materials for the noncontent words.

Having covered the two major groups of words, we can now proceed to the final major component in reading instruction—the books that your child reads.

chapter 8

Teaching Through Books

The Skills of Reading

Sequencing	Writing	Phonology	Semantics	Syntax	Text

Learning how to read words and sentences is only a starting point. The obvious goal is to be able to read books. Books represent the heart and soul of reading. Even in this high-tech age, children find those bound sets of pages to hold an almost magical attraction.

Well before they can read, children choose to spend hours with books. They love turning the pages, they love being read to, they love keeping books on their shelves, and they love returning to these books time and time again. Most of all, they yearn for the day when they can read on their own. Using books they have learned by heart, children often pretend to have reached that miraculous point long in advance of actually getting there. The motivational power of books is tremendous.

The Limits of Motivation

The question then naturally arises, if children are so motivated to read, why do so many experience problems? Aren't we taught that if we want something enough, it will happen?

The answer is simple. Motivation is not the whole story. It never has been. It never will be. For many years, though, people were convinced that it might be. Whole language is grounded in this appealing proposition. It maintains that reading happens naturally if the standard, dreary, drill-type exercises that hold back learning are eliminated and replaced by attractive books that capitalize on children's natural interest.

Sadly, that is not how things work. Any parent whose child struggles with the printed page will tell you the real story. Motivation, like a rainbow, is magnificent. And like a rainbow, it exists only when the conditions are right. With repeated failure, motivation vanishes into thin air—to be replaced by dark clouds of fear, tension, and misery. Children who start out loving books can begin to avoid them like the plague. Children will love reading only if they can read the messages on the printed page easily and effortlessly.

Books: Critical but Neglected

As we discussed in Chapter Two, books—the very core of reading—receive relatively little attention in reading instruction today. For example, in the report on a prestigious, government-sponsored study undertaken for "promoting optimal literacy instruction," you will find the index to contain over 200 references to phonology and related sound analysis activities, but only about sixty references to books of any sort (Snow, Burns, & Griffin, 1998). Books just do not have anywhere near the clout in reading instruction that you might expect them to have.

Whole language adherents assume that children innately have the capacity to deal with appealing books once those books are provided. As a result, they see no need to carry out an in-depth analysis of how books should be structured.

Phonics adherents see decoding of individual words as essential. It is taken as a given that once children can decode the individual words, they will automatically transfer these skills to the books they see—so long as they have been taught all the sounds contained in the words.

The end result of both these approaches is that many of the books that children are eventually given to read on their own fall short of what children need for success. Instead of supporting the reading process, they present hurdles that contribute to failure.

How Is Your Child Doing?

Before we outline how books should be designed, you probably want to get a measure of how well your child is currently doing in this realm. The most efficient way to do this is to carry out a set of brief writing activities that reflect the sorts of sentences contained in books across a range of levels.

Step 1. Start by preparing three sheets of paper with the following sets of sentences, one set per sheet:

Set 1	Sentence	# Correct
1.	The kid is not a girl.	_____
2.	Some rockets are flying.	_____
3.	This robot cannot jump.	_____
4.	Can they walk here?	_____
5.	Some more boys are swimming.	_____
	Criterion: 20 correct	Total _____

Set 2	Sentence	# Correct
1.	That is the only kid who wants to clean this place.	_____
2.	The mice would not move out of the hole.	_____
3.	Which of the two kids pushed the rocks out here?	_____
	Criterion: 24 correct	Total _____

Set 3	Sentence	# Correct
1.	The girl was never scared to go out by herself.	_____
2.	Do most of the kids know how to read their names?	_____
3.	When the computer went down, the girl really started to yell.	_____
	Criterion: 26 correct	Total _____

Step 2. When you have the material ready, sit down with your child at a desk in a quiet room. Provide blank sheets of lined paper along with a pencil or marker, and say, "I'm going to say some sentences and I would like you to write them. But first, listen." Say the first sentence in set 1. Then say, "Now I'll say it again, one word at a time and you write each word." Dictate the words of the sentence—one word at a time—until the sentence is complete. Do not offer any help or guidance. If your child is unable to write a particular word, say, "Let's move on," and dictate the next word.

Step 3. As your child writes each sentence, circle on your sheet each word he or she writes correctly. To be scored as correct, the word has to be error free. Errors include omitting a letter, introducing a letter that is not in the word, putting a letter in the wrong place, or using the wrong case (the first letter of the first word in each sentence should be uppercase; all other letters should be lower-case).

Step 4. When you have finished set 1, add up the number of correct words to see if your child has met the criterion for that set, which is writing twenty or more of the words correctly.

Step 5. If your child has not achieved the criterion, stop the writing and end the session. If your child has achieved the criterion, move on to set 2 and repeat the process. Continue in this manner until your child fails to meet a criterion or until set 3 is completed. (If you and your child cannot complete the writing in a single session, continue in another session a day or so later.)

Step 6. Evaluate the results using the following guidelines. If your child has met the criterion on

- Set 1, his or her level is about mid-first grade.
- Set 2, his or her level is about mid-second grade.
- Set 3, his or her level is about third grade.

Keep in mind that this assessment is brief and does not cover the full range of skills needed for dealing with text. For example, it gives you no indication of your child's comprehension. Still, it is useful in indicating whether or not your child is meeting many of the demands of the grade he or she is in. If your child, for example, is in second grade and has met the criterion on set 2, that suggests he or she is moving along at the expected rate. You may also find that your child has advanced skills relative to his or her grade level.

If your child scores below his or her grade level, do not be concerned. Through the Phonics Plus Five system, you can provide your child with the success you both long for.

Books involve two major skill components, one that is familiar through our earlier discussions and one that is new. The familiar component is decoding, or translating the printed words into their spoken equivalents. The new component is comprehension, or understanding the message that the words convey.

Ensuring Success in Decoding

As I mentioned above, books have not received anywhere near the attention that they should. Their problems in relation to reading instruction start with the number of words they contain. Admittedly, beginner books are not chock-full of words. But even *easy readers* have what amounts to a lot of words for a child.

When a Little Is Still Too Much

Books for the earliest levels of reading will often proudly advertise that they contain "ONLY thirty words!" To experienced readers that seems like a very small number. But as you will recall from your experience with the twenty-six-word foreign letter passage in Chapter One, for a child at the start of the process, that many words can be overwhelming.

Of course for kids who are "born readers" and can immediately identify the words, the reading is easy. For those who must still rely on sounding out, however, the situation is difficult because of the challenge imposed by sounding out twenty-plus words.

Even when the words are in the end sounded out correctly, slow sounding out poses major problems. Words must be read at a steady clip if their message is to be understood. This is a must for successful reading.

To   get
a   sense
of   what   happens
with
                    slow
reading,   try
          remembering
the
                                        words
in   this
segment   when
you
                    have
to   deal
                              with
gaps
          in
space   that
     partially   convey
the
     painful
pauses   that
                    mire   the
young
reader   in
failure.

Slow even though accurate reading is problematic enough. When errors occur, as they inevitably do, the difficulties escalate. Misreading just a single word can render a message incomprehensible. Consider this text:

Ben's friend got a new dog.

His name was Spot.

Spot was very nice and

Ben wanted to play with the dog.

Now consider what would happen if the single word *play* were misread as *pay*. The error is easily dealt with if you happen to be there, listening to your child read aloud. You point out the mistake, your child corrects it, and the reading moves on. If your child is reading independently, though, he or she has no idea where the breakdown occurred. The only solution is to stop, reverse gears, and reread the entire text, hoping to identify what has gone wrong.

An occasional cycle of incomprehension, pausing, and rereading is of no concern once a child's confidence and skill have been established. In the earliest stages, though, when a child is still insecure, errors should be avoided if at all possible.

Small Numbers and Known Words

These decoding problems in beginner books can be minimized by

- Constructing books so they contain fewer words than is typically the case
- Having children learn all the words in a book prior to seeing them in that book, so that slowness and errors are reduced to as close to zero as possible

You can see how these ideas are implemented in the first book of the Phonics Plus Five system, which appears on the next two facing pages. This book is from the Boarding program, and it is titled *Some Kids*. The book tells the story of a group of children coming together to build a snowman, and it does so with a vocabulary of only eight different words, and a total word count of twenty.

Through the word-training activities completed earlier, the children reading this book know every word that appears, permitting the immediate word recognition that underlies smooth decoding. The child's feeling is one of total triumph.

The number of words children know is steadily and rapidly expanded as the children progress through the programs. In addition, relevant words learned in earlier sessions are incorporated into the new material, fostering integration and review. As a result, at the higher levels, a book may contain over 150 different words and around 400 words in all. You can see the increase in complexity by reviewing a sample of four pages from a book used in the highest level, the Soaring program. In this story—*Not a B, But a Bee*—a baby bee is unhappy because she believes her name is a single letter and not a *real* name.

Book 1: Some Kids

some   kids

1

Book 1: Some Kids

some   girls,

some   boys

2

Book 1: Some Kids

a   girl

3

Book 1: Some Kids

a   boy

4

Book 1: Some Kids

more   girls

5

Book 1: Some Kids

some   more   girls

6

Book 1: Some Kids

some   more   boys

7

Book 1: Some Kids

some   kids

8

Book 27: Not a B, But a Bee

Once upon a time, there was a bug. She was like other bugs, and did a lot of the things they did. She would fly, she would eat, and she would drink.

Book 27: Not a B, But a Bee

Sometimes she would do things that people did not like. She would bite. But she would only do that when she was scared.

Book 27: Not a B, But a Bee

Most of the time, she was a nice, happy bug. Then one day, the bug was not happy anymore. She would not smile. All she would do was cry.

Book 27: Not a B, But a Bee

Her mother went to her and asked her why she was crying. She said, "You were such a happy bug. Now your face looks so sad. Can I help? I do not want you to be so sad."

Using Real Books

Beginner texts, even when they exceed the optimal number of words, are still quite short. They are so short that it hardly seems worthwhile putting them in a book. That's why many phonics programs present their texts not as independent books but as segments of workbook pages. The consequences are most unfortunate.

Books hold a magical appeal for children that goes far beyond the stories they contain. Reading the identical text in a workbook simply doesn't provide this exhilaration.

To tap into this motivation, the texts children see must be packaged in book form—a linked set of pages that stands alone and contains a complete message. And these books must be offered to children as early as possible. In Phonics Plus Five, this goal is achieved by offering the child with no previous reading skills a book after he or she has learned only eight words. Within two weeks of starting to read, your child has the thrill of reading a complete book.

Books hold a magical appeal for children that goes far beyond the stories they contain. For a child, being able to read a book is like winning an Olympic medal. A six-year-old who had been floundering in early reading started the Phonics Plus Five programs. Within three weeks, he read his first book. After smoothly and accurately completing its twenty words, he exultantly exclaimed: "I did it! I did it! I read a whole book!"

Anticipating What Is to Come

Once I was in the middle of creating a book and so it still lacked some of its illustrations. A child who was just beginning to read happened to pick it up. When he came to a page of text with no picture, he gasped and said, "I can't read that. Those are just words," and he immediately put the book down. Because I knew he had learned the words, I prevailed upon him to try. He reluctantly agreed, ending up with a perfect reading that both surprised and delighted him.

I subsequently found that many children show similar sorts of reactions. Because they are accustomed to pictures accompanying words, pictureless, word-only text frightens them, and this means they are ill-prepared for the shift to the chapter books that appear in second and third grades.

Fortunately, this problem is easy to overcome. Even though pictures are attractive and necessary, there is no reason for them to appear on every page. Phonics Plus Five books have been designed to provide regular exposure to simple, pictureless texts that children can easily read, and this prepares them for the text-only books that are shortly to follow.

You can see an example of a pictureless book page in the following two pages from the second level—the Runway program. This book—*A Puppy Who Can Run*—tells a story about a puppy who is too small to run but still wants to run.

Book 9: A Puppy Who Can Run

Here is the puppy. The puppy is looking at the big dogs. It also wants

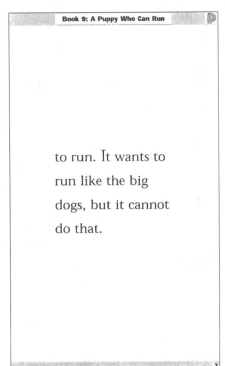

Book 9: A Puppy Who Can Run

to run. It wants to run like the big dogs, but it cannot do that.

Letting Noncontent Words Do Their Work

In the earlier chapters we saw how traditional phonics-based books avoid noncontent words in an attempt to protect children from seeing words that do not "follow the rules." The harm this inflicts on text cannot be emphasized enough. It twists and limits language in ways you would never anticipate.

You have seen here, and probably in your child's homework too, lots of these sentences that aim to restrict words from the noncontent realm. Just to remind you, here is an example of the type of text I am referring to.

Ted has a hat.

Tig hid the hat.

Flit is a bug.

Flit is fast.

Bill has a soft bed.

Bob has a big belt.

Bud has a cut leg.

—Rowland, 1995, workbooks 12 and 14

The problems in such texts are many. For a start, in these texts your child is typically presented with a world of single individuals. Plurals do not seem to exist.

Why do these beginning books depict the world in this way? Surely it's not because children do not understand plurals. Children begin using plurals in their speech when they are about two years old.

It's not children who need to be protected from plurals. It's the reading method that has to be protected. For traditional phonics-based systems, plurals add complications that these systems prefer to postpone. The *s* that attaches to English words to form the plural is another of those pesky *exceptions* that refuse to abide by having a single sound. Depending on the word it attaches to, a final *s* or *es* can be pronounced as *zzz* (as in *dogs*), as *sss* (as in *cats*), or as *ezz* (as in *dishes*).

When sounds become just one of the many components of reading, the difficulties evaporate. Taught correctly, children find it no harder to read *boys* than *boy* or *cats* than *cat*. The benefits for text are clear. The words the children are reading can depict a real world—one where singular and plural coexist. The totally artificial world where plurals have vanished can be avoided.

If you look back to the *Some Kids* book shown previously, you can see that even in the very first book, children in the Phonics Plus Five system are shown how to deal with both singular and plural forms. This is simply one example of the way in which the inclusion of noncontent words leads children to decode more meaningful language.

The Comprehension That Books Require

We now turn to the issue of comprehension. Comprehension is critical to the world of books, and it calls on a set of skills totally different from the skills used in decoding. Books must be structured to enable children to master this component. A major source of difficulty for children is that in working with books, they must deal not simply with words and sentences but with sets of sentences.

Connecting Sentences: An Amazing Skill

Children are used to conversations that span large numbers of sentences. The sentences they are used to in speech, though, are unlike the ones they see in early reading books. In these texts the *simplified sound patterns* invariably combine to form a distorted language. I call it distorted because, unlike real language, these texts often do not transmit meaningful messages.

To understand the difficulties, we need to consider a unit of language we've barely dealt with up to this point. It is the unit known as *connected sentences.* That term refers to the fact that meaningful language, whether in books or in conversation, is made up of sets of sentences that connect with one another. Examples of connected sentences are everywhere.

Imagine, for instance, a person entering a room and saying, "It's cold in here," and then following that up with the question, "Could you please close the window?" If this were to happen, you would not be at all confused, because when you put the two sentences together they make sense.

Now imagine a person entering a room and saying, "It's cold in here," and then following that up with, "Do you wear sunglasses?" At the very least, you would be surprised, because the sentences do not make sense together. Although it may seem strange, currently no one—not even the best linguists—understands just how we develop the remarkably sophisticated system that enables us to recognize in an instant when certain sets of sentences "make sense" and when they do not. It is yet another of the seemingly miraculous and hidden abilities that enable us to choose reliably among the infinite possibilities for structuring language.

Oddly enough, beginning reader books typically offer texts permeated with disconnected and meaningless language. The sentences in those books mirror few of the patterns of language as they are actually used. Instead, in the effort to "simplify" the words, children are offered confusing combinations of sentences.

To see the difficulties, let's reconsider the Dan and Sam text that we discussed in earlier chapters.

Human beings have a phenomenal skill in their knowledge of how to connect one sentence to another. As with so many hidden abilities, the ties are invisible, and no one fully understands how they work. But they do work—and because they do, we can use and understand long stretches of language.

Dan has an ax.

Has Dan an ax?

Sam has ham.

Has Sam ham?

Dan has land and sand.

Has Dan sand?

Sam sat.

Dan sat.

In this text the first sentence is *Dan has an ax.* If realistic language were being used, you would expect a second sentence to continue the theme by possibly talking about characteristics of the object (for example, *It is sharp*), Dan's relationship to the object (for example, *He just bought it*), or a comparison between Dan and others (for example, *Sam does not have an ax*).

Given the range of options, we do not know precisely what the next sentence will be. Still, it is a forgone conclusion that when a person has just asserted that Dan possesses an ax, the next sentence would never be one in which that person questions what he or she has just said by asking, *Has Dan an ax?*

With the third sentence, in this example, the juxtaposition gets even more confusing. After saying that Dan has an ax, it would be ludicrous for a person to continue by saying that *Sam has ham.* Reasonable alternatives might be, *Sam does not have an ax, Sam has a hammer,* or *Sam envies Dan.* In a real-life conversation or written text, we might say a lot of different things about Sam within the context of Dan's having an ax, but the chances of our mentioning that Sam has ham are infinitesimally small.

As we proceed through this text, we find that each sentence is plagued with similar problems. *Land* and *sand* are about as disconnected as they could possibly be from *ax* and *ham.* The only justification for linking them comes from phonics— it is either that they share the letter *a* (thereby restricting the words used to a single vowel) or that they end with the same cluster of letters (thereby teaching rhyming). Similarly, the only justification for the strange questioning of each assertion (*Has Dan an ax? Has Sam ham? Has Dan land?*) is that the statement and question use identical words, thereby limiting the number of words the children must deal with.

By disregarding message meaning and focusing exclusively on parameters for individual words, initial reading instruction has allowed itself to present children with books that are inherently meaningless—a surefire way to create confusion. This problem of using disconnected, rather than connected, sentences is not new.

Using Texts That Make Sense

In any text, meaning should always be preeminent. There's no purpose in constructing a book that conveys a meaningless message. Fortunately, when sounds are no longer permitted to dominate the text, the obstacles to meaningful stories vanish. Gone is the need to confine the message to a *cat* and a *rat*, or to *Sam* and *ham*. That is what permits the thirty books of the Phonics Plus Five system to have a quality totally different from that of most early reading books. Even in the early levels they mirror the characteristics of published texts—both fiction and nonfiction—and convey the message that texts are meaningful. Anything less is detrimental to children's progress.

To see the richness and meaning that an instructional text can convey, the following illustration shows the last eight pages from a book offered in the fourth level, the Airborne program. Titled *Birds and Flying,* this book exposes children to nonfiction text that lays the groundwork for reading books on science. The theme is that most birds move by flying, but the book then moves on to point out that there are some flightless birds.

This text is quite a step up from the twenty-word text offered in the first book, but children following the Phonics Plus Five programs are systematically prepared to advance to this level in a relatively short period of time.

The Ability to Predict

As I said earlier, we do not understand much about the remarkable skills we have for connecting sets of sentences so they make sense, but one factor that does seem critical is predictability.

As a message comes in, people have an amazing power to take that message and predict what is coming next—before it is actually stated. That's why, after hearing "It's cold in here," you are not surprised to hear the question "Could you please close the window?" This skill is based on your hidden ability to predict the kinds of ideas that can sensibly follow one another. This is what is meant by predictability.

It is a bird. Birds are animals that can move by flying. They do not have to fly all the time and they do not fly all the time. But they can fly any time they want.

All kinds of birds can move that way. Big birds can fly and small birds can fly.

Birds that stay in hot places can fly, and birds that stay in cold places can fly.

Birds that eat small bugs can fly, and birds that eat big animals can fly.

Birds with small legs can fly, and birds with big legs can fly. Birds that go in the water can fly, and birds that do not go in the water can fly.

8

All those birds have wings, and they use their wings to fly.

Some kids think that all birds can fly. It seems like that. It seems that all birds fly. Still there are some birds that cannot fly.

What birds are those?

9

Here are some of those birds. Do these birds have wings? Yes, they do. But their wings are very small. Their wings are too small for them to fly. These birds still move, but they do not fly.

10

Are there still some kids who think that all birds fly? Yes, there are.

But now you can say, "It seems that way and most of them do. But some do not."

11

Published books—even those for young children—steadily demand this skill. For example, consider the following sequence from the classic tale of the Pied Piper.

> Hamelin was a lovely town.
>
> It had pretty little houses
>
> and cobblestone streets.
>
> And it was next to
>
> a great wide river.
>
> But Hamelin had a problem.
>
> —_Hautzig, 1989, p. 5_

In this story, as in any real story, the sentences are marked by enormous variation. Most do not share even a single word, let alone sets of words. But this is how words and sentences appear in real life. Predictability rests not in the repetition of words or sounds but in the meaning that links the sentences together. We accept the combination, "Hamelin was a lovely town. It had pretty little houses and cobblestone streets," because it makes sense. Having heard that a town is lovely, it is reasonable to expect that the town has pretty houses and nice streets. Meaning, not word repetition, is _the_ factor that determines the predictability of real sentences in the real world.

Unique Materials: Books to Enact

It has long been known that skill in predicting an oncoming message, or in knowing where "the text is leading" (Snow et al., 1998, p. 195), is a phenomenal advantage in reading, and readers who develop this skill find it far easier to understand what they are reading, and they can read at a faster rate (Blank, 2002). The ability to predict language is phenomenally complex, and children vary greatly in this skill. Further, as with so many of the other skills in reading, this one has been cast aside in early reading instruction, so that nothing systematic is included to help children develop it. In Phonics Plus Five this skill is addressed through an innovative technique of having children read books with incomplete messages. These books have gaps in their wording. The holes on the page, just like the holes in a partially completed jigsaw puzzle, stimulate children's natural interest, and they want to fill them in.

Puzzles stimulate visual skills, such as color and shape recognition. Filling in missing words, in contrast, stimulates language skills, such as predictability.

Consider a simple example such as having to come up with the missing word in a text like, "Here is a boy. He __ __ walking." Turning to your knowledge of language, you can predict that *is* is the missing word. That is why this method is so effective.

Each of the five reading programs (Boarding, Runway, Liftoff, Airborne, and Soaring) in the Phonics Plus Five system contains six books. The first, third, and fifth books feature complete texts (*books intact*), and as with conventional texts, your child has only to read the story. The second, fourth, and sixth books at each level have blank spaces to be filled in (*books to enact*), and your child has to complete the missing words before reading the story.

The material that follows from the book *The Bugs, the Kids,* which is used in the first level (the Boarding program) is a sample of this type of innovative text.

There are two ways for children to accomplish the insertions:

1. With material they feel they can predict, they can use the code to confirm each prediction. For example, on the page showing some kids and the text

    Here are

    _____ kids.
    ♥

    children might suggest—correctly—that the missing word is *some.* But before writing in that word, they can check their guess by looking at the code at the bottom of the page:

    ∪ = can   ♠ = jump   ♥ = some   ⇐ = the

2. With less familiar material, children can go directly to the code and find the words they need. For example, on the second page, the children see

    _____ can
    ∪∪

    _____.
    ♠

Book 4: The Bugs, the Kids

Here are
some _____.
⊃⊃

⊃⊃ = bugs   ⇐ = not   ◆ = swim

1

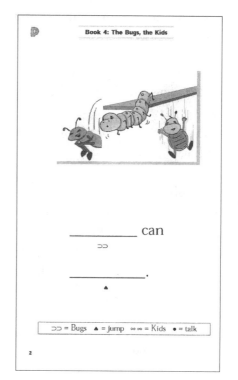

Book 4: The Bugs, the Kids

_____ can
⊃⊃

_____.
▲

⊃⊃ = Bugs   ▲ = jump   ∞∞ = Kids   • = talk

2

Book 4: The Bugs, the Kids

Here are
_____ kids.
♥

∪ = can   ▲ = jump   ♥ = some   ⇐ = the

3

Book 4: The Bugs, the Kids

_____ kids
⇐

_____ jump.
∪

⊃⊃ = bugs   ∪ = can   ∞ = not   ⇐ = The

In a situation with a number of possible options, children are better served when they look down at the choices to get the words they need.

In other words, depending on their skill level, in any book and even on any page, children can switch between these two modes of responding. In combination, they allow children, even at the earliest stages of reading, to carry out a sophisticated prediction and completion task in an errorless manner that is invaluable to the learning process.

The Main Idea

The final aspect of comprehension that we will consider can be referred to as the *main idea*. It is the ability to take the set of ideas in a story and succinctly summarize the essence, omitting all but the essential details.

This is a primary goal of reading instruction across the grades. It's the reason why teachers regularly ask students: What was the story about? Can you give me a summary of what you read? or, What was the main idea? In response to these requests, children are expected to "analyze, critique, abstract, and reflect on text" (Snow et al., 1998, p. 10) so as to get at the core of the issues and condense them into brief, coherent statements.

These demands to summarize increase as children advance in their grades. That is why many kids' reading scores plummet in about the fourth grade. At this time there is a shift in emphasis as the instruction moves from decoding to comprehension. Problems in this area are among the major forces responsible for the poor reading scores that the states are reporting. Vast numbers of children are stymied when they have to cull and convey the meaning of what they have read.

These difficulties, though disturbing, are not surprising, because children receive almost no systematic teaching in this area. Identifying the main idea requires them to bypass details, when almost all their training has been focused on the recall of details. They are used to being asked questions about specific points, such as "the color of the man's car," "the name of the girl's pet," and "the toy that the boy received." They are not at all used to combining the details so as to succinctly summarize the total message. As a result, many simply do not know what to do when faced with calls for a main idea.

One bright fourth grader who was struggling with the main idea candidly explained the situation. His explanation reveals not only his coping strategy, but the way that strategy had been fostered by the dominant educational practices: "The main idea? I have no idea what a main idea is. But it's not so bad. Eight out of ten questions are on details and only one or two are on the main idea. That means I can still get 80 percent or 90 percent on my tests. So it doesn't matter if I figure out the main idea."

You can admire this child's ingenuity, but ultimately, his strategy won't work. As books get longer and more complex, the details pile up beyond manageable levels. If children do not learn how to summarize, their comprehension never reaches adequate levels. We must offer children the training they need to master this key skill in reading.

"The main idea? I have no idea what a main idea is. But it's not so bad. Eight out of ten questions are on details and only one or two are on the main idea. That means I can still get 80 percent or 90 percent on my tests. So it doesn't matter if I figure out the main idea" [comment of a fourth-grade student].

Gleaning Meaning

Fortunately, effective training can begin early on and provide children with a solid base for comprehension. Once past the first two reading levels in the Phonics Plus Five system, your child is introduced to the *Gleaning Meaning* activity that sets him or her on the path to early and effective comprehension.

This activity provides your child with a prototype, or model, of a short text that summarizes the story he or she has just completed. The model, however, contains gaps that your child fills in to make the summary complete.

For example, in the book *Birds and Flying* (segments of which you saw earlier), your child sees the summary illustrated here. Selecting one word at a time from the words at the bottom of the page, he or she fills in the blanks and then reads the full summary.

> **Book 19: Birds and Flying**
>
> ## Gleaning Meaning
>
> Animals are not like plants. Plants
> cannot move, but animals
> _____. They have many ways of
> _____. Some move by
> walking, some by _____, and
> some by _____.
> Birds are a kind of animal, and
> _____ of them move by flying.
> They fly by using their _____.
> But some birds cannot fly. Their
> wings are too _____ for them
> to fly.
>
> can flying most moving small swimming wings
>
> 12

This task looks simple and it is. It has been designed to be that way. Children who are still novices at reading find it easy, and their confidence skyrockets. At the same time, the regular encounters with well-constructed summaries, without pressure or fear of failure, foster the hidden abilities that lead children to create summaries on their own. By the time they reach the highest-level programs, most children are accomplishing this with ease.

Key Features of the Programs

At all five levels—the Boarding, Runway, Liftoff, Airborne, and Soaring programs—the books of the Phonics Plus Five system are designed to facilitate both decoding and comprehension.

Decoding is taught through the following techniques:

• Tightly limiting the total number of words in the initial books

• Restricting the books to words the children have learned

• Providing all the texts in the form of independent (stand-alone) books

- Incorporating features, such as pictureless text, that help children prepare for the conventions of the more advanced, published books they will soon encounter

- Including noncontent words in ways that mirror natural language

Comprehension is fostered by the following methods:

- Providing texts with meaningfully connected sentences

- Offering incomplete texts (books to enact), where children make entries that foster skills such as predictability

- Including comprehension activities that initiate children at the earliest levels into formulating main ideas

Chapter Twelve provides the directions for creating the books for all five reading programs (Boarding, Runway, Liftoff, Airborne, and Soaring).

PART 3

Constructing the Programs

Materials for the Teaching

All the materials that follow will allow you to create the entire reading system. However, if you prefer a fully prepared set of materials of Phonics Plus Five, you can order it by calling 1-866-DRBLANK (866-372-5265) or by visiting http://www.phonicsplusfive.com.

Sequences in Sight

The first program in the Phonics Plus Five system is Sequences in Sight. It is one of the two programs at the Get Set level that prepares your child for reading. This chapter presents the material you need to create and use the program.

Depending on the skills your child has already developed, he or she may not need this program. The activities outlined in Chapter Four under How Is Your Child Doing? will tell you whether you should carry out this program with your child. Generally, for children who are nonreaders or are just beginning to recognize some words, this program is an excellent one to use.

If your child does not need this program, you can bypass this chapter and go to Chapter Ten, where the Letters to Write program is described.

If your child needs both of the Get Set programs (Sequences in Sight and Letters to Write), you can carry out these programs simultaneously, with the first half of each session devoted to one program and the second half to the other.

Effective sequencing skills can best be developed prior to formal reading instruction. That is the goal of Sequences in Sight.

Preparing the Materials for Sequences in Sight

Be sure to prepare all the materials in advance, before you start the teaching. To do this, make copies of the following set of pages and follow the directions they contain.

The Symbols

What to do: Copy the table of symbols and then cut and paste each symbol onto a small, separate cardboard square (so that it resembles a chip used in board games).

δ	γ	φ	λ	π
σ	ϖ	ξ	ψ	ζ
δ	γ	φ	λ	π
σ	ϖ	ξ	ψ	ζ
δ	γ	φ	λ	π

σ	ϖ	ξ	ψ	ζ
δ	γ	φ	λ	π
σ	φ	ξ	ψ	ζ
θ	ϖ	δ	φ	θ
θ	φ	θ	φ	σ

In addition, prepare a $8\frac{1}{2}$-by-11-inch cardboard sheet with three lines (following the pattern shown here).

The Record Form

What to do: Complete all twenty items in a session. As each item is completed, if your child's first response is correct, place a ✓ in the appropriate space; if the response is not correct, place an X in the space, and repeat the item until your child completes it correctly. Make several copies of the following Record Form so you will always have one available. One form can be used for two sessions.

Sequences in Sight: Record Form

Date _____ Session # _____ | Date _____ Session # _____

What to do: Enter ✓ if correct; X if incorrect. | (Repeat item until it is correct.)

Sequence from Level _____ | Sequence from Level _____

1 ___	11 ___	1 ___	11 ___
2 ___	12 ___	2 ___	12 ___
3 ___	13 ___	3 ___	13 ___
4 ___	14 ___	4 ___	14 ___
5 ___	15 ___	5 ___	15 ___
6 ___	16 ___	6 ___	16 ___
7 ___	17 ___	7 ___	17 ___
8 ___	18 ___	8 ___	18 ___
9 ___	19 ___	9 ___	19 ___
10 ___	20 ___	10 ___	20 ___

Total ✓s _____ | Total ✓s _____

Moving on: Enter a • in the Summary of Session chart below if there are 14 or more ✓s in a session. When your child achieves a • in 3 successive sessions, move to the next level.

Summary of Session   Level ____

Session	1	2	3	4	5	6	7	8	9	10	11	12	13	14	15	16
•																

The Sequences to Be Used

What to do: The following sheets provide the sequences you will be using in each session. During a session, always have these patterns nearby to guide you in putting out the symbols.

Sequences for Levels 1 and 2

Sequence	Symbols for Selection	Sequence	Symbols for Selection
Sessions 1, 5, 9, 13		_Sessions 2, 6, 10, 14_	
λπ	θλξπ	δφ	δγφλ
φλ	φπλγ	λπ	θλξπ
λπσ	γλπσ	σδλ	ϖφσδλ
φλσ	θϖφλσ	φλ	φπλγ
θπλ	θφπξλ	λπσ	γλπσ
ψλ	φψλξ	φλσ	θϖφλσ
πψδ	πψζσδ	πψ	ξπψσλ
σψ	ζσγψ	θσλ	θφσλσ
λφ	λξφψ	φδ	θφδπ
σφϖ	λσφϖσ	πσδ	ψπζσδ
λζ	γπλδζ	σδ	φσπδ
φψφ	θφψγφ	πσδ	ζπσϖδ
σφλ	πσϖφλ	πλσ	ψπλϖσ
ψδ	ψφξδ	φψφ	φϖψφ
λφφ	ξλφφπ	σφλ	ξλσφλ
δσσ	δπσσ	ψδ	ψδπσ
ζφ	δζφλ	λφφ	λϖφψφ
σψζ	σϖψδζ	δσσ	δϖσψσ
σφσ	ψσφζσ	ζφ	ζφψφ
λπ	λξπφ	σψζ	θσψθζ

Sequence	Symbols for Selection	Sequence	Symbols for Selection
Sessions 3, 7, 11, 15		*Sessions 4, 8, 12,16*	
δδπ	σδδπθ	δφδ	δσφϖδ
σφ	πψγσφ	σπ	φσπζ
φφ	φθφλ	θλπ	σθλδπ
πσψ	ϖπδσψ	λφ	ππλφ
φδπ	λφδθπ	πσλ	ζπδσλ
σλσ	σφφλσ	λφσ	θλφπσ
ζφφ	γζπϖφφ	πψ	πϖψσ
φψσ	φγψλσ	σσλ	σφσϖλ
φσ	φξλσζ	λφ	λφσσ
δφλ	φδφγλ	πσδ	πλσδλ
———	———	———	———
φσδ	δϖφσδ	ϖσδ	ϖφσπδ
λφπ	σλφπγ	φπσ	φλπϖσ
ψσζ	ψσϖζσ	πλ	θδπλ
πφφ	πφπλφ	φφψ	φπφλψ
σδλ	σϖφδλ	φλσ	λλφλσ
ψσπ	ϖψσζπ	δψ	δφψφ
σφσ	ζσφζσ	φλφ	ϖφπλφ
ψλ	ψγλ	σδσ	πλσδσ
σδ	σξδφ	σφ	σδσδ
δσλ	δσγλ	σζψ	φσζφψ

Sequences for Levels 3 and 4

Sequence	Symbols for Selection	Sequence	Symbols for Selection
Sessions 1, 5, 9, 13		*Sessions 2, 6, 10, 14*	
δφψ	δγφγψ	φδλ	πφγδλ
λπδ	θλπδξ	φψψπ	φψψπσσ
δσδ	δϖϖσδ	φδ	ξφξδ
φλ	φπλγ	δσλ	δππσλ
λπσψ	θλπσψθ	πψψλ	πθψσψλ
φλσ	θϖφλσ	δπσ	δπψσψ
πψ	ξπψσ	σψσψ	γσψσψγ
φσδ	θφσδπ	πδδφ	θπδδφσ
πσδδ	ψπζσδδ	δλψψ	θδθλψψ
πλψσ	θπθλψσ	φλσ	ζφζλσ
———	———	———	———
σδπ	σξδφπ	δγφλ	δσγφλσ
δσ	λδξσ	θλξ	θπλξπ
φππδ	λφππϖδ	ϖφδλ	ϖφσδζλ
λψλ	γλψλϖ	φπλ	φπφλγ
δσπψ	ζδσπζψ	γλπσ	γθλπσ
σπδ	ϖξσπδ	θϖφ	θλϖφσ
δπλλ	δγγπλλ	ξψσξ	ξπψσξλ
λσψ	ζλσψγ	θφ	θφσλ
δπψσ	ξδπψσξ	φδπ	θγφδπ
δλψλ	δλϖϖψλ	ψπζσ	γψπζσδ

Sequence	Symbols for Selection	Sequence	Symbols for Selection
Sessions 3, 7, 11, 15		**Sessions 4, 8, 12, 16**	
δλφ	δπλφπ	δφϖ	δφϖδ
σπφψ	σπγγφψ	φσπζ	φδδσπζ
δπ	δξπξ	σθλδ	σπθλδπ
δλσσ	δλδδσσ	ππλ	φππλφ
πλσ	πθλσθ	ζπδδ	ζσπδσδ
σππ	ψψσππ	θλ	θφπλ
φσψψ	πφσψψ	πψσ	πλϖψσ
πδφ	θπδφθ	σφσλ	σγφσϖλ
λψδ	θθλψδ	λσσ	λϖφσσ
φλλσ	ωφλωλσ	πλσδ	πζλσδλ
————	————	————	————
πλσσ	ϖλπθσσ	ϖφσ	ϖφσπδ
φψψπ	λφλψψπ	φλπφ	φλπφγσ
ψφ	ψσφλ	θδπ	θψδπλ
λππλ	φλφππλ	πφλψ	φπφλπψ
λφψ	λφγλψ	λφ	λφλσ
δφππ	δφϖππ	δφψ	δσφψφ
λσπ	λδσφπ	ϖφπλ	ϖφξπλφ
σλ	σλσγ	πλσλ	πλσλδσ
ψλψ	ψπλδψ	σδφ	σϖδφδ
σλδφ	ξσλδφξ	φζφψ	φσζφψδ

The Levels

The program consists of four levels, with level 1 always serving as the starting point. Every session contains twenty sequences. Once your child has mastered a level, move on to the next one. This pattern is repeated until all four levels have been completed.

Level 1: What to Do

Using the cardboard squares with symbols that you prepared earlier and following the symbol sequences in the Sequences to Be Used chart, you set out two sequences on the $8\frac{1}{2}$-by-11-inch lined cardboard sheet. The top row contains a sequence of two or three symbols that you place on the line in left-to-right order. The bottom row contains the symbols for selection; these are symbols identical to those in the top row along with additional symbols. A typical arrangement might appear as follows:

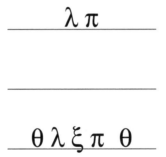

You point to the sequence in the top row and say to your child, "Look at these." Then pointing to the middle row, you say, "You are going to make another sequence here that is just like the one on top."

Point to the first symbol on the left in the bottom row and say, "Use these to make the matching sequence. Start here."

In creating the matching sequence, your child always has to work from left to right. In the sequence above, for example, the λ has to be entered before the π.

When the sequence is completed correctly, you say, "That's right," and remove from the sheet the symbols in the bottom row that were not used. The sheet then appears as follows:

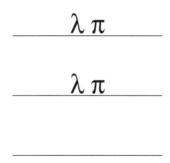

$\lambda \pi$

$\lambda \pi$

If your child makes an error (including not placing the symbols in left-to-right order—even if the symbols themselves are correct), you immediately stop him or her and say, "No, that is not right." Then you model the correct sequence (that is, you take, one at a time from the bottom row, the correct symbols in the correct left-to-right order and move them to the middle row). After that, you replace the symbols in their original bottom row positions and say, "Now try that again."

After each sequence is completed, you enter the score on the Record Form. You continue in this manner until all twenty sequences for the session have been completed.

Level 2: What to Do

At this level, your child has to match the patterns from memory. First you set out a model in the top row such as the following:

$\psi \pi \pi$

You then say to your child, "Look at these." Following this, you cover the symbols with a blank card. Then, you set out the Symbols for Selection in the bottom row so that your child sees the following arrangement:

Then you point to the bottom row and say, "Find the symbols that are the same as the ones you just saw, and [*pointing to the middle line*] put them here. [*Pointing to the symbol on the left*] Start here."

If your child's selection (including left-to-right order) is correct, say, "That was great," and move to the next sequence. If there is an error, stop your child immediately and say, "No, that isn't right." Then show both patterns and allow your child to redo the sequence while both patterns are in view. Then repeat the activity once again, but this time, with the top pattern covered.

Level 3: What to Do

For this level you follow the same procedure as for level 1. However, the sequences contain up to four symbols.

Level 4: What to Do

The final level uses the same memory activity as in level 2. However, the sequences are longer and include patterns containing up to four symbols.

The Sessions

Once the materials are ready, you can start the sessions. They should be carried out at a desk or table in a quiet room where you can be alone with your child. You might like to try a short practice session with someone—child or adult—who is not going to be working with the program so that you can become comfortable with the material.

There are twenty sequences in a session. You create them by following the symbols outlined in Sequences for Levels 1 and 2 and Sequences for Levels 3 and 4. The material is designed so that after completing sessions 1 to 4 at a level, you reuse the same patterns for the sessions that follow. For example, the sequences used for session 1 are then reused for sessions 5, 9, and 13. Similarly, the sequences used for session 2 are then reused for sessions 6, 10, and 14.

During each session you need to have the sheet of sequences close at hand so that you can easily create the patterns you need. However, you should always position the paper so that your child cannot see the patterns you are following.

At the start, sequencing demands are novel, and it may take your child a few sessions to adjust to them. If this happens in the initial sessions of a level, do not be concerned. The accuracy is likely to improve in short order.

Each session takes about ten to twenty minutes to complete. You should schedule no more than one session a day. In the course of a week, you can arrange to have between three and seven sessions. It is important to have at least three sessions a week, but I recommend more if you have the time to do so. If your child has already experienced some difficulties in reading, it is best to schedule six to seven sessions a week, because that enables the child to attain as quickly as possible the success he or she has been longing for.

Moving On

Your child remains at a level until he or she shows mastery of that level. This means completing three successive sessions with fourteen or more (of the twenty) sequences correct on a first attempt. When this happens, you move to the next level. At the end of level 4, your child has finished the Sequences in Sight program. He or she can then move on to the Boarding level—if he or she has also finished the Letters to Write program or does not require that program.

Although the time will vary according to the number of sessions in a week, most children complete Sequences in Sight in three to six weeks. However, with some younger children this may not happen. An occasional "off day" is not a problem. But if after the first five sessions at a level you find that your child does not steadily achieve at least twelve correct responses in a session, you should stop the program. It is likely that your child is not yet ready for Sequences in Sight. You can then wait a month or two and try the program again.

chapter 10

Letters to Write

This chapter presents the program components for Letters to Write, the Phonics Plus Five program that teaches the motor skills needed for handwriting. Your child's performance on the activities in Chapter Five in the section titled How Is Your Child Doing? tells you whether he or she needs this program.

Your child may need both the Sequences in Sight and the Letters to Write programs. If that is the case, these programs can be carried out simultaneously (with the first half of a session devoted to one program and the second half to the other).

If you are working on Sequences in Sight or Letters to Write, do not begin the reading and writing programs. However, if your child does not need either of these Get Set programs, you can move ahead to Chapter Eleven.

Effective handwriting skills are essential to enabling a child to carry out the writing that supports and extends reading skills. That is the goal of Letters to Write.

Preparing the Materials for Letters to Write

Before starting the teaching, prepare all the materials in advance, as described in the following pages. You may make copies of these pages so that you have the instructions for producing the letters at hand during the sessions.

Creating the Worksheets

What to do: All the writing is done on worksheets you create. Each worksheet looks like this:

To make the worksheet, take a blank $8\frac{1}{2}$-by-11-inch sheet of white paper, and draw two rows of six black lines on it, as illustrated. You will be using three to five of these worksheets in each session, so make sure you have enough copies made up in advance. In addition, you will need a thin, colored marker (blue, green, or red) for writing the letters. Markers are easier to use than pencils, and the colored writing stands out against the black lines.

Creating the Letters

What to do: The teaching is designed so that your child sees not just a final, completed letter but also the process by which the letter is created. You show this by creating the letter while your child observes what you are doing. This allows your child to see such features as the point where you start the letter and the places where you change the direction of the strokes.

On every worksheet, you start by producing a letter on the top left-hand space. Your child, on the line directly below, then immediately copies what you have done. For example, after the first letter has been written, the worksheet might appear as follows:

C __ __ __ __ __

C __ __ __ __ __

After the second letter has been written, it might appear like this:

c l __ __ __ __

c l __ __ __ __

You continue in this manner until you and your child have completed all the letters in a session. These letters are outlined in the Letters in a Session guide that follows.

The Letters in a Session

What to do: The following guide presents the order in which the letters are to be produced in each session. Have this sheet available during each session so that you will know which letters to present.

Letters for Level 1

Sessions 1, 4, 7, 10, 13, 16

| c | j | l | o | c | j | o | i | o | c | l | o | c | c | j | l |

Sessions 2, 5, 8, 11, 14, 17

| l | o | l | j | c | i | c | i | c | l | j | o | l | i | j | o |

Sessions 3, 6, 9, 12, 15, 18

| j | c | o | l | i | o | i | l | j | o | l | i | c | o | i | o |

Letters for Level 2 (letters produced in a series of steps are underlined the first time they appear)

Sessions 1, 4, 7, 10, 13, 16

| <u>e</u> | e | c | <u>f</u> | f | <u>i</u> | i | <u>s</u> | s | <u>k</u> | k | <u>e</u> | e | o | <u>j</u> | j |

Sessions 2, 5, 8, 11, 14, 17

| l | <u>t</u> | t | o | <u>k</u> | k | c | <u>f</u> | f | <u>j</u> | j | <u>e</u> | e | <u>s</u> | s | c |

Sessions 3, 6, 9, 12, 15, 18

| c | <u>e</u> | e | o | <u>f</u> | f | <u>k</u> | k | l | <u>i</u> | i | <u>t</u> | t | <u>s</u> | s | l |

Letters for Level 3

Sessions 1, 4, 7, 10, 13, 16

| e | o | c | f | s | i | j | s | t | k | j | e | c | o | j | l |

Sessions 2, 5, 8, 11, 14, 17

| l | t | o | c | k | s | t | f | o | j | i | e | o | s | e | c |

Sessions 3, 6, 9, 12, 15, 18

| c | e | t | o | f | s | k | l | j | i | l | t | i | s | e | l |

Letters for Level 4 (letters produced in a series of steps are underlined the first time they appear)

Sessions 1, 4, 7, 10, 13, 16

<u>d</u>   d   c   <u>n</u>   n   <u>h</u>   h   <u>a</u>   a   <u>n</u>   n   <u>b</u>   b   e   <u>x</u>   x

Sessions 2, 5, 8, 11, 14, 17

e   <u>q</u>   q   f   k   <u>u</u>   u   <u>g</u>   g   f   i   <u>z</u>   z   <u>r</u>   r   t

Sessions 3, 6, 9, 12, 15, 18

c   <u>y</u>   y   o   <u>w</u>   w   <u>p</u>   p   l   <u>m</u>   m   <u>v</u>   v   <u>h</u>   h   j

Letters for Level 5

Sessions 1, 4, 7, 10, 13, 16

e   d   c   n   s   h   j   s   t   a   m   e   c   n   g   p

Sessions 2, 5, 8, 11, 14, 17

l   q   f   w   k   s   t   v   o   u   i   e   r   b   a   o

Sessions 3, 6, 9, 12, 15, 18

c   y   t   o   f   m   g   l   d   z   h   b   i   n   e   l

Scoring the Letters

What to do: Each letter is evaluated on the following four points:

Scoring Criteria

Point A	Starting point	The letter is produced by starting at the top.
Point B	Placement	The letter is placed correctly relative to the line (*c*, *s*, *u*, *o* touch the line; *j* and *p* go below the line).
Point C	Size	The letter is similar in size to the model at the top.
Point D	Shape	The letter is the correct shape (for example, *c* is rounded; *j* has a straight line ending in a curve; *o* is circular; *u* has an open, *cup* shape; *p* has a straight line with a circular shape in the appropriate place; *s* has 2 curves in correct orientation).

To be considered correct, a letter must meet all four points. Although there is obviously a level of subjectivity in the scoring, do not be overly concerned. Just let your first impression guide you, because it usually is the right one.

The Record Form

What to do: Complete all sixteen items in a session. As each item is completed, if your child's first response is correct, place a ✓ in the appropriate space; if it is not, place an X in the space, and repeat the item until your child completes it correctly. Make several copies of the Record Form so that you will always have one available. One form can be used for two sessions.

Letters to Write: Record Form

Date _____ Session # _____	Date _____ Session # _____
Level _____	Level _____
1 __ 9 __	1 __ 9 __
2 __ 10 __	2 __ 10 __
3 __ 11 __	3 __ 11 __
4 __ 12 __	4 __ 12 __
5 __ 13 __	5 __ 13 __
6 __ 14 __	6 __ 14 __
7 __ 15 __	7 __ 15 __
8 __ 16 __	8 __ 16 __
Total ✓s _____	Total ✓s _____

Scoring criteria: Enter a ✓ for a letter if it meets the following four points:
1. Each stroke starts at the correct point.
2. The letter is placed correctly relative to the line.
3. The size of the letter is similar to the size of the model.
4. Each line or stroke has the correct shape.

Moving on: Enter a • in the Summary of Session chart below if there are 12 or more ✓s in a session. When your child attains a • in 2 successive sessions, move to the next level.

Summary of Session   Level _____

Session	1	2	3	4	5	6	7	8	9	10	11	12	13	14	15	16	17	18
•																		

The Levels

Letters to Write has five levels, with each level containing sets of lowercase letters that advance from simple to complex. All children start with level 1.

Level 1: What to Do

Level 1 teaches the letters *c, i, j, l,* and *o,* which are restricted to single shapes.

As shown in the diagram below, you create each of these letters by starting at the top point and moving down. In the case of the *o* and the *c,* the movement is to the left. The letter *j* is important in teaching your child from the outset that some letters break the horizontal guide line. Aside from the *j,* each letter at this level must end up "resting" on the horizontal line. Omit the dots above the *i* and the *j* for now; they will be introduced at the second level.

The letters are constructed in two steps.

Step 1. With your child watching, say, "Look at this." Then you make one of the letters on the top left-hand line of a copy of the worksheet you made earlier. (Do not give your child a marker for this step; he or she needs to just watch you and not attempt to write along with you.)

Step 2. After you have completed the letter, you hand the marker to your child. Then point to the bottom left-hand line, and say, "Make the same letter here." Your child then replicates the letter on the bottom line.

In producing the letter your child must (1) follow the same sequence of movement you used and (2) achieve the same final product (so that his or her letter contains all the key features your letter contains). The Scoring Criteria chart guides you in determining the adequacy of your child's production.

When your child's letter is correct, you say, "Yes, that's right," and then move on to the next letter. When your child's letter is not correct, you immediately stop him or her and provide feedback, saying, "No, that's not right." Then, saying, "Let's try

Letters at Level 1

that again," you move to the next line to the right and repeat the process (so that you again produce the model letter on the top line and your child has to reproduce that letter on the bottom line). If a problem is arising because your child is not starting the letter at the correct point, move your child's hand to the appropriate place and say, "Start here."

Level 2: What to Do

At this level, along with the letters from level 1, your child also produces the double shapes *e, f, k, s,* and *t.* The Letters for Level 2 guide provides the order to follow. The diagram below shows you how to create the new letters.

The new letters are constructed in the following steps.

Step 1. You make the first stroke (with an *e,* for example, the first stroke is the short horizontal line; with an *s,* it is the top half, *c*-shaped segment, of the letter; and so on). (The previous illustration shows the first strokes for level 1.)

Step 2. Your child copies that first stroke.

Step 3. Working in the same space where you produced your first stroke, you add the second stroke to complete the letter (for an *e,* you attach the curved, *c*-shaped stroke; for an *s,* you add the bottom, ⊃ shape, and so forth).

Step 4. Your child copies the second stroke, thereby completing his or her letter.

Letters at Level 2

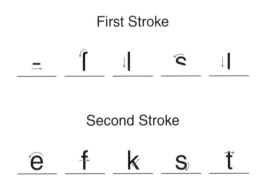

First Stroke

Second Stroke

Step 5. You move to the empty line to the right, and you create both strokes of the same letter you've been working on, without a pause.

Step 6. Your child copies your model, so that he or she is also producing the complete letter without a pause.

A completed worksheet for this level might appear as follows:

e e o l f f

e e o l f f

In level 2 the letters from level 1 (*c, i, j, l, o*) are constructed as before—with the exception of the letters *i* and *j*. At this level, the dot is added to each of these two letters, in steps 3 through 6.

Use the Scoring Criteria and the Record Form to assess your child's production and to offer positive or corrective feedback as appropriate.

Level 3: What to Do

At this level, no new letters are added. You use the same letters you used in level 2, but now all these letters are produced in a single step without pausing (so that you create a complete letter and then your child does the same). The Letters for Level 3 guide tells you the order to follow. Once again, use the Scoring Criteria to assess your child's production and offer positive or corrective feedback as appropriate.

Level 4: What to Do

At this level, along with the letters from levels 1 and 2, your child produces all the remaining letters of the alphabet. The Letters for Level 4 guide tells you the order to follow. The illustration that follows shows how to create the new letters.

Most of the new letters require retracing, which means that you go over again, or retrace, one of the lines in the letter. As with the level 2 letters, the new letters are created in a series of steps.

Step 1. You make the stroke (with *p*, for example, you start at the top and go down to construct the long vertical line that "breaks," or crosses, the guide line).

Step 2. Your child copies the stroke.

Letters for Level 4

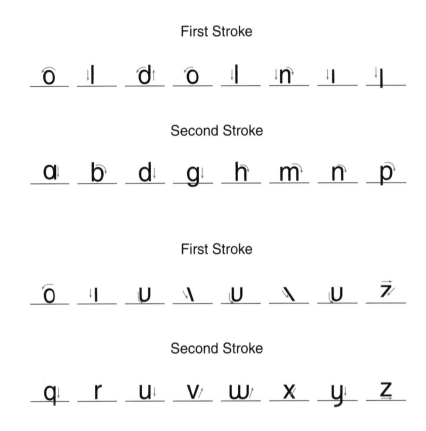

First Stroke

ô l d̂ ô l în̂ ll ll

Second Stroke

a b d g h m n p̂

First Stroke

ô l U ＼ U ＼ U ⃗z

Second Stroke

q r u v w x y z

Step 3. Working in the same space where you produced your first stroke, you create the second stroke, retracing where necessary (with the *p*, you start at the bottom of the vertical line and retrace it; near the top, you turn the line and add the circular form that completes the letter).

Step 4. Your child replicates your stroke.

Step 5. You move to the next line on the worksheet and create both lines of the letter without a pause.

Step 6. Your child replicates your letter.

A completed sheet at this level might appear as follows:

<u>b</u> <u>b</u> <u>f</u> <u>t</u> <u>g</u> <u>g</u>

<u>b</u> <u>b</u> <u>f</u> <u>t</u> <u>g</u> <u>g</u>

Once again, use the Scoring Criteria and the Record Form to assess your child's production, and then offer positive or corrective feedback as appropriate.

Level 5: What to Do

This level adds no new letters. You now construct the retraced letters from level 4 in a single step, without pausing, and your child does the same. The Letters for Level 5 guide tells you the sequence to follow. Use the Scoring Criteria and the Record Form to assess your child's production, and then offer positive or corrective feedback as appropriate.

The Sessions

In each session, follow the appropriate Letters in a Session guide until you complete all the letters listed. Start the program with level 1, session 1. After you have completed three sessions at a level, you go back and reuse the same order of letters for the sessions that follow. For example, you will be using the one set of letters for sessions 1, 4, 7, 10, 13, 16 and another set for sessions 2, 5, 8, 11, 14, 17.

The work should be carried out at a desk or table in a quiet room where you can be alone with your child. You might like to try a short practice session with someone—child or adult—who is not going to be working with the program so that you can become comfortable with the material.

It's best to work at a desk or table that offers firm support. You should sit next to your child, making sure that he or she can readily see the models you are producing. Place the worksheet on a hard surface (such as a triangular block or a loose-leaf binder) that is angled up about 20 degrees from the desk. Raising the paper in this way eases the physical demands that writing places on young children. Your child's feet should be touching the floor. If necessary, put a box under his or her feet so that they are supported. Also make sure that your child is holding the marker in a correct and comfortable manner.

Throughout the writing, do not name the letter, though it's fine if your child chooses to do so. When your child's production of a letter is not correct, you move to the line to the right and repeat the process. Your child stays with each letter until he or she completes it correctly. When errors occur, it means that your child will not complete all the letters listed for a session. Unless your child makes many errors, this is not a problem. The key to success is accuracy, and the immediate feedback and correction are more important than the number of letters that is completed.

Each session takes about ten minutes to complete. You should schedule no more than one session a day. In the course of a week, you can arrange to have between three and seven sessions. It is important to have at least three sessions a week, but I recommend more if you have the time and inclination. If your child has already experienced some difficulties in reading, it is best to schedule six to seven sessions a week, because that enables your child to move as quickly as possible into the success he or she has been longing for.

As discussed in Chapter Five, it can be extremely useful to support your child's wrist when he or she is writing. With the wrist supported, stability is ensured, and your child is free to focus on the central issues—namely, shape and movement. The support is provided by lightly placing your palm under the child's wrist and your index finger under his or her thumb, as shown here. If your child is right handed, you might sit to your child's right and use your left hand to provide the support; if your child is left handed, you might sit to your child's left and use your right hand to provide the support. Feel free to modify the position so that you and your child are most comfortable.

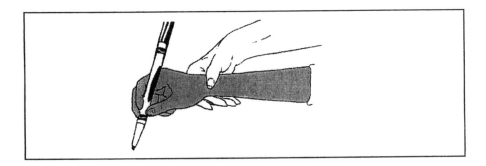

Moving On

For each letter your child constructs, use the Scoring Criteria to determine whether the letter has been made correctly. If a letter meets all the points in the scoring criteria, record a ✓ in the appropriate space on the Record Form and move to the next space on the worksheet to model the next letter. If the letter does not meet the criteria, record an **X** and move to the next space on the worksheet to repeat the same letter.

Your child remains at a level until he or she shows mastery of that level. The criterion for moving on is for your child to complete two successive sessions where twelve or more of the sixteen items receive a ✓. When this occurs, you move to the next level.

At the end of level 5, your child has finished the Letters to Write program. He or she can then move on to the Boarding program—so long as he or she has also completed or does not need the Sequences in Sight program.

Although the time will vary according to the number of sessions in a week, most children complete Letters to Write in four to six weeks. However, in some cases, particularly with younger children, difficulties are encountered. Generally, you will find that the problems are resolved by supporting your child's hand (as discussed earlier). Should you find the difficulties continuing, you should stop and review what is happening. An occasional "off day" is not a problem. But if after the first ten sessions your child does not achieve a correct response on at least ten of the sixteen items in a session, you should stop the work and try the program again in a month or two.

Teaching Activities for the Words

There are five reading and writing programs in Phonics Plus Five: Boarding, Runway, Liftoff, Airborne, and Soaring. Each contains a set of content words, noncontent words, and books. This chapter offers the information you need for teaching the words.

An Overview of the Teaching Sequence

All the words taught in the five programs are listed on the charts that follow. It is useful to make a copy of these charts so that you have them at hand throughout the teaching. The unshaded words are the content words; the shaded words are the noncontent words. The words are taught in the order listed. For example, if your child is starting the Boarding program, the first word taught is *kid,* the next word is *girl,* the next is *kids,* and so on. As you can see in the charts, the content and noncontent words are interwoven during the teaching (for example, after teaching the content word *girls,* the next word taught is the noncontent word *some*).

The Words and Books of the Boarding Program

✓X	✓X	✓X	✓X	✓X	✓X
kid	cat	the	bug	is	doll
girl	bird	eat	swim	walk	they
kids	pet	fly	talk	plane	rocket
girls		rest	jump	-ing	sit
some		can		toy	
a		are		but	
boys		here		this	
more		not		robot	
				it	
Book 1	Book 2	Book 3	Book 4	Book 5	Progress check Book 6

The Words and Books of the Runway Program

✓X	✓X	✓X	✓X	✓X	✓X
thing	like	one	man	my	duck
she	what	run	of	need	by
big	frog	other	yes	you	these
baby	to	which	fix	wing	water
who	does	there	have	hop	way
also	want	dog	good	all	and
that	many	look	he	no	both
do	those	at	arm	their	move
I		puppy	has	use	in
am		now	leg	stop	for
we			truck		
Book 7	Book 8	Book 9	Book 10	Book 11	Progress check Book 12

The Words and Books of the Liftoff Program

✓X	✓X	✓X	✓X	✓X	✓X
was	help	play	them	park	clean
sad	where	face	hole	nice	will
rocks	his	most	find	place	bag
hurt	very	food	out	pool	put
-ed	see	her	be	still	make
only	go	ate	push	ground	would
did	think	happy	us	dirt	said
time	me	any	then	-y	with
on	near	fat	mice	say	stay
could	cry		get	two	
-'s				had	
				swing	
				were	
Book 13	Book 14	Book 15	Book 16	Book 17	Progress check Book 18

The Words and Books of the Airborne Program

✓X	✓X	✓X	✓X	✓X	✓X
plant	happen	safe	drink	mouth	sky
animal	rain	-er	n't	after	moon
another	fall	why	mother	claw	earth
kind	each	ant	own	teeth	people
cold	house	work	lot	take	start
seem	again	nest	sea	funny	our
hot	sun	because	live	back	until
small	saw	together	come	part	day

(continued)

The Words and Books of the Airborne Program, Cont.

✓X	✓X	✓X	✓X	✓X	✓X
too	same	group	how	tongue	than
	rainbow	up	salt		
	when	long	land		
	about	dig			
	just				
Book 19	Book 20	Book 21	Book 22	Book 23	Progress check Book 24

The Words and Books of the Soaring Program

✓X	✓X	✓X	✓X	✓X	✓X
home	fish	ask	cliff	penny	bull
as	so	such	ever	tell	never
scare	ray	bite	daisy	every	head
over	top	your	from	kite	slow
hungry	sand	sure	change	hand	-self
open	float	name	computer	idea	tree
yell	better	letter	even	high	down
luck	try	three	nothing	true	
went		know	sleep	hear	
bad		real	got	told	
candy		smile			
much		once			
him					
Book 25	Book 26	Book 27	Book 28	Book 29	Progress check Book 30

After a set of words is taught, you move on to the book that is listed under that set of words. For example, after teaching the word *more* in the first set of words in the Boarding program, you then offer your child Book 1.

At the end of each program, just before the sixth book, you take your child through a *progress check* that tells you how well he or she has learned the material. The results enable you to determine whether you should move on to the next level or stay at the same level so as to provide your child with additional practice.

Identifying the Words to Teach: The Mini Skills Check

In all the programs, you teach only the words your child does not already know. To find out which words these are, before teaching a word you carry out a series of mini skills checks. Your goal is to identify the first five words that your child does not yet know. (If you are certain that your child does not yet know how to read and write a word, you can bypass the mini skills check and go directly to the teaching.)

The mini skills check works as follows. Provide your child with lined paper and a pencil or thin marker. Using the list of words in, for example, the Boarding program chart, you ask your child to write the first word (for example, *kid*). Do not show the word; simply say, "Try to write *kid*." Though you may be tempted, do not offer any assistance.

If your child writes the word with total accuracy and ease, count it as correct and place a ✓ next to the word on your copy of the chart; if there is any error (such as leaving out a letter, adding a letter, or switching the order of the letters), count it as incorrect and place an **X** next to the word. In addition, if your child takes a long time trying to figure out how to write a word, even if the word is ultimately produced correctly, it is best to place it in the group of words to be taught. Slowness is a sign that the reading and writing are not yet automatic and additional teaching is worthwhile.

You continue the pattern just outlined until you have a list of the first five words in a program that your child does not know. These are the words you will use in starting your teaching. For example, of the words in the Boarding program, you may find that your child knows *kid, girl, some,* and *a,* but does not know *kids, girls, boys, more,* and *cat.* These last five words are the ones you will teach.

Once you have identified these words, you prepare the teaching materials for them. This process continues until you complete all the words in all five reading programs.

After you have completed teaching three of the five words you have identified, you repeat the mini skills check to find the next set of five words that you will be teaching. In this way, you can always be ready with the materials you need to keep the teaching moving at a steady pace.

The process is the same whether your child is just starting to read or is at a more advanced level. The only difference is in the particular words you will find yourself teaching. For example, suppose that your child is relatively far along in reading and can accurately write all the words in the Boarding and Runway programs. In that case you will find the first set of words you will be teaching in the Liftoff program.

In all the reading programs, you teach only the words your child does not already know. So create only those materials you need for the words you are going to teach.

The Sessions

Once you have created the materials you will be using (as described after these overview sections), you can start the sessions. You might like to try a short practice session with someone—child or adult—who is not going to be working with the program, so that you can become comfortable using the material.

You teach one word a session, and in each session your child completes four activities for that word. At the end of the session, you turn to your copy of the charts given at the start of this chapter and draw a line through the word. This indicates that the word has been completed. In the next session, you move on to the next word that the mini skills check shows that your child needs to learn.

Each session takes about fifteen to twenty minutes to complete. In the course of a week, you can arrange to have between four and seven sessions. It is important to have at least four sessions a week, but I recommend more if you have the time and inclination. If your child has already experienced some difficulties in reading, it is best to schedule six to seven sessions a week, because that enables your child to move as quickly as possible into the success he or she has been longing for.

It's best to work at a desk or table that offers firm support. You should sit next to your child and make sure that he or she can readily see the material you have prepared. Arrange the seating so that your child's feet are touching the floor. If this is not possible, put a box on the floor so that his or her feet can rest on a firm surface. Make sure that your child is holding the pencil or marker in a correct and comfortable manner. If your child still needs it, continue supporting his or her hand as you did in the Letters to Write program.

Dealing with Error

The activities have been designed to limit the number of errors your child will make. Still, mistakes will happen, and you need to respond to them in a way that helps your child progress in the smoothest manner.

Errors tend to be of three types:

1. *Failure to recognize a word.* For example, you ask your child to find a word (as in the activities Savvy Sounds or Spot 'n Sort), and he or she selects the wrong word or overlooks the correct word. When this happens, stop your child, tell him or her the correct word, and then repeat the activity. For example, if your child selects *gild* in place of *girl* in Savvy Sounds, point to *girl,* and say, "This is *girl.*" Then say, "Let's do that again. Find *girl.*"

2. *An error in reading a word.* For example, you ask your child to read a word (as in Symbol Search and Spot 'n Sort), and he or she comes up with the wrong word or fails to come up with any word. In this case, stop your child, tell him or her the correct word, and then repeat the activity. For example, if your child reads *plays* as *play* in Spot 'n Sort, say, "No, that is *plays.* Say *plays.*" Then say, "Let's do that again. Tell me that word."

3. *An error in writing a word.* For example, you ask your child to write a word (as in Symbol Search or Find 'n Fill), and he or she includes wrong letters, omits correct letters, enters letters in the wrong sequence, or does not know what letters to enter. In dealing with writing errors on single words (as in Find 'n Fill), stop your child, turn the page over, show the target word that you have written there, and say, "This is how you write that word." Then turn the page back and say, "Now correct the word." In dealing with errors in sentences (as in Symbol Search), show the complete sentence that is on the worksheet and say, "Find the word you need." Then cover the sentence, provide a fresh piece of paper, and say, "Now let's start from the beginning and rewrite the whole sentence." In other words, no matter how far along your child is in the writing of the sentence, he or she is asked to redo the entire sentence. This technique is ultimately far more productive than allowing your child to correct a single word or letter.

Moving On

Your child remains at a level until he or she completes all the words for that level that he or she does not know. After each set of words is completed, your child reads a book containing those words along with words previously learned (the books are listed on the charts that appeared earlier).

After your child completes the final word for a level, you carry out a brief progress check to see how well he or she has mastered the material. The material you need for this progress check is in Chapter Thirteen. If the progress check shows that your child is retaining the material effectively, you move on to the next level. If it shows that your child is not retaining the material at the level that is needed, you carry out the review activities that are described in that chapter.

The Activities for the Content Words

The materials for all the activities are arranged as follows:

- The format for the activity is presented, filled in with a sample word. This is your model for setting out the other words.

- A blank format is provided. Use this to make the copies you need to serve as activity material.

- The content of the teaching for the first five words in each program is offered. This content is your model for creating the remaining material.

Savvy Sounds: Sample Content

The charts on pages 191–193 contain the content to be used with the Savvy Sounds format for the first five content words in each program (Boarding, Runway, Liftoff, Airborne, and Soaring). Use these charts as models in setting up this format for the other words in the programs.

Savvy Sounds Activity: Sample Word—*kid*

What to do: (1) Write the target word (*kid*) on the back of the page you have prepared, which is arranged as in the following illustration. Point to the target word and say, "This is *kid*." (2) Turn the page over. (3) Arrange the paper so your child sees only one row at a time. (4) Point to *ki* in the first row. Say, "This starts the word *kid*." (5) Point to the choices in the first row. Say, (a) "Find the whole word *kid*"; (b) "Circle it"; (c) "Say *kid*." (6) Repeat for each row.

ki		kid		kiss
ki		kink		kid
ki		kid		kiln
ki	kick		kid		kiss
ki	kiln		kin		kid

Savvy Sounds: Blank Format

What to do: (1) Write the target word on the back of the page. Point to it and say, "This is _____." (2) Turn the page over. (3) Arrange the paper so your child sees only one row at a time. (4) Point to the part word (incomplete word) in the first row. Say, "This starts the word _____." (5) Point to the choices in the first row. Say, (a) "Find the whole word _____"; (b) "Circle it"; (c) "Say _____." (6) Repeat for each row.

Initial Part of Word

Choices

Savvy Sounds: Boarding Program Sample Content

Target Word	Initial Part	Line 1	Line 2	Line 3	Line 4	Line 5
kid	ki	kid kiss	kink kid	kid kiln	kick kid kiss	kiln kin kid
girl	gir	girl gild	gill girl	gift girl	give girl gig	gird giddy girl
kids	kid	kids kind	kite kids	kids kiss	kinds kids kiss	kids kilt kick
girls	girl	gifts girls	girls gills	gives girls	grill girds girls	girth girds girls
boys	boy	boys bond	boys born	bows boys	boys boy bond	boss boys boats

Savvy Sounds: Runway Program Sample Content

Target Word	Initial Part	Line 1	Line 2	Line 3	Line 4	Line 5
things	thing	things thin	thick things	thief things	thinks things third	thin things thighs
big	bi	bill big	bird big	big bit	big bid bib	bind big bite
baby	ba	baby bad	baits babies	base baby	bays babies balls	band baby bald
frog	fro	frog front	frost frog	from frog	front frog frond	froth frog frown
run	ru	run rub	rust run	run rug	run rush rude	rut ruse run

Savvy Sounds: Liftoff Program Sample Content

Target Word	Initial Part	Line 1	Line 2	Line 3	Line 4	Line 5
sad	sa	sad sap	said sad	sad sack	sag sad sat	sad salt sand
rock	ro	root rock	rock rook	roil rock	rocket rock roost	roam room rock
hurt	hur	hurry hurt	hurt hustle	hurt hurl	hush hunt hurt	hurt hull hurl
time	ti	time tile	tie time	tidy time	time tide tie	tine time tire
help	hel	heels help	help helm	held help	hen help head	herd hefty help

Savvy Sounds: Airborne Program Sample Content

Target Word	Initial Part	Line 1	Line 2	Line 3	Line 4	Line 5
animal	ani	animal animate	animate animal	angle animal	anger animal angel	angle ankle animal
rock	ro	root rock	rock rook	roil rock	rocket rock roost	roam room rock
kind	ki	kin kind	kink kind	kids kind	kind kick kiln	kite kind kilo
cold	co	cold coat	cold cope	coal cold	cook cold corn	cold comb coop
hot	ho	hot hop	hot hole	host hot	hose hop hot	hock hot hood

Savvy Sounds: Soaring Program Sample Content

Target Word	Initial Part	Line 1	Line 2	Line 3	Line 4	Line 5
home	ho	home holy	hole home	hoop home	hold hole home	hood hope home
scared	scare	scrape scared	scald scared	scared scored	scared scaled scab	scarce scat scared
hungry	hun	hungry hurray	hungry husky	hurrah hungry	hunt hungry hurry	hungry hunch hurler
open	op	open oppose	open offend	opal open	open offend opera	object open oath
yell	ye	yellow yell	yells years	yearns yells	yields yells yeast	yells yelps yellow

Find 'n Fill: Sample Content

The charts on pages 197–199 contain the content to be used with the Find 'n Fill format for the first five content words in each program. The hyphens (-) represent the spaces to be supplied for the missing letters in each word; the slashes (/) separate the words. Use this content as a model in setting up this format for the other words in the programs.

Find 'n Fill Activity: Sample Word—*park*

What to do: (1) On the back of the page with the activity format (see the following sample illustration), write the target word (*park*). Point to it and say, "This is *park*." (2) Turn the page over and point to the first row, saying, "Find any word in this row that can become *park*." (3) Say, "Add the letters to make it say *park*." (4) Say, "Now say *park*." (5) Make sure your child works from left to right across the row. Immediately correct any error. (6) Repeat for each row.

p _ g	h _ t	p _ _ k	p _ d
_ a _ _	b _ g	m _ t t	_ e r k
s a _	p _ l l	p _ r _	p _ _
u _ _	p r _ _	p _ _ k	p _ _ t
_ a n _	p a _ _	d a _ _	_ a r p

Find 'n Fill: Blank Format

What to do: (1) On the back of the page, write the target word. Point to it and say, "This is _____." (2) Turn the page over and point to the first row, saying, "Find any word in this row that can become _____." (3) Say, "Add the letters to make it say _____." (4) Say, "Now say _____." (5) Make sure your child works from left to right across the row. Immediately correct any error. (6) Repeat for each row.

Find 'n Fill: Boarding Program Sample Content

Target Word	Line 1	Line 2	Line 3	Line 4	Line 5
kid	k-d/ s-n/ d-d/ -id	m-th/ k-d/ bu-/ ki-	s-n/ -id/ li-/ d-d	k-/ k-n/ kn--/ ki-	m-n/ k--/ ki-e/ --d
girl	gi-l/ di--/ gi-t/ g--l	t-ol/ li-e/ -irl/ g--l	g-ve/ gi--/ g-r-/ dir-	g-st/ g--/ g--d/ gu-l	r-n/ r-le/ g-r-/ l-g
kids	kid-/ d-t/ k--d/ -id-	b-g/ k-d-/ ki-k/ kis-	s--k/ --ds/ kn--/ b-d	---s/ k-n/ k--t/ ki--	k--s/ k--s/ ki-s/ --d
girls	gi-l-/ bi--/ gi--s/ g-ll-	d-ep/ gi-l-/ -urn/ m--k	h-ve/ g--d/ g-r--/ dir-	g-t-/ g---s/ h--d/ -a-l	r-n/ r-le/ g-r-/ l-g
boys	boy-/ b--l-/ -d/ boy-	b-y-/ g--g/ bo--/ y-s	sa-e/ -oy-/ k--d/ -ay	sa-e/ -oy-/ k--d/ -ay	g--l/ bu -s/ b-ys/ k--

Find 'n Fill: Runway Program Sample Content

Target Word	Line 1	Line 2	Line 3	Line 4	Line 5
thing	th---/ s--s/ p-y/ t--n	t-i--/ b-ll-/ g--/ m-t	t--ng/ to-gh/ d-t/ p-ts	s-im/ th-ng/ tr--/ gn--	t--/ ro--/ t-ing/ s-ng
big	r-g/ b-t/ b--/ b-d	--g/ t-ig/ nea-/ sea-	ri-e/ b-g/ l-g/ --g	bu-/ r-g/ w-t/ b--	b--/ st--/ b--/ be-t
baby	b-b-/ b--r/ r--/ b-by	a-t/ b-a-/ s--/ bl--t	r-t/ ba-e/ fac-/ b--y	b-t/ b--y/ cr--/ b--n	clu--/ -s-y/ do--/ y--
frog	fr--/ p--s/ s-y/ f--t	f-o-/ p-ll/ g--f/ c-t	s-ng/ f-og/ -o-gh/ b-ts	b-ins/ th-ng/ fr--/ g-m-	t--/ -ro-/ t-igs/ f-og
run	r--/ r-n/ st--/ b-r	p--/ su-s/ b--/ -un	ta-k/ r-n/ d-/ g-	r-n/ r-b-t/ --n/ m--k	re-t/ r--/ r-n/ r-b

Find 'n Fill: Liftoff Program Sample Content

Target Word	Line 1	Line 2	Line 3	Line 4	Line 5
sad	s-d/ s--r/ r--/ r-bbi-	t-a/ s--/ b--/ sl--t	s-t/ ba-e/ --d/ b--y	m-t/ s--/ d--/ d--n	stru-/ ai-/ s-d/ s-i-
rock	b-se/ e--k/ ri-g/ l-ck	ra-/ d---s/ w-rk/ r-ck	--ck/ cl--k/ ros-/ w-g	-ins/ r--/ ma-t/ r-n-	r--/ b--y/ r--k/ -i-gs
hurt	h-g/ h-t/ h--t/ f-d	--ge/ th-re/ hea-/ h---	-u--/ b-g/ h-t/ --rt	sa-/ h-ll/ h-rt/ p--	u--/ fr--/ r-t-/ h--t
time	t-m-/ w--p/ t-y/ t--e	t-le/ s--ls/ t--e/ --m-s	r-pe/ -i--/ st-m/ t--e	to-s/ t-ne/ p--r/ -p-t	t--e/ st--/ --e/ r---
help	h-g-/ h-l-/ h--p/ h-d	--ap/ h-ir/ pea-/ h--p	pe--/ f-d/ p-ts/ --lp	su-/ h-lp/ h-rt/ l--p	c--/ fr-sh/ -e-p/ l--p

Find 'n Fill: Airborne Program Sample Content

Target Word	Line 1	Line 2	Line 3	Line 4	Line 5
plant	pl-n-/ w--r/ s--g/ --nt	c-t/ pa-e/ p-a-t/ g-ing	pl-n-/ p--/ r-ns/ s--g	c-t/ pa-e/ p-a-t/ g-ing	s-ing/ --ant/ p-a--/ s-nt
animal	an-mal/ ani---/ si-g/ c-tch	fa-e/ g--s/ ---mal/ -ct-	a-i-a-/ d-sk/ hos-/ a--s	-ins/ a---al/ a--er/ an----	wi-gs/ -ni--l/ fi-es/ r---
kind	d--/ k-te/ k-n-/ b--k	k--d/ s-e/ k i--/ d-m	ki-gs/ --nd/ pl--y/ k-ys	se-k/ t-ink/ --nd/ s-w-ng	kin-/ -i--/ m-nd/ din-
cold	c--l/ k-te/ c-l-/ c--d	b--d/ c--d/ s-y/ c-d	ki-gs/ s-nd/ pr-yl/ --l-	le-f/ c---/ --nd/ c-ws	c-l-/ c-c-/ b-nd/ con-
hot	t-g/ h-t/ h--t/ k-d	--ge/ h-re/ rea-/ h--	-a--/ h--/ h-t/ y-rn	-o-/ h-ll/ h-rr-/ f--	o--/ pr--/ m-r-/ --t

Find 'n Fill: Soaring Program Sample Content

Target Word	Line 1	Line 2	Line 3	Line 4	Line 5
home	h-me/ b-d/ --me/ h-d	-o--/ al-o/ s--th/ --n-	--t/ --uth/ h-m-/ h--e	c-t/ h-s-/ --me/ ---t	-o-e/ man-/ h-me/ m-ts
scare	sc-r-/ c-aw/ s-a--/ -rcs	cr-ws/ scar-/ bl-e/ b--	sa--y/ -aw/ -cr--/ b-t-	dr--/ ca--e/ sta--/ r-a-	-tar-/ m--y/ -ag-/ sc-r-
hungry	h-ngry/ s-fe/ h-r-y/ p--t	kn-w/ h-ste/ s-at/ -ung-y	he-ps/ h--gry/ --r-/ s--g	an-gry/ --rt/ hun-ry/ f---	t-e/ p---/ --ngry/ thunde-
open	-pen/ p-d/ --me/ h-d	--t/ --uth/ -p-n/ o--n	r-pe/ -i--/ st-m/ t--e	to-s/ t-ne/ p--r/ -p-t	-ome/ man-/ o-en/ m-ts
yell	-el-/ s-at/ s-r-e/ y--	y--r/ y--l/ bl-e/ b--	-e-l/ -ar/ -ca--/ b-t-	dr--/ ye--/ sta--/ r-a-	--ar/ m--y/ -ag-/ y--l

Spot 'n Sort: Sample Content

The charts on pages 203–207 present the content to be used with the Spot 'n Sort format for the first five content words in each program. Use these materials as models in setting up the format for this activity with the other words in the programs.

Spot 'n Sort Activity: Sample Word—*play, plays*

What to do: (1) On the back of a prepared page (see the following illustration), write the target word and its variant. Point to it, saying, "This is *play, plays*." (2) Turn the page over and say, "Some words here say *play* or *plays*, and some do not." (3) Point to the first row. Say, "Cross out any word that does *not* say *play* or *plays*." Make sure your child works from left to right across the row. Immediately correct any error. Repeat for each row. (4) When the crossing out is completed, say, "Now read all the words that are not crossed out." Immediately correct any error.

poor		hits		play		does
pear		play		plate		plays
flay		great		plot		pays
plays		plays		yelps		treat
silt		plants		plays		pats
ploys		pelts		play		plays

Spot 'n Sort: Blank Format

What to do: (1) On the back of the page, write the target word (and any variant if the ending has been taught). Point to it, saying, "This is _____." (2) Turn the page over and say, "Some words here say _____, and some do not." (3) Point to the first row. Say, "Cross out any word that does *not* say _____." Make sure your child works from left to right across the row. Immediately correct any error. Repeat for each row. (4) When the crossing out is completed, say, "Now read all the words that are not crossed out." Immediately correct any error.

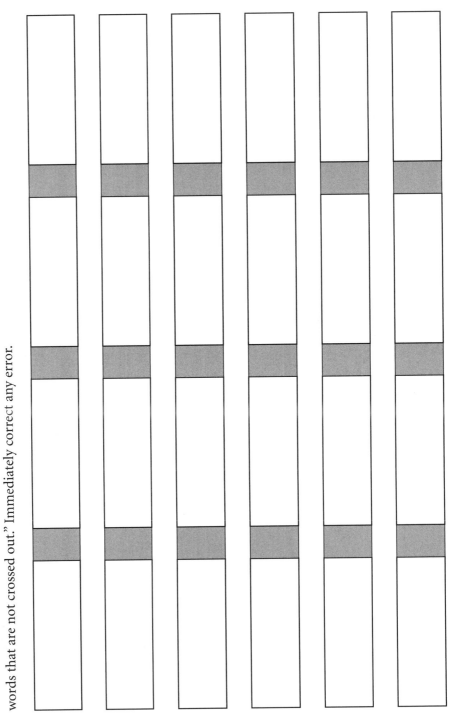

Spot 'n Sort: Boarding Program Sample Content

Target Word	Line 1	Line 2	Line 3	Line 4	Line 5	Line 6
kid	kite kid bin ace	kid star book kid	kin dike kid lid	kite kid sit kick	stop kid dig kid	apple kid kiss toy
girl	gate girl rag girl	road girl little girl	guy list girl girl	guest girl grill gaze	girl grass girl girl	get girl yell girl
kids	kite kids kids kind	kite kids kids kind	bike pick kids kids	men kids dikes dirt	kids man take kids	dips hides kids kilt
girls	gifts goes isle girls	girls goals mall girls	lifts girls wins girls	grill grow girls gaze	gibe girls gulls goes	gum rules girls gift
boys	buys boys days paid	toys girls books bout	boats boys bolt barks	boys balls boys bake	kid flag boys bolts	bays bolt boys says

Spot 'n Sort: Runway Program Sample Content

Target Word	Line 1	Line 2	Line 3	Line 4	Line 5	Line 6
thing/things	thing toys tough ten	bats things thin pets	thing thread toll thin	cut things tot thing	toss thick robot thong	third thing things runs
big	bud big gab road	swims bird big big	bag need dots going	beams cats big bit	boss big talks wins	big boar rats big
baby/babies	cats baby do barb	babies jump baits hats	able babies daily baby	goes come start baby	babies baby barely berry	puppy babble baby do bait
frog/frogs	frog fret got spot	foggy bat frog frogs	foes frog cot long	toes frog runs girl	frogs rags van frog	forge rest frog rage
run/runs	roots looks run rust	runs suns runs real	coat runs run near	run turn barn runs	runs run rib rind	rent runs raft look

Spot 'n Sort: Liftoff Program Sample Content

Target Word	Line 1	Line 2	Line 3	Line 4	Line 5	Line 6
sad	said car kid sad	funny sad days ray	sad bad race buy	goat hat sad sad/cats	sad hot late daze	run has not go
rock/rocks	root rock sake roam	rocks rock year time	rakes back rocks raking	takes rocks safe clock	dock rock get rocks	buck pull rocks rock
hurt/hurting	huts huge bib hurts	wins herd hurt hurting	hurl deed hot being	reams hurt dirt dip	hurt hat turn hurt	hurt huffs hurting hip
time/times	bring times talk time	still time top stop	times ties time ticks	sale items hop times	toss thin time times	tills mime slump ton
help/helped	hoots helped run hurts	sun belt help hops	real coat help wheel	pleads held help grant	jump urns holds helped	trucks spot high heels

Spot 'n Sort: Airborne Program Sample Content

Target Word	Line 1	Line 2	Line 3	Line 4	Line 5	Line 6
plant/plants	pans land plants said	long talk plants paints	plants panes lake puts	sinking plant punts	cold plants planted got	plot pills plant rocket
animal/ animals	alert spark animal angry	animals murals gain annual	fish animal mauls nicely	goat mate minimal coal	animals monkey label male	alphabet wait normal animals
kind	kin fish kind blend	kink hush bean kind	king kind walk drink	face kind din rest	know hop rink wet	ghost kind kind dish
cold	done cold kite coop	cold bold curl sent	bird cold cold coal	cold kick teach coast	old cold corn king	kind hurt cold sold
hot	hut hot bib hip	swim hot hot hurl	home feed hot since	read hug dot hot	hole have talks hot	hot hip hull hot

Spot 'n Sort: Soaring Program Sample Content

Target Word	Line 1	Line 2	Line 3	Line 4	Line 5	Line 6
home/homes	home mutt pant homes	bees home moth moan	house hotel homes mode	home other home none	home hone meal seen	mound fend home some
scare/scared	some scared split bare	scared homey scary soap	house scare gone care	scared other soared scare	score hail scared been	sound scare care space
hungry	hound howl hungry hunt	nest hungry bets party	help need hungry hugging	petty hungry pear lath	hungry harms near hustle	hungry pint hungry part
open/opens	opens mutt occurs home	bees opening moth open	odors hotel omits opened	opposed opens home open	open hone organs orbits	pounds opens poems open
yell/yelled	years going yelled saying	yelled yield soaps jell	house yell yelled gone	yell other soared seen	scored hail yells been	sold yelled care yell

Symbol Search Activity: Sample Word—*come, comes, coming*

What to do: (1) Write the target word and all its variants on the back of a prepared page (see the sample in the following illustration), and point to them, saying, "This is *come, comes, coming*." (2) Turn the page over, arrange the paper so that your child sees only the first sentence, and say, "Words are missing. The symbols tell you what they are." (3) Point to the first symbol above the line and say, "Find the word for this first symbol and say it." (4) Cover the word and say, "Write it on the line." (5) Repeat this until all the words have been filled in. (6) Say, "Read the sentence." Immediately correct any error. Repeat steps 1 through 6 with the second sentence. (7) Cover both sentences and say, "Now you'll write a sentence." Provide lined paper. Dictate the words of the first sentence, one word at a time. If there is any error (including an error in capitalization or punctuation), stop. Show the sentence, cover it, provide fresh paper, and have your child redo the sentence from the first word. Then repeat step 7 with the second sentence.

♣

He is _____ here with his _____ to swim in the sea.

♣ = coming   • = group

♣

She _____ here all the _____ ⊃ ∅ she is sad.

♣ = comes   ⊃ = time   ∅ = when

Symbol Search: Blank Format

What to do: (1) On the back of the page, write the target word and its variants. Point to them, saying, "This is _____." (2) Turn the page over, arrange the paper so that your child sees only the first sentence, and say, "Words are missing. The symbols tell you what they are." (3) Point to the first symbol above the line and say, "Find the word for this first symbol, and say it." (4) Cover the word and say, "Write it on the line." (5) Repeat this until all the words have been filled in. (6) Say, "Read the sentence." Immediately correct any error. Repeat steps 1 through 6 with the second sentence. (7) Cover both sentences and say, "Now you'll write a sentence." Provide lined paper. Dictate the words of the first sentence, one word at a time. If there is any error (including capitals and punctuation), stop. Show the sentence, cover it, provide fresh paper, and have your child redo the sentence from the first word. Then repeat step 7 with the second sentence.

Symbol Search: Sample Content

The charts that follow present the content to be used with the Symbol Search format for the first five content words in each program. Use these materials as models in setting up this format with the other words in the programs. The Symbol Search activity is not used with the first four words of the Boarding program. In the sentences shown in these charts, the underlined words are the ones that you omit and replace with symbols. Here are some of the symbols you could use in creating the sentences: • ♣ ♦ ♥ ↔ ∩ ⊇ ∇ ∨ □ ⇔ ⇑ ⇒

Symbol Search: Boarding Program Sample Content

Target Word	Sentence 1	Sentence 2
boys	some <u>boys</u>, some <u>girls</u>	a <u>boy</u>, some <u>boys</u>
cat	a <u>cat</u>	a <u>cat</u>, some <u>more cats</u>
bird	a <u>bird</u>	some <u>more birds</u>
pet	a <u>pet cat</u>	some <u>pets</u>, some <u>more</u> pets
eat	<u>Eat</u> some <u>more</u>!	A <u>bird eats</u>.

Symbol Search: Runway Program Sample Content

Target Word(s)	Sentence 1	Sentence 2
thing/things	Some <u>things</u> are <u>robots</u>.	Is the <u>thing</u> a <u>bird</u>?
big	The <u>big</u> bird is <u>eating</u>.	<u>Do</u> the <u>big</u> kids <u>walk</u> here?
baby/babies	The <u>baby</u> can<u>not</u> walk.	Some <u>babies</u> are <u>swimming</u>.
frog/frogs	The <u>frogs are</u> not <u>jumping</u>.	<u>What things</u> can <u>frogs</u> do?
run/runs/ running	The <u>boy</u> does not <u>want</u> to <u>run</u> here.	<u>What</u> is she <u>doing</u>? She is <u>running</u>.

Symbol Search: Liftoff Program Sample Content

Target Word(s)	Sentence 1	Sentence 2
sad	<u>Which</u> boy has a <u>sad look</u>?	<u>Yes,</u> both <u>puppies</u> are <u>sad</u> now.
rock/rocks	<u>These other</u> things are <u>rocks</u>.	<u>There</u> are <u>many rocks</u> in the water.
hurt/hurting	It <u>hurts</u> to <u>jump like</u> that.	The big <u>bird</u> is <u>hurting</u> the baby <u>frog.</u>
time/times	<u>Those</u> are not the <u>times</u> to fly.	What <u>time</u> is <u>good</u> for <u>swimming</u>?
help/helped	<u>That</u> man <u>helped</u> many of my <u>pets</u>.	<u>Only</u> some kids are <u>helping</u> to <u>fix</u> the toys.

Symbol Search: Airborne Program Sample Content

Target Word(s)	Sentence 1	Sentence 2
plant/plants/ planting/ planted	He is <u>planting</u> some <u>things</u> now in the <u>ground</u>.	<u>Did</u> the man put all the <u>plants</u> on the <u>truck</u>?
animal/animals	<u>There</u> are no other <u>animals facing</u> them.	What <u>animal</u> was <u>getting</u> out of the <u>hole</u>?
kind	He <u>could</u> also be <u>kind</u> to their <u>pets</u>.	What <u>kinds of</u> animals are <u>those</u>?
cold	It <u>was cold</u> on the <u>ground</u>.	That <u>food</u> is <u>still</u> not <u>cold</u>.
hot	It <u>seems hot</u> here, but they said it <u>would</u> not be hot.	The <u>rocks</u> are <u>hot,</u> but the <u>plants</u> do not seem to be that <u>way</u>.

Symbol Search: Soaring Program Sample Content

Target Word(s)	Sentence 1	Sentence 2
home/homes	The people were in their <u>home because</u> they <u>needed</u> to rest.	How many <u>homes</u> do you <u>think</u> are in this <u>place</u>?
scare/scary/ scared	That <u>animal</u> seems <u>very scary</u> to me.	Are many <u>people scared</u> to go into that <u>house</u>?
hungry	The kids <u>said</u>, "We are as <u>hungry</u> as can <u>be</u>."	The cat over there <u>looked hungry</u>, but he <u>wasn't</u>.
open/opens/ opened/ opening	That part of the pool was not <u>open when</u> we were <u>there</u>.	The cat is <u>opening</u> her <u>mouth</u> because she wants to <u>drink</u>.
yell/yells/ yelling/yelled	The mother said, "Could you stop all that yelling for now?"	Why does he <u>yell</u> over and over <u>again</u> when there is <u>nothing</u> to yell <u>about</u>?

The Activities for the Noncontent Words

As with the activities for the content words, the materials for the noncontent word activities are arranged as follows:

- The format for the activity is presented, filled in with a sample word. This is your model for setting out the other words.

- A blank format is provided. Use this to make the copies you need to serve as activity material.

- The content of the teaching for the first five words in each program is offered. This content is your model for creating the remaining material.

Write In to Read Activity: Sample Word—*she, She*

What to do: (1) Write the target word(s) on the back of a prepared page (see the sample in the following illustration), starting each word with an uppercase or lowercase letter as appropriate. Point to the word(s) and say, "This is *she*." (2) Turn the page over, arrange the page so your child sees only one box at a time, and say, "Write the word I showed you on this line." (3) Ask your child to read the sentence(s). (4) Repeat steps 1 through 3 with each box. Immediately correct any error (including capitalization). (5) Cover all the sentences, provide lined paper, and say, "Now we have more writing to do." Dictate the words in the first box, one word at a time. If there is any error, stop. Show the words, cover them, provide fresh paper, and have your child redo the writing from the first word.

The girl is not here. _____ is resting.

Here _____ is a girl. Girls can sit. Is _____ sitting?

Here is _____ a kid. _____ is not a boy. _____ is a girl.

Write In to Read: Blank Format

What to do: (1) Write the target word(s) on the back of the page, starting each word with an uppercase or lowercase letter as appropriate. Say, "This is _____." (2) Turn the page over, arrange the paper so your child sees only one box at a time, and say, "Write the word I showed you on this line." (3) Ask your child to read the sentence(s). (4) Repeat steps 1 through 5 with each box. Immediately correct any error (including capitalization). (5) Cover all sentences, provide lined paper, and say, "Now we have more writing to do." Dictate the words in the first box, one word at a time. If there is any error, stop. Show the words, cover them, provide fresh paper, and have your child redo the writing from the first word. (6) Repeat step 5 for the second box. (For the illustrations, you may use those provided in Chapter Twelve, pictures from magazines, or drawings you and your child create.)

Write In to Read: Sample Content

The charts that follow contain material for the first five noncontent words in each program. The words in italics are to be omitted and filled in by your child. A plus sign (+) next to a phrase or sentence indicates that illustrations are required. (You may also illustrate the text without a +, but it is not essential to do so.)

Write In to Read: Boarding Program Sample Content

Target Word(s)	Frame 1	Frame 2	Frame 3
some	+ *some* girls	+ *some* kids	
a	+ *a* boy	+ *a* girl	+ *a* kid
more	+ a boy some *more* boys	+ a girl *more* girls	+ a kid + *more* kids
the	+ *the* kids	+ *the* girls	+ *the* boy
can/Can	Some pets *can* fly.	+ The bird *can* rest.	*Can* kids eat?

Write In to Read: Runway Program Sample Content

Target Word(s)	Frame 1	Frame 2	Frame 3
she/She	The girl is not here. *She* is resting.	+Here is a doll. Dolls can sit. Is *she* sitting?	+Here is a kid. *She* is not a boy. *She* is a girl.
who/Who	+*Who* is sitting here? She is a baby.	+ Here is a doll *who* can walk.	+ *Who* are they? They are big birds.
also	Boys are kids. Girls are *also* kids.	+ Here is a cat. She is *also* a pet.	+ The robot is a toy. + The plane is *also* a toy.
that/That	+ *That* kid is not big. She is a baby.	+ The kids can pet *that* cat.	+ Some things are here but *that* toy is not.
do/Do	*Do* not do that! *Do* not jump here!	Some bugs *do* swim.	*Do* rockets fly? They *do* that.

Write In to Read: Liftoff Program Sample Content

Target Word(s)	Frame 1	Frame 2	Frame 3
was/Was	A boy *was* here. Now he is not.	+ *Was* someone moving this truck? No, no one *was* doing that.	+ This frog *was* not jumping. It *was* swimming.
-ed	A man *fixed* some toys for these kids.	The bird was not flying. It *needed* to move its wings.	+ These ducks *jumped* in the water. They *wanted* to jump. They also *rested* in the water.
only/Only	The boy has *only* one toy.	What was the *only* thing in there?	There was a duck. The *only* thing it wanted to do was to eat and eat.
did/Did	+ This baby *did* not want to move. She only wanted to sit.	*Did* the bug fly there? No, it *did* not. It hopped there.	*Did* all the kids want to swim? Yes, they *did*, but only some of the kids *did* that.
on/On	+ Many bugs hopped *on* that man. He did not like that at all.	The arm was not *on* the doll. The doll was not good at all.	Can kids jump *on* those rocks? Yes, they can. Are any kids jumping *on* the rocks now? No, they are not.

Write In to Read: Airborne Program Sample Content

Target Word(s)	Frame 1	Frame 2	Frame 3
another/Another	Some kids walked to the park, but then they did not like it there. They said they wanted to go to *another* park.	"I liked that place. Can we go there *another* time?"	That is not the duck that was here. That is *another* duck.
too/Too	That bird can fly. It can also do other things. It can swim *too*.	Some girls wanted to go to the park. Some boys wanted to go there *too*.	The baby cannot run. He is *too* small to run. He can sit, but he is *too* small to run.
each/Each	There are some girls who would like to go to a pool. *Each* of them wants to swim, but not one of them can do that.	+ *Each* one of these toys can fly, but there is no one here now to make them fly.	*Each* of the kids has a pet, but their pets are not here.
again	It rained *again* and *again*. It did not seem to stop raining.	A boy jumped and hurt his leg near here. He could not jump *again*.	The kids are not happy. They were at the pool and the pool was very dirty. They are not going to go to that pool *again*.
saw (a content word better suited to noncontent formats)	The baby *saw* a dog who was hurt, but she could not say that. She could not talk. She was only a baby.	All the kids *saw* what happened. They did not like what they *saw*. They *saw* some mice jumping on all the things.	A man *saw* the kid's toy on the swing.

Write In to Read: Soaring Program Sample Content

Target Word(s)	Frame 1	Frame 2	Frame 3
as/As	*As* this cat gets older, she does not like to do things. She only wants to sit and to eat.	That place was *as* cold *as* any place could be. Anyone who was there said that about it.	That dog is *as* good *as* any dog can be.
over/Over	There was something *over* the house, but we could not see it.	The man wanted to look *over* the plans for fixing the pool.	*Over* and *over* again, the mother said, "Do not play there. It's not safe."
much	The man did not say how *much* time it would take to fix the truck.	"How *much* candy did the kids want?" "They wanted a lot, but they didn't get *much*. Those kids were not very happy about that."	+ "Do not open it too *much*. The bird will fly out."
him	A girl was looking for a man but she did not see *him*.	Some people have a dog, but they are still not used to *him*.	"Where is the boy who was willing to clean this place? Can you find *him* for me?"
so	All the kids wanted *so* much to be here, but they could not get here. Something happened and they could not get here.	+ The frogs are *so* happy because they can go back in the pool.	"Was the water dirty?" "No, it was *so* clean you could drink it."

Detect 'n Select Activity: Sample Word—*also*

What to do: (1) On the back of a prepared page (see the following illustration), write the target word and say, "This is *also*." (2) Turn the page over, point to the left-hand box, and say, "Circle the first word that says *also*." (3) Say, "Now say the word." (4) Repeat for each instance of the target word in the box. Do *not* have your child read any of the other words. Repeat steps 1 through 3 for the boxes in the middle and on the right. Make sure your child works from left to right across rows.

| That girl can do so many things. She can sing. She also can dance. She also plays the piano. Her sister is also able to do those things. | The bird is big. It is also blue. What else is it like? It is also smart. It knows how to go on long trips and also how to get back here. | The girl is going to sit here for now. She is also going to keep score. Another boy will also keep score with her. We don't know if they will also be doing other things. |

Detect 'n Select: Blank Format

What to do: (1) On the back of the page, write the target word(s), starting with both lowercase and uppercase letters, if appropriate, and say, "This is _____." (2) Turn the page over, point to the left-hand box, and say, "Circle the first word that says _____." (3) Say, "Now say the word." (4) Repeat for each instance of the target word in the box. Do *not* have your child read any other words. Repeat steps 1 through 3 for the boxes in the middle and on the right. Make sure your child works from left to right across rows.

Detect 'n Select: Sample Content

The following charts contain material for the first five noncontent words in each program.

Detect 'n Select: Boarding Program Sample Content

Target Word(s)	Frame 1	Frame 2	Frame 3
some/Some	A girl had some books. Some of the books had pictures and some did not.	Some kids went shopping. They got some candy and some toys.	There were some kids here. Some looked at cars and some looked at trucks. They looked for some time.
a/A	The kid put on a hat, a coat, and a scarf. Those are the things she likes.	Some girls had a party for a friend. They gave her a present. It was a lot of fun.	My pet is a cat. She is a white cat. She wears a pink collar with a bell on it.
more/More	More animals are here now. They want more food. The dogs want more meat and the cats want more fish.	A girl wanted to play some more. She wanted more time on the slide and more time on the swings.	Do more kids like summer? Yes, more kids do. The sun shines more and there are more things to do then.
the/The	The cat was not here, but the dog was. The dog liked it here. It was a good place to be.	The cups and the plates were on the table. The spoons were still in the box.	"I go to the beach. I jump in the waves and on the sand. The beach is great."
can/Can	Can the kids do that? They can if they can get the things they need, but they may not get them.	He can play the piano and he can play other things too. What other things can he play?	Some girls can rest here and some boys can rest there. Then they can play together again.

Detect 'n Select: Runway Program Sample Content

Target Word(s)	Frame 1	Frame 2	Frame 3
she/She	Is she the girl who drew the picture? Yes, she is that girl. She loves to draw and she does it all the time.	Here is my sister. She takes care of me and she is nice to me. I think she is the best sister there is.	She wants to play with the toys. Can she do that? Can she play with them? She will be careful and she will not harm anything.
who/Who	I need someone big who can help me carry these boxes. Who can do that? Are you someone who can do that?	We know some kids who can swim and some kids who can run, but we don't know any kids who can fly.	Who is at the door? Who is it? We will not open the door until we know who it is.
also	That girl can do so many things. She can sing. She also can dance. She also plays the piano. Her sister is also able to do those things.	The bird is big. It is also blue. What else is it like? It is also smart. It knows how to go on long trips and also how to get back here.	The girl is going to sit here for now. She is also going to keep score. Another boy will also keep score with her. We don't know if they will also be doing other things.
that/That	That thing is not a bird. It looks like a bird but that is not a bird. I think that is just a big bug. That is what I think it is.	Who is that boy? Is he the one that did all those nice things? Is he the one that also brought all that food to the party?	That baby can sure cry. That is all he seems to do and that is all he seems to want to do. He does that from morning to night.
do/Do	What do the kids do when they are there? Do they play or do they work? Do they like the things they do there?	Those birds do fly there in the winter but the other birds do not. They do not need to go there.	What are the men doing? They are doing all they can to help. They do not want anyone to be hurt.

Detect 'n Select: Liftoff Program Sample Content

Target Word(s)	Frame 1	Frame 2	Frame 3
was/Was	Was the boy here? It looks like he was here, but I am not sure if he was. Could you tell me if he was?	"Who was at the meeting? Was my friend there? She said she would be there, but I do not know if she was there."	Their dog was not a good pet. He was always jumpy and he was always a pest. I was glad he is not with them anymore.
-ed/ looked/ jumped/ walked	The man looked into the car for a tool. Then he looked into the truck. He looked and looked but he could not find the tool.	Some boys jumped onto the truck. They jumped on it because it was so high. Some of the girls also jumped on it.	The dog walked behind some rocks. The kids walked there too. All of them walked in that place when they could.
only/Only	Was she the only girl here? I know he was the only boy here, but I did not think she was the only girl here. Sometimes being the only one can be fun and sometimes it can be scary.	"I am only going to the store and my friend is only going to the meeting. We wanted to go to more places but we each can only go to one thing."	That girl knows how to play only one thing on the piano. She does not like knowing only one thing, but that song is the only one she knows.
did/Did	The bugs did a lot of bad things. Did all of them do that, or did only some of them do that? What did they do?	Did any of the kids need your help? Yes, they did seem to need help. But they did not want to take help from anyone, did they?	Who did the baby look like? Did she look like her mother or did she look like her father?
on/On	The men were not on time. They were planning to be on time, but they got on a bus that was late and so they were not on time. They were upset that they could not be on time.	On their way, the kids stopped for a while. They were on a rough road and they had to rest. Then they went on their way again. They were tired when they finished their hike.	The guide said, "Do not go on the rocks and do not go on those trees. We are not allowed to go on those things so please don't do it." Everyone did what the guide said.

Detect 'n Select: Airborne Program Sample Content

Target Word(s)	Frame 1	Frame 2	Frame 3
another/Another	Another girl is coming so we need another seat. Can someone find another seat for her? Please try to get it quickly.	Do you want another cookie? I will get another one for you. Does your friend want another cookie too? I will get one for him.	She keeps wanting more and more! She wants another pet, she wants another toy, she wants another TV! She just wants too many things.
too/Too	The baby is too little to talk and he is too little to walk, but he is not too little to cry. He does that all the time.	That cat is too big and too mean to keep. He just does too many nasty things. I do not want him in the house.	There are too many things here. There are too many boxes, too many bottles, too many cans. There is just too much.
each/Each	I can see that each one of those kids has something. What does each one have? Each has a pet. Each one has either a cat, a dog, or a bird.	We have a problem here. Look at all those chairs. Something is wrong with each one of them. Each of them is broken. Each one has either a broken seat or a broken arm.	Each of the rooms has lots of things. Each one has a bed, each one has a chair, and each one has some lamps. So each one is all right to stay in.
gain/Again	He went to that place again and again. Each time, the man would say, "Are you here again?" Then he would smile, but he would not say anything.	The man likes to start everything he says with, "I have said this again and again and again." He doesn't seem to know how to say anything else.	The girl was here again. Her sister was here again as well. We did not expect to see them again, but we were lucky that they were able to come.
saw	They saw it! I tell you that they saw it. They saw a monster even though everyone says that you can't see monsters. Still, I think they saw it. What do you think?	The group was walking and they saw lots of things. They saw strange birds, they saw some big trees, and they saw beautiful plants. They liked all that they saw.	"Who saw the storm?" "The boys who were in the woods saw it. The girls saw it too. It scared all of them. It was really a bad storm. I'm glad I didn't see it."

Detect 'n Select: Soaring Program Sample Content

Target Word(s)	Frame 1	Frame 2	Frame 3
as/As	Do you agree that they are as smart as anyone else? They work as hard as anyone else. We are lucky to have them here.	How can we make this place as safe as can be? It is not as safe as we would like. This has to be changed. Who can help us do that?	As he told us, they are not going to get things done as fast as we had thought. So, as I said before, we have to make plans about what we can do.
over/Over	How often can someone go over the same idea over and over again? It's good to go over things, but this is too much.	Over here, there's going to be a garden. Over there, there's going to be a pond. Can we add anything else over there?	Are we over that problem? Yes, we are over it. It's good that we are over it and don't have to deal with it anymore.
much/Much	They are so difficult. They do not know much, they do not care much and they do not do much. They are no help.	How much does that toy cost and how much does the other toy cost? I think they will both cost too much.	Much as he wants to go and much as she wants to go, they will not be able to go. They have too much to do here.
him	"We can see him. He's right there. Can't you see him? You will be able to see him if you move over just a little bit. Try doing that."	A girl was with the boy, but then she left him. She just went off without him and now she wants to get back to him, but she cannot find him.	At his party, we're going to give him lots of things. We'll give him a truck and we'll give him a plane. We'll also give him some books.
so/So	"How can you be so quiet? How can you be so still?" "I am usually not so quiet. I just feel like being quiet today."	That man is so big and so strong. It is hard to believe anyone can be so strong. Did you ever see anyone as strong as he is?	There was so much food there and so much to drink. I had never before seen so much on one table. And it looked so pretty.

Letter In: Sample Content

The charts on pages 229–230 contain the material for the first five noncontent words in each program. A hyphen (-) in a word indicates the letter to be omitted.

Letter In Activity: Sample Word—*each*

What to do: (1) On the back of a prepared page (see the sample in the following illustration), write the target word and say, "This is *each*." Ask your child to repeat the word. (2) Turn the page over. Say, "All these words can become *each* when you add the right letters." (3) Arrange the paper so your child sees only one word at a time. Say, "Add the letters here that you need." (4) Say, "Say the word you just completed." Immediately correct any error. (5) Repeat for each set of boxes. (6) For the last box, say, "Now write the whole word here."

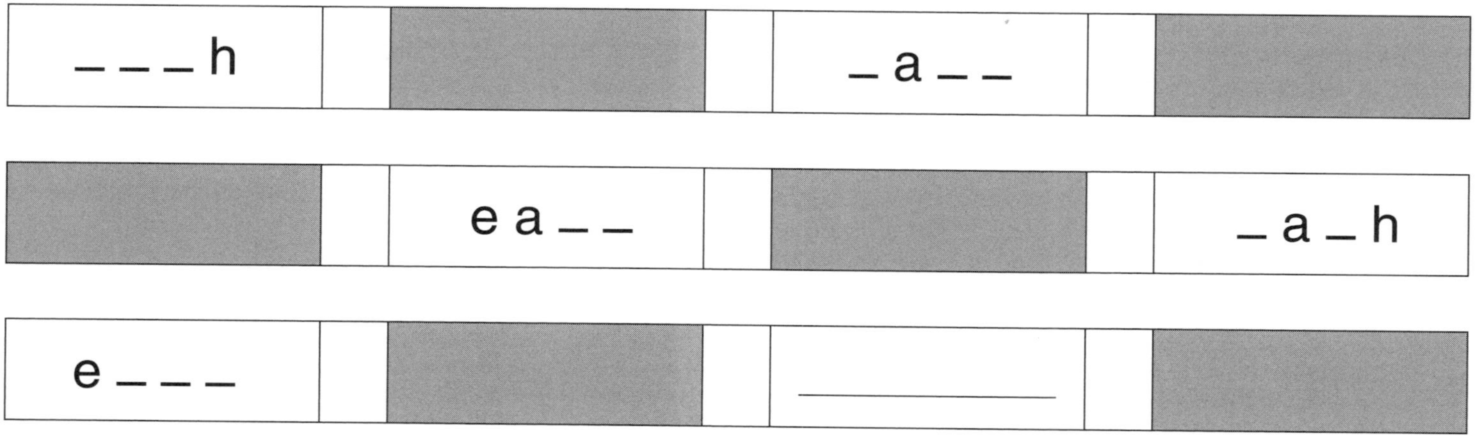

– – – h

e a – –

e – – –

– a – –

– a – h

Letter In: Blank Format

What to do: (1) On the back of the page, write the target word and say, "This is _____." Ask your child to repeat the word. (2) Turn the page over. Say, "All these words can become _____ when you add the right letters." (3) Arrange the paper so your child sees only one word at a time. Say, "Add the letters here that you need." (4) Say, "Say the word you just completed." Immediately correct any error. (5) Repeat for each set of boxes. (6) For the last box, say, "Now write the whole word here."

Letter In: Boarding Program Sample Content

* Single-letter word is paired with the word *girl*.

Target Word	1	2	3	4	5	6
some	som-	s--e	so-e	s--e	-o-e	_____
a*	- g--l	- --rl	- g-r-	- gi--	- --r-	_____
more	m--e	mo-e	m-r-	m--e	m-r-	_____
the	t--	t-e	--e	-h-	--e	_____
can	c--	--n	c--	--n	-a-	_____

Letter In: Runway Program Sample Content

Target Word	1	2	3	4	5	6
she	s-e	s--	sh-	s-e	--e	_____
who	w--	--o	w-o	wh-	--o	_____
also	a--o	-l-o	--s-	---o	a-s-	_____
that	-h-t	-h--	-hat	t--t	---t	_____
doing	d-in-	d----	do--g	---ng	--in-	_____

Letter In: Liftoff Program Sample Content

*Two-letter word is paired with the word *it*.

Target Word	1	2	3	4	5	6
was	w--	--s	-a-	--s	w-s	_____
-ed (jumped)	j-m---	-u-p--	-umpe-	-u-p--	j-m---	_____
only	on--	-n-y	--l-	o---	o-l-	_____
did	-i-	--d	-id	-i-	d--	_____
on*	o- i-	o- --	-- it	-n -t	-- i-	_____

Letter In: Airborne Program Sample Content

Target Word	1	2	3	4	5	6
another	an---er	a-o--er	anoth--	an-th-r	--oth--	_____
too	t--	--o	t-o	--o	-o-	_____
each	e--h	--c-	-a--	e---	e--h	_____
again	a---n	-ga--	--ai-	a--in	a-a-n	_____
saw	s--	-a-	--w	-aw	s--	_____

Letter In: Soaring Program Sample Content

* Two-letter word is paired with the words *near to*.
** Two-letter word is paired with the word *good*.

Target Word	1	2	3	4	5	6
as*	a- ne-- -o	as ne-- --	-s n--r --	-- near --	-- -ea- --	_____
over	-ve-	--er	o--r	--e-	-v--	_____
much	m--h	--c-	-u--	m---	m--h	_____
him	--m	-i-	--m	-im	h--	_____
so**	s- ---d	-o go--	s- g--d	-o -oo-	s- goo-	_____

Cipher Wiz Activity: Sample Word—*also*

What to do: (1) Point to the top line (as shown in the following illustration) and say, "You need to write in words and punctuation marks here. The numbers tell you what to write." (2) Point to the first number in the top box and say, "Look under the line and find the one for this number." (In this case, it is the word *Are.*) (3) (If the item is a word and not a punctuation mark) say, "Read the word(s)." (4) Cover the word or mark, point to the line, and say, "Write that here." (5) Repeat the sequence until the write-ins are all completed. (6) Say, "Now read what it says." Immediately correct any error. Complete the second set in the same manner. (7) Cover the sentences, provide clean lined paper, and say, "Now you'll write the whole sentence again." Dictate the words of the first sentence one word at a time. If there is any error in words or punctuation, stop. Show the words, cover them, provide fresh paper, and have your child redo the writing from the first word. (8) Repeat for the second sentence in the same manner.

| 2 | 4 | 1 | 3 | 5 |

_____

_____

1 = also   2 = Are   3 = swimming here   4 = the boys   5 = ?

| 5 | 1 | 3 | 6 | 2 | 1 | 4 | 6 |

_____

_____

1 = cannot   2 = She also   3 = sit   4 = talk   5 = The baby   6 = .

Cipher Wiz: Sample Content

The charts on pages 234–238 contain the material for the first five noncontent words in each program.

Cipher Wiz: Blank Format

What to do: (1) Point to the lines and say, "You need to write in words and punctuation marks here. The numbers tell you what to write." (2) Point to the first number in the top box and say, "Look under the line and find the one for this number." (3) (If it is a word and not a punctuation mark) say, "Read the word(s)." (4) Cover the word or mark, point to the line, and say, "Write that here." (5) Repeat the sequence until the write-ins are all completed. (6) "Now read what it says." Immediately correct any error. Complete the second set in the same manner. (7) Cover the sentences, provide clean lined paper, and say, "Now you'll write the whole sentence again." Dictate the words of the first sentence one word at a time. If there is any error in words or punctuation, stop. Show the words, cover them, provide fresh paper, and have your child redo the writing from the first word. (8) Repeat for the second sentence in the same manner. (Use two sheets for this activity.)

Cipher Wiz: Boarding Program Sample Content

Target Word	Sentence 1	Sentence 2
some	1 2 1 = some 2 = kids	2 1 1 = girls 2 = some
a	2 3 1 1 = a girl 2 = some girls 3 =,	1 2 4 3 1 = a kid 2 = some kids 3 =,
more	3 1 4 2 1 1 = kids 2 = more 3 = some 4 =,	1 2 6 5 4 3 1 = a 2 = boy 3 = boys 4 = more 5 = some 6 =,
the	2 1 1 = bird 2 = the	4 1 5 3 2 1 = girl 2 = girls 3 = some 4 = the 5 =,
can	1 4 3 2 5 1 = Can 2 = fly 3 = pet 4 = the 5 = ?	1 3 2 4 5 1 = A 2 = can 3 = girl 4 = rest 5 = .

Cipher Wiz: Runway Program Sample Content

Target Word	Sentence 1	Sentence 2
she	5 3 6 1 2 7 1 = but she 2 = is not resting 3 = rest here 4 = she 5 = She can 6 =, 7 = .	1 2 3 4 1 = Is she 2 = petting 3 = the cat 4 = ?
who	3 2 1 4 1 = here 2 = is walking 3 = Who 4 = ?	2 1 3 1 = is swimming 2 = Who 3 = ?
also	2 4 1 3 5 1 = also 2 = Are 3 = swimming here 4 = the boys 5 = ?	5 1 3 6 2 1 4 6 1 = cannot 2 = She also 3 = sit 4 = talk 5 = The baby 6 = .
that	4 3 2 1 5 1 = is jumping 2 = that 3 = the kid 4 = Who is 5 = ?	6 2 5 7 1 3 4 8 1 = but it 2 = can also 3 = cannot 4 = jump 5 = talk 6 = That bird 7 =, 8 = .
do	4 1 2 6 5 1 3 6 1 = do 2 = not sit here 3 = that 4 = The boys 5 = The girls 6 = .	5 3 6 2 1 4 7 1 = are not 2 = but the robots 3 = do walk 4 = doing that 5 = Some robots 6 =, 7 = .

Cipher Wiz: Liftoff Program Sample Content

Target Word	Sentence 1	Sentence 2
was	6 1 3 2 10 5 7 9 4 8 10 1 = a boy 2 = also a girl 3 = and there was 4 = but the girl 5 = The boy 6 = There was 7 = was running 8 = was walking 9 =, 10 = .	6 2 8 7 10 1 9 3 5 4 9 1 = it was 2 = moving 3 = The truck 4 = this way 5 = was moving 6 = Was the truck 7 = Yes 8 = ? 9 = . 10 =,
-ed	4 6 2 1 5 3 7 1 = also 2 = in the water 3 = like this 4 = That duck 5 = walked 6 = who is 7 = .	3 1 2 5 4 6 1 = needed 2 = some things 3 = Those kids 4 = their robot 5 = to fix 6 = .
only	3 2 1 4 5 6 1 = does not 2 = of the puppies 3 = Only one 4 = want to eat 5 = now 6 = .	4 5 1 7 6 2 3 7 1 = can fly 2 = cannot 3 = do that 4 = Many 5 = of the planes 6 = Only some 7 = .
did	1 3 7 4 9 6 5 2 8 1 = Did all the kids 2 = did that 3 = jump in the water 4 = No 5 = of the kids 6 = only some 7 = ? 8 = . 9 =,	7 5 1 6 9 3 4 1 2 8 1 = at the 2 = birds 3 = but it 4 = did look 5 = did not look 6 = puppies 7 = The cat 8 = . 9 =,
on	1 8 5 9 2 3 7 10 6 4 10 1 = A bug 2 = but she 3 = did not 4 = looked at it 5 = on the girl 6 = She only 7 = stop it 8 = was hopping 9 =, 10 = .	6 2 5 3 1 4 7 1 = in the water 2 = of their puppies 3 = on the rocks 4 = that time 5 = was jumping 6 = Which one 7 = ?

Cipher Wiz: Airborne Program Sample Content

Target Word	Sentence 1	Sentence 2
another	3 5 4 7 6 9 1 2 8 1 = Did another one 2 = go with them 3 = He thinks that 4 = of the girls 5 = only two 6 = to the park 7 = went 8 = ? 9 = .	6 5 4 2 7 1 3 8 1 = Can another 2 = cleaning the place 3 = girl help her 4 =one girl 5 = still only 6 = There is 7 = . 8 = ?
too	5 11 10 9 1 8 2 7 12 6 1 8 4 3 12 10 1 = are 2 = big to go on 3 = for you 4 = small for you 5 = The man said 6 = They 7 = those swings 8 = too 9 = You 10 = " 11 =, 12 = .	7 2 4 10 5 9 1 6 10 5 3 8 10 1 = and it can 2 = can move 3 = hop 4 = in many ways 5 = It can 6 = jump 7 = That robot 8 = too 9 = walk 10 = .
each	5 9 6 7 10 3 4 2 1 8 10 1 = a big help 2 = could be 3 = Each one 4 = of them 5 = Some kids 6 = to help fix 7 = the swings 8 = to us 9 = would like 10 = .	7 1 4 2 8 5 6 3 9 1 = each of 2 = go 3 = near us 4 = the animals 5 = They need 6 = to stay 7 = Where did 8 = ? 9 = .
again	3 4 2 5 1 9 8 7 6 9 1 = again 2 = are going 3 = Do you think 4 = the bugs 5 = to fly this way 6 = to stop them 7 = we do 8 = What can 9 = ?	4 9 8 6 5 1 3 2 7 8 1 = again 2 = have rested 3 = now that they 4 = She said 5 = seem very happy 6 = The two babies 7 = . 8 = " 9 =,
saw	6 3 4 1 2 5 7 1 = getting out 2 = of the hole 3 = of the kids 4 = saw the mice 5 = that time 6 = Which one 7 = ?	5 2 3 1 7 4 6 8 1 = many good places 2 = said that 3 = she saw 4 = swim anytime 5 = The girl 6 = we wanted to 7 = where we could 8 = .

Cipher Wiz: Soaring Program Sample Content

Target Word	Sentence 1	Sentence 2
as	7 4 2 1 6 8 3 5 9 1 = any animal 2 = as nice as 3 = Don't you think 4 = happens to be 5 = it is 6 = on earth 7 = That animal 8 = . 9 = ?	7 6 9 8 3 1 4 5 1 2 10 8 1 = as 2 = I can 3 = I will get 4 = many mice 5 = out of their holes 6 = said 7 = The man 8 = " 9 = , 10 = .
over	3 4 1 6 9 5 8 10 2 7 11 1 = get over 2 = He is going 3 = How can 4 = the boy 5 = They are 6 = those rocks 7 = to fall 8 = very big 9 = ? 10 = ! 11 = .	3 7 6 1 2 9 5 4 8 6 1 = Can you 2 = move over 3 = The kid said 4 = too near me 5 = You are sitting 6 = " 7 = , 8 = . 9 = ?
much	1 2 7 4 9 3 10 8 11 5 2 11 1 = Is there 2 = much dirt 3 = No 4 = of the pool 5 = There isn't 6 = there 7 = to dig out 8 = you are lucky 9 = ? 10 = , 11 = .	2 7 3 6 8 4 1 5 8 1 = and they 2 = Much of the time 3 = the boys 4 = They were hungry 5 = were eating 6 = were not playing 7 = , 8 = .
him	1 4 2 7 5 6 3 8 1 = After the kids 2 = crying 3 = him 4 = saw the baby 5 = they wanted 6 = to help 7 = , 8 = .	6 4 8 2 10 7 5 1 3 9 1 = after he jumped 2 = in that place 3 = over the rocks 4 = the kid 5 = to him 6 = We couldn't see 7 = What happened 8 = when we were 9 = ? 10 = .
so	4 3 6 5 2 1 7 1 = and eat there 2 = had to stop 3 = in the group 4 = So many people 5 = that we 6 = were hungry 7 = .	5 8 1 3 6 9 7 3 2 4 9 1 = because they could 2 = one 3 = see 4 = so much 5 = The kids 6 = the rainbow 7 = They had wanted to 8 = were so happy 9 = .

chapter 12

Creating the Books

There are thirty books in the system, six from each of the five reading and writing programs: Boarding, Runway, Liftoff, Airborne, and Soaring. Half are *books intact*—complete books that your child reads, and half are *books to enact*—incomplete books that your child helps to create. Each book is offered after your child learns a set of words. The charts at the start of Chapter Eleven, containing the words and books of the reading and writing programs, tell you at what point each book should be introduced. In addition, in the material that follows, each book description lists the set of words that should be mastered before the book is presented.

Preparing the Materials

In developing the books, it's best to focus only on the books in the program your child is in at a particular time. For example, if your child is in the Boarding program, develop the six books for that program; if your child is in the Runway program, develop the six books for that program, and so on. Although you skip over words that your child knows, you do not skip over any books. So prepare all the books in the level at which your child is working.

To construct the books, take standard $8\frac{1}{2}$-by-11-inch blank white paper. Fold the sheets in half so they look like a booklet. Each sheet can then serve as four pages of the booklet. You also need a cover page for the title. So if a book has text extending over eight pages, use three sheets of paper. One will serve as the cover and the others will contain the text pages. If a book has text extending over twelve pages, use four sheets, and so on. If you prefer to use bigger sheets of paper, feel free to do so.

There will generally be several days, and at times a week or two, between the time your child begins reading one book and then begins the next. So don't feel rushed to get the books done all at once. Generally, it is best to set up a schedule that allows you to prepare two books a week. In that way, you will always have the material you need ready to go.

Creating the Texts

You can find the words and sentences for the books in the section of this chapter titled Materials for the Books. When you have the sheets of paper prepared, enter the text on the relevant pages. You can do this in a number of ways. It's usually easiest to use a computer and type the text, in a large font size. Then, after printing it out, you can paste the various segments onto the appropriate pages. Remember to leave room for illustrations. Alternatively, if your printing is clear, you can write directly on the pages, once again making sure to leave room for the graphics.

Starting with the Liftoff program, each book contains a comprehension activity, called Gleaning Meaning, that appears as the last page in the book. This activity presents a set of sentences that summarizes the story. The sentences contain blank spaces that your child has to fill in, using the set of choices at the bottom of the page. At the end of Chapter Eight, you can see an example of the way in which Gleaning Meaning is arranged.

Adding the Illustrations

Along with the words, the books contain illustrations. These are provided at the end of this chapter and are designed for copying and using in a range of cutting and pasting activities. For example, Book 1 has pages with text referring both to individual children (for example, *a girl, a boy*) and groups of children (for example, *some kids*). For the pages where you need a single child, you can use the picture of a group and cut out a figure that will fit the text. In making copies, you may find it useful to enlarge the pictures. Children also enjoy having the opportunity to color them in.

Do not feel that you should limit yourself to the illustrations provided here. Many children love to create their own pictures, making them with computer programs, downloading artwork from the Internet, or drawing them themselves. Regardless of the route you select, it is useful to go over the text of a page with your child, and together decide on the illustration that best suit the material.

As you prepare the material, keep in mind that some pages should be left without illustrations. As we discussed in Chapter Eight, pictureless text is valuable in helping children to increase their understanding of the words on the printed page.

The Sessions

When you have completed teaching the set of words that precedes reading a book, you offer your child the book. This can be done in the same session in which the last word of the set has been taught, or it can be done in the next session.

The first, third, and fifth books in each program are books intact while the second, fourth, and sixth books are books to enact.

Books Intact

For books intact, you present the book to your child and carry out the following steps:

Step 1. Open to page 1. Say, "Read this book to me."

Step 2. If there is an error, immediately correct it by telling your child the correct word.

Step 3. After supplying the correct word, say, "Now start here" (pointing to the first word on the page), so that your child rereads the page from the first word of the page.

Step 4. Repeat steps 1 through 3 for each page.

Books to Enact

For books to enact, you present the book to your child and carry out the following steps:

Step 1. Open to page 1. Say, "There are missing words here. Use the symbols to find the missing word, and then write the word on the line."

Step 2. If there is an error, immediately correct it. If the spelling is incorrect, erase it and say, "Start again"; if the choice is incorrect, erase it and say, "Find the right word that goes there."

Step 3. When all the words on a page are filled in, say, "Now read the page to me." Repeat steps 1 through 3 with each page of text.

Step 4. Repeat steps 1 through 3 for each page.

Step 5. After the last page has been completed and read, say, "Now read the whole book to me."

Step 6. If there is an error, immediately correct it by telling your child the correct word.

Step 7. After supplying the correct word, say, "Now start here" (pointing to the first word on the page), so that your child rereads the page from the first word of the page.

Gleaning Meaning

For the Gleaning Meaning activity, carry out the following steps:

Step 1. Say to your child, "This tells a summary of the story, but you need to fill in some of the words. Use the words at the bottom of the page to do that."

Step 2. Immediately correct any error.

Step 3. When all the words are filled in correctly, say, "Now read this page to me."

Step 4. Immediately correct any error.

Once a book has been completed, give it to your child to keep and to read whenever he or she chooses to do so. The books of the Liftoff program are designed to be read in sets of two (Books 13 and 14; 15 and 16; 17 and 18). For these books, each time you get to an even-numbered book, first have your child reread the preceding odd-numbered book, and then immediately go on to the even-numbered book.

Moving On

After your child has read a book, return to teaching the next set of words in the program. (These are the words listed in Chapter Eleven and also in the following book descriptions.) Before your child reads the sixth book in each program, carry out a Progress Check to determine how well your child has learned the material. You can find the Progress Check in the next chapter. It tells you whether your child is ready to move on to the next program or whether he or she needs some review at the current level.

Materials for the Books

Boarding Program

Book 1

Theme: Children coming together to build a snowman.

Words taught before reading book: *kid, girl, kids, girls, some, a, boys, more.*

Page	Text	Page	Text
Cover	**Some Kids**	1	some kids
2	some girls, some boys	3	a girl
4	a boy	5	more girls
6	some more girls	7	some more boys
8	some kids		

Book 2

Theme: A boy has some pets: some are cats; the others are birds who increase in number as their eggs hatch.

Words taught before reading book: *cat, bird, pet.*

Note that this is the first book to enact. In this type of book, your child enters words to complete the text. The sample page displayed here shows how the material is arranged.

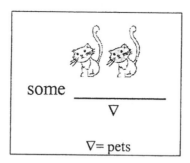

In the text for these books, the underlined words are the ones that are to be replaced by symbols.

Page	Text	Page	Text
Cover	**Some Pets**	1	a <u>boy</u>
2	some <u>pets</u>	3	a <u>cat</u>
4	some <u>more cats</u>	5	<u>some</u> pets
6	some <u>birds</u>	7	<u>more</u> birds
8	<u>some more</u> birds		

Book 3

Theme: Similarities and differences among birds and kids.

Words taught before reading book: *the, eat, fly, rest, can, are, here, not.*

Page	Text	Page	Text
Cover	**The Pets, The Kids**	1	Here are some pets.
2	The pets can eat.	3	Here are some kids.
4	The kids can eat.	5	Pets can rest.
6	The kids can rest.	7	The pets can fly.
8	Kids cannot fly.		

Book 4

Theme: Similarities and differences among bugs and kids.

Words taught before reading book: *bug, swim, talk, jump.*

Page	Text	Page	Text
Cover	**The Bugs, The Kids**	1	Here are some <u>bugs</u>.
2	<u>Bugs</u> can <u>jump</u>.	3	Here are <u>some</u> kids.
4	The kids <u>can</u> jump.	5	The <u>bugs</u> can <u>swim</u>.
6	The kids can <u>swim</u>.	7	Kids can <u>talk</u>.
8	Bugs can<u>not</u> <u>talk</u>.		

Book 5

Theme: Child with a toy robot that cannot fly and a plane that can.
Words taught before reading book: *is, walk, plane, -ing, toy, but, this, robot, it.*

Page	Text	Page	Text
Cover	**The Toys**	1	Here is a toy.
2	The toy is a robot.	3	The robot can walk. It is walking.
4	The robot can jump. It is jumping.	5	The robot can walk, the robot can jump, but it cannot fly.
6	Here are more toys.	7	This toy is a plane. It cannot walk,
8	it cannot jump, but it can fly. The plane is flying.		

Book 6

Theme: Different features of toy robots and dolls.
Words taught before reading book: *doll, they, rocket, sit.*

Page	Text	Page	Text
Cover	**The Bugs, The Kids**	1	Here are some toys. The toys are
2	dolls. The dolls can walk. They are walking.	3	The dolls can sit. They are sitting. The dolls
4	can walk, they can sit, but they cannot talk.	5	More toys are here. The toys
6	are rockets. Rockets cannot walk.	7	They cannot walk, but they can
8	fly. The rockets are flying.		

Runway Program

Book 7

Theme: Interaction between two babies who cannot speak, but who can still communicate.

Words taught before reading book: *thing, she, big, baby, who, also, that, do, I, am, we.*

Page	Text	Page	Text
Cover	**The Babies**	1	"Who are they? They are
2	kids. Who am I? I am also a kid but I am not a big kid. I am	3	a baby. I am also a girl. I am a baby girl."
4	"Who is that? That is a kid. She is not a big kid.	5	She is also a baby. She is a baby girl."
6	"I am a baby. She is a baby. We are babies. We are baby girls."	7	"Babies cannot do some things. Babies cannot
8	walk. Babies cannot jump. Babies cannot talk. But we can eat. We are eating."		

Book 8

Theme: The "lifestyle" of a lazy frog.

Words taught before reading book: *like, what, frog, to, does, want, many, those.*

Page	Text	Page	Text
Cover	**What Does the Frog Like?**	1	What is <u>that</u>? That is a <u>frog</u>.
2	Frogs <u>can</u> do <u>many</u> things, but that frog does not like to <u>do</u> those <u>things</u>.	3	Frogs can <u>jump</u>, but this frog does not <u>like</u> to jump.
4	It <u>does</u> not <u>want</u> to jump. It does <u>not</u> jump.	5	Frogs can <u>walk</u>, but this <u>frog</u> does not like to walk. It does not want to walk.
6	<u>It</u> does not walk. It does not do <u>that</u>.	7	The frog is not jumping. The frog is not walking.
8	<u>The</u> frog is resting. That is <u>what</u> it likes to <u>do</u>.		

Book 9

Theme: Pets in action, including a puppy who gets to run (by riding on the back of a bigger dog).

Words taught before reading book: *one, run, other, which, there, dog, puppy, look, at, now.*

Page	Text	Page	Text
Cover	**The Puppy Who Can Run**	1	Here are some things. One is a thing that can fly. It is not a plane, but it can fly like a plane. What is it? It is a bird.
2	Which one is the bird? This one is the bird. Now it is flying. It likes to fly.	3	What are those other things? Some are things that can run. They cannot fly, but they can run.
4	What are they? They are dogs. The ones that can run are dogs.	5	Those dogs are not babies. But there is a baby dog. It is a puppy. Which one is the puppy?
6	Here is the puppy. The puppy is looking at the big dogs. It also wants to run.	7	It wants to run like the big dogs, but it cannot do that.
8	Now the puppy is running.		

Book 10

Theme: Man fixing a broken robot.

Words taught before reading book: *man, of, yet, fix, have, good, he, arm, has, leg, truck.*

Page	Text	Page	Text
Cover	**The Man Who Can**	1	Who is <u>that</u>? Is that a <u>man</u>? Yes, it is a man. The man is one <u>who</u> likes toys.

(continued)

Page	Text	Page	Text
2	<u>He</u> is a man who likes to fix toys. He <u>fixes</u> toys that are not <u>good</u>. He can fix <u>trucks</u>. He can	3	<u>also</u> fix dolls. Those are some <u>of</u> the things he can fix. He also fixes <u>robots</u>.
4	Here is one of the <u>toys</u>. It is a robot. The robot is not good. The robot has its <u>legs,</u>	5	but it does not have its <u>arms</u>. Is the man <u>looking at</u> the robot? Yes, he is.
6	<u>Can</u> the man fix the robot? <u>Yes</u>, he can. He can do that. He can fix <u>it</u>.	7	That is what he is <u>doing now</u>. The man is fixing <u>the</u> robot.
8	Now the robot <u>has</u> its arms. Now it is a <u>good robot</u>.		

Book 11

Theme: A boy with an "independent" pet frog who is trying to get away, and the boy pulls him back.

Words taught before reading book: *my, need, you, wing, hop, all, no, their, use, stop.*

Page	Text	Page	Text
Cover	**The Boy's Frog**	1	Here is a boy. He has some things. What does he have? The boy has many toys. He also has some pets. The pets are here.
2	"These are my pets. I like my pets. One of my pets is a frog. Can my frog fly? No, it cannot. You need wings to fly and frogs do not have wings."	3	But they have other things. What other things do they have? They have legs. They can use their legs to do many things.
4	Can they use their legs to jump? Yes, they can do that. They can use their legs to jump.	5	Can they also use their legs to hop? Yes, they can do that. They can use their legs to hop.

Page	Text	Page	Text
6	Can they use their legs to walk? Yes, they can also do that. They can use their legs to walk.	7	Frogs can do all those things. They can jump. They can hop. They can walk.
8	"My pet is doing something now. What is it doing?	9	It is hopping." The boy does not like the frog doing that.
10	"You cannot do that. You can hop, but you cannot hop there. You have to stop that."	11	The frog does not want to stop. It does not stop. But the boy does stop the frog.
12	Now he has his frog.		

Book 12

Theme: Capabilities of some animals.

Words taught before reading book: *duck, by, these, water, way, and, both, move, in, for.*

Page	Text	Page	Text
Cover	**Flying and Swimming**	1	Ducks are <u>birds</u>. Like other birds, they have wings and <u>those</u> wings are good <u>for</u> flying. Can this duck fly? Yes, it can. What is it <u>doing</u> now? It is flying.
2	Ducks can also <u>move</u> in other ways. They can move by swimming. But they do not <u>use</u> <u>their</u> wings to swim. They use <u>their</u> legs to do that.	3	<u>These</u> ducks are doing that now. They are <u>using</u> their legs to move in the <u>water</u>. Ducks can move by flying and by swimming. They can move in <u>both</u> ways.

(continued)

Page	Text	Page	Text
4	Are there other things that can also do <u>that</u>? Yes, other things can fly and <u>swim</u>. <u>Which</u> things can do that? Some bugs can do that. Water bugs can do that. <u>Like</u> birds, water bugs have wings that are good for flying.	5	They use their wings to fly. They also <u>have</u> legs that are good for swimming. Now they are <u>not</u> swimming. These bugs are flying.
6	Here is <u>something</u> that cannot fly, but it can swim. What is it? It is a frog. The frog is swimming now. It is <u>in</u> the <u>water</u>	7	and it is <u>swimming</u>. Frogs can <u>move</u> by swimming, but they cannot move <u>by</u> flying.
8	Do frogs have <u>other</u> <u>ways</u> to move? Yes, they do. Frogs can move in many ways. They can <u>hop</u> and they can jump.		

Liftoff Program

At this level the texts extend across two books so that Books 13 and 14 tell one story; Books 15 and 16 another; Books 17 and 18 another.

Book 13

Theme: The start of a story about a frog who wishes only to jump.

Words taught before reading book: *sad, rock, hurt, -ed, only, did, time, on, could, -'s.*

Page	Text	Page	Text
Cover	**The Jumping Frog 1**	1	There was a frog. Did that frog like to do things? Yes, he did. What did the frog like to do? The frog liked to jump.
2	All frogs like to jump and this frog also liked to do that.	3	Did he also like to do other things? No, he did not. He did not like to sit, he did not like to run, he did not like to swim.

Page	Text	Page	Text
4	Could the frog swim? Yes, he could swim. Could the frog run? Yes, he could run. Could the frog sit? Yes, he could sit.	5	But the frog did not like doing those things.
6	This frog was not like other frogs. He only liked to jump. The frog did not stop jumping. He jumped all the time.	7	He jumped and jumped and jumped.
8	Now the frog is doing what he likes to do. He is doing what he does all the time. He is jumping.	9	The frog is jumping in some water. The water has many rocks in it.
10	The frog jumped on the rocks. That was not a good thing to do. The rocks in the water hurt the frog's leg.	11	Now the frog has stopped jumping. He cannot jump. The frog's leg hurts.
12	Here is the sad frog. This is the frog that was jumping all the time. Now he is not doing that. The frog cannot move. He can only rest. He has to rest.		

(After reading this book, put it aside and return to it again when ready to read *The Jumping Frog 2*. Then have your child read both books, one after the other.)

Book 14

Theme: The jumping frog changes his view of life.

Words taught before reading book: *help, where, his, very, see, go, think, me, near, cry.*

Page	Text	Page	Text
Cover	**The Jumping Frog 2**	1	Here is the frog who was hurt. <u>Where</u> is that frog? He is <u>near</u> the water. He is not in the water, but he is near the <u>water</u>. What is the frog doing? The frog is sitting.

(continued)

Page	Text	Page	Text
2	He does not like to sit, but at this time that is all he can do. The frog is very sad. His leg hurts and he cannot move. Now he is crying.	3	The frog could not move, but he could think. What was he thinking? He was thinking, "I cannot move. I cannot jump. I need help, but no one is here to help me."
4	The frog thinks that no one is there, but someone is. A girl is walking near the water. The girl sees the frog and the frog sees the girl.	5	The girl stopped walking. Where did she stop? She stopped near the frog. The frog could not go to the girl. The frog could not move.
6	But the girl could go to the frog. She does that. Now she is near the frog.	7	The girl could not talk to the frog, but she could help the frog.
8	The girl looked at the frog's leg. She was thinking "You cannot talk, but I can see that you need help. I can help you."	9	The girl did that. She fixed the frog's leg and now the leg does not hurt the frog.
10	Now the frog is not sad and he is not crying. He is also doing more thinking.	11	He is thinking, "I am not going to/jump the way I did. I am not going to jump and jump and jump. I am only going to jump like the other frogs do."

12   **Gleaning Meaning**

There was a frog who liked to _____. One time, that frog was

hurt and he was _____. He could not move. A girl

_____ near the frog. She fixed his _____.

That helped the _____. His leg was _____

and he was not sad. He also stopped jumping all the _____.

* * *

frog   good   jump   leg   sad   time   walked

Book 15

Theme: The start of a story of a lazy cat who loves to eat.

Words taught before reading book: *play, face, most, food, her, ate, happy, any, fat.*

Page	Text	Page	Text
Cover	**The Cat Who Liked to Eat 1**	1	Cats like to play. These are some cats. What are they doing? They are playing.
2	Cats also like to rest. Most cats like to rest and they rest most of the time. But there was a cat that did not like to do that. She did not like to rest and she did not like to play. Did she like to do anything?	3	Yes, she did. What did she like to do? She liked to do only one thing. She liked to eat. All she liked to do was to eat. Anytime there was food, she ate it. She ate and she ate and she ate. Where is that cat?
4	Here she is. What is she doing? Is she eating? Yes, she is. She is doing what she does most of the time. She is eating and she is happy. She is also fat. Her face is fat. Her legs are fat. All of her is fat.	5	Can the fat cat move? Yes, she can, but she does not like to move. She only likes to sit and eat.
6	Now the cat has stopped eating. She does not have anything more to eat. She is not happy now. She wants more food.	7	She was looking for some food. She looked and looked, but there was no food anywhere near her.
8	The cat thinks, "I want more food, but there is no food near here. I have to look for some food." The cat does not like to move, but now she has to do that.		

(After reading this book, put it aside and return to it again when ready to read *The Cat Who Liked to Eat 2*. Then have your child read both books, one after the other.)

Book 16

Theme: The fat cat gets stuck in a mouse hole and has to change her view of food.

Words taught before reading book: *them, hole, find, out, be, push, us, then, mice, get.*

Page	Text	Page	Text
Cover	**The Cat Who Liked to Eat 2**	1	You can see the fat cat who <u>wanted</u> more food. She was <u>looking</u> for <u>some</u>, but she could not find any. She was not at all happy.
2	Then the cat sees a <u>hole</u>. She thinks, "Sometimes <u>mice</u> can be in holes. Can there be any mice in there? I <u>think</u> there can. Some mice can be in that hole." The cat <u>gets</u> to the hole. Then she looks in and sees some mice.	3	She likes seeing the mice, but they do <u>not</u> <u>like</u> seeing her. They think, "That cat wants to eat us. We do not want her to eat <u>us</u>. We do not want her to be near us." To get the mice, the cat has to get into the hole.
4	To do that, the cat has to push and <u>push</u> and push. She does that. Now she is in the hole, but she cannot get <u>out</u> of the <u>hole</u>. She cannot move. She is near the mice, but she cannot get to them.	5	The mice look at the cat. They see that she cannot move. They think, "<u>We</u> can be here. The cat cannot get to us. She cannot eat us." Then the mice are <u>happy</u>, but the cat is not. She is sad.
6	The cat <u>has</u> to be in the hole for some time. All that <u>time</u>, she cannot eat. Now the cat is not fat <u>anymore</u>. Her face is not fat. Her legs are not fat. She can get out of the hole. She does that.	7	Now the cat does not eat all of the <u>time</u>. She does not eat most of the time. She eats <u>only</u> some of the time.

8   **Gleaning Meaning**

There was a fat cat who only liked to _____. One time, she did

not have any _____. She looked for some in a

_____. In the hole, she could see some _____.

She wanted the mice but she could not get to _____. The cat

pushed into the hole but then she could not _____. She could

not eat for some time and then she was not _____. She could

get _____ of the hole and she did that. She also stopped

eating all the time.

* * *

eat   fat   food   hole   mice   move   out   them

Book 17

Theme: The start of a story about some kids going to a park to play.

Words taught before reading book: *park, nice, play, pool, still, ground, dirty, -y, say, two, had, swing.*

Page	Text	Page	Text
Cover	**Getting a Nice Place to Play 1**	1	Here are some kids. These kids had wanted to play ball, but they did not have a ball. They had also wanted to go swimming, but they did not have the things you need for swimming.
2	Still, the kids want to do something, but they cannot think of what they can do. The kids walk and they walk and they still cannot think of what to do.	3	Then two of the kids stop and they say, "We could go to a park. Parks are nice places. We could play there. There are many things to do in a park."

(continued)

Page	Text	Page	Text
4	The other kids liked that. There was a park nearby and they all wanted to go there. They were all thinking that the park was going to be nice. They were thinking that it was going to look like this.	5	But in the park things did not look nice. The kids looked at the swings. They could see that the swings were not good. They also looked at the pool. They could see that the pool was not good to swim in. They looked at the ground. The ground was dirty. It had many things on it.
6	The kids are not happy. Look at their faces. You can see that they do not like where they are.	7	They wanted a good place to play in and a park like this was not a good place for doing that.
8	But two of the kids do not say that. They think that there is a way to fix the park. The two kids want to do that.		

(After reading this book, put it aside and return to it again when ready to read *Getting a Nice Place to Play 2.* Then have your child read both books, one after the other.)

Book 18

Theme: The kids work together to restore the park to a good state.

Words taught before reading book: *clean, will, bag, put, make, would, said, with, stay, her.*

Page	Text	Page	Text
Cover	**Getting a Nice Place to Play 2**	1	There was a park that the kids did not think looked nice. Some of the kids did not want to <u>fix</u> the park, but <u>two</u> kids did. They wanted to <u>fix</u> the park.

Page	Text	Page	Text
2	The two kids were saying to the other kids, "We can fix this park. It does <u>not</u> have to be this <u>way</u>. We can fix the swings, we can move all the dirty things on the <u>ground</u> into bags. It can be nice. Will you help us? Stay here with us and help us clean the park."	3	<u>That</u> makes the other <u>kids</u> stop and think.
4	They had wanted to go and they had not been <u>thinking</u> about fixing and cleaning the park. But now they are thinking that way. They are thinking it would be <u>nice</u> to clean the park. Then they would have a good <u>place</u> to play.	5	Are the kids going to <u>stay</u> to help clean the park? <u>Yes</u>, they are. They go to the two kids and say, "Yes, we <u>will</u> stay with you and help you. We <u>would</u> like to make the park a nice place to be."
6	The kids are doing what they said. They fixed the swings. Then they get all the things on the <u>ground</u> and put them in <u>bags</u>.	7	The <u>kids</u> did all the things they said they <u>would</u> do. Now, they have the nice park that they had wanted to have.

8   **Gleaning Meaning**

There was a park that was very _____. Some kids wanted to

get _____ of the park. But some other kids wanted to stay

and _____ the park. All the kids did stay and they cleaned it.

They _____ all the dirty things into _____.

Then the park was a nice _____ for _____.

* * *

bags   clean   dirty   out   place   playing   put

Airborne Program

Book 19

Theme: A science-type text on common features of birds and some of their differences (that some birds, such as the kiwi, cannot fly).

Words taught before reading book: *plant, animal, another, kind, cold, seem, hot, small, too.*

Page	Text	Page	Text
Cover	**Birds and Flying**	1	The plants you see here are like other plants. They cannot move. They have to stay in one place.
2	Animals are not like that. Animals can move. They can move where they like. Animals can also move in many kinds of ways. Some move by walking, others move by swimming, and still others move by hopping.	3	There is a kind of animal that moves in all those ways. But it can also move in another way. In what other way can it move? It can move by flying.
4	What kind of animal is that? It is a bird. Birds are animals that can move by flying. They do not have to fly all the time and they do not fly all the time. But they can fly any time they want.	5	All kinds of birds can move that way. Big birds can fly and small birds can fly.
6	Birds that stay in hot places can fly and birds that stay in cold places can fly.	7	Birds that eat small bugs can fly and birds that eat big animals can fly.
8	Birds with small legs can fly and birds with big legs can fly. Birds that go in the water can fly and birds that do not go in the water can fly. All those birds have wings and they use their wings to fly.	9	Some kids think that all birds can fly. It seems like that. It seems that all birds fly. Still, there are some birds that cannot fly. What birds are those?

Page	Text	Page	Text
10	Here are some of those birds. Do these birds have wings? Yes, they do. But their wings are very small. Their wings are too small for them to fly. These birds still move, but they do not fly.	11	Are there still some kids who think that all birds fly? Yes, there are. But now you can say, "It seems that way and most of them do. But some do not."

| 12 | **Gleaning Meaning** |

Animals are not like _____. Plants cannot move, but animals

_____. They have many ways of _____.

Some move by walking, some by _____, and some by

_____. Birds are a kind of animal and _____

of them move by flying. They fly by using their _____. But

some birds _____ fly. Their wings are too

_____ for them to fly.

* * *

can   cannot   flying   most   moving   plants   small   swimming   wings

Book 20

Theme: A story of children in the rain recognizing properties of a rainbow.
Words taught before reading book: *happen, rain, fall, house, each, again, sun, saw, same, rainbow, when, about, just.*

Page	Text	Page	Text
Cover	**In the Rain**	1	Some kids are playing in a park. Each of them is having a good time. Some are swimming and some are running.

(continued)

Page	Text	Page	Text
2	But then something happens that the kids do not like. What has <u>happened</u>? Rain is falling. It is <u>raining</u>. The kids did not like to play in the rain.	3	They were thinking about going to another place. They were thinking about going to one of their houses. They were <u>about</u> to go when one kid said,
4	"It can <u>stop</u> raining. Then, we could play again. We do not have to go. We <u>just</u> have to get out of the rain."	5	<u>What</u> did the kids do? They stayed in the park and <u>looked for</u> a place to stay.
6	They could see a <u>small house</u> in the park. The kids could stay there and be out of the rain. They did <u>that</u>.	7	In that place, the rain did not <u>fall</u> on <u>them</u>. They could look at the rain and not have the rain falling on <u>them</u>.
8	It was still <u>raining</u> when they saw the sun. The sun was out <u>again</u>. There was rain and there was sun at the <u>same</u> time.	9	Then the kids saw <u>one</u> more thing. The thing they saw was <u>very</u> nice. What was it? It was a <u>rainbow</u>.
10	Sometimes when there are rain and <u>sun</u> at the same time, there can be a rainbow. When there is just sun, there is no rainbow. When there is just rain, there is <u>no</u> rainbow. But the sun and rain were there	11	at the same time, and the kids did see a rainbow. It was very, very nice. They were happy they did not go to their <u>houses</u>. They <u>were</u> happy <u>they</u> stayed in the park. By staying there, they saw a <u>rainbow</u> and that is a very nice thing to see.

12   **Gleaning Meaning**

Some kids were in the park when they saw that it was _____.

They were going to go away, but they did not do that. They stayed in the

_____ and walked to a place where they would be out of

the _____. It was still raining when they saw that the sun was

out _____. Then the kids also saw a _____.

There are not many rainbows, but they can _____ when there

are sun and rain at the same _____.

* * *

again   happen   park   rain   rainbow   raining   time

Book 21
Theme: Life in an ant colony.
Words taught before reading book: *safe, -er, why, ant, work, next, because, together, group, up, long, dig.*

Page	Text	Page	Text
Cover	**Some Animal Workers**	1	All animals need places to stay. They do not have houses, but the places they stay in are like houses to them. Why do they need
2	places to stay? They need them because they need places where they can rest. They need places where they can be safe. They also need places where their babies can be safe.	3	Some kids do not think that ants are animals, but they are. They also need places to stay. Like many other animals, ants make the places that they need. They make nests. Their nests are not like the nests of birds.
4	Most ants make their nests in the ground. Ants stay together in groups and the groups work together to make the nests. They dig into the ground where they can make long holes.	5	Ants do many things to fix their nests. Why do they do that?

(continued)

Page	Text	Page	Text
6	They do that because they want their nests to be clean. The work of some of the ants in the group is to just do the cleaning.	7	They also fix the nest when the group gets bigger. When there are more ants in the group, the ants need
8	to make the nests bigger and they do that. Ants do many things to make the nests just the way they want. The nests can get too hot. What do the ants do then?	9	The nests can also get cold. When that happens, the ants move up and get to places which are nearer to the sun. Those places are hotter and then the ants are not cold. The ants do not just stay
10	in their nests. They need to go out for many things. One of the things they need is food. Most of the time, they do not eat the food when they are out of the nest. They get the food and put it in the nest. That is where they put the food and that is where they eat the food.	11	Ants are small but they can do many, many things.

12   **Gleaning Meaning**

Animals need places to _____ and many of them make those

places. Ants are small animals and they make the _____ that

they stay in. The ants work to fix the nests to be just the way they

_____ them to be. They can dig to make them

_____ and they can clean them too. They go out of the nests

to get _____. They put the food in the nest and then they eat

it _____.

* * *

bigger   food   nests   stay   there   want

Book 22

Theme: Mother and baby bear searching for drinkable water.

Words taught before reading book: *drink, -n't, mother, own, lot, sea, love, come, how, salt, land.*

Page	Text	Page	Text
Cover	**All Water Is Not the Same**	1	Animals have <u>babies</u> and their babies need many things like food to eat, water to <u>drink</u> and good places to stay. <u>Those</u> are some of the things they need.
2	Most of the time, babies cannot <u>get</u> those things on their <u>own</u>. <u>Why</u> can't they do that? Why can't they get the things they need?	3	They can't get them because they are <u>too</u> small to do many things on their own. <u>How</u> do they get the things they need? <u>Someone</u> helps them. Most of the time, their mothers are the ones to <u>help</u>.
4	Here is a baby bear with his mother. The mother and the baby have many <u>of</u> the things they <u>need</u>. They have a good place to stay and <u>they</u> also have food. But they do not have any water.	5	Animals have to have <u>water</u> and these animals don't have any. They <u>used</u> to get water from a water <u>hole</u> that was near them, but now there is no water in that hole.
6	What are the mother and baby bear going to do? They are going to <u>look</u> for water. <u>How</u> are they going to do that? They are going to <u>walk</u>.	7	They walked a <u>long</u> way and they have come near the <u>sea</u>. The sea is a place with lots and lots of water. But that water is not good for them. <u>Why</u> is the water not good?

(continued)

Page	Text	Page	Text
8	Sea water is very <u>salty</u>. Some animals who <u>live</u> in the sea can use that water, but most <u>land</u> animals cannot. Land animals cannot drink salty water. It is not good for them to <u>drink</u> sea water.	9	The mother bear and the baby bear <u>moved</u> on. They looked in lots and lots of <u>places</u>, but they still did not find water they could <u>drink</u>.
10	Now they have come to a place that has many <u>rocks</u>. They walk on the rocks and they do not <u>find</u> any water. But they see a <u>hole</u>. They look into the hole and find just what they have been looking for. They find water.	11	Is the water <u>salty</u>? No, it is not. The <u>water</u> is not salty and the <u>two</u> bears were happy. They had all the water they needed.

12   **Gleaning Meaning**

All living things need to have water to _____. A baby bear

was with his _____ and they did not have any

_____. They looked for some, but the only water they could

find was in the _____. Land animals can not drink that kind of

water because it is _____. The mother and baby bear looked

in lots of places. Then they saw a _____, which had water that

was not salty. Then the two bears had all the water they

_____.

* * *

drink   hole   mother   needed   salty   sea   water

Book 23

Theme: Features of anteaters.

Words taught before reading book: *mouth, after, claw, teeth, take, funny, back, part, tongue.*

Page	Text	Page	Text
Cover	**The Anteater**	1	Many animals have teeth. But some do not. One kind is a funny looking animal. It is the anteater. It does not have teeth, but like other animals, it does have a mouth.
2	Its mouth is very small and when it wants to eat, it has to get things that can go into a small mouth. Many bugs are small and that is the food that anteaters eat most of all.	3	How does it get its food? Bugs stay in nests and anyone who wants them has to get into their nests. That is what anteaters do. They get their food by going into the nests of bugs.
4	They are too big to go into the nests all the way. Only some parts of them can get into the nests. Those parts are	5	their tongues and their claws. The anteater does not have any teeth, but it does have big claws and a long tongue. It uses these things to get its food. How does it do that?
6	It uses its claws to dig into the nests of bugs. After that, it uses its long tongue to take the bugs into its mouth.	7	Anteaters are big and bugs are small. They have to eat lots and lots of bugs to get the food they need. The anteater eats all kinds of bugs but the bugs it likes most of all are ants. After all, it is an ANTEATER!

(continued)

Page	Text	Page	Text
8	Do anteaters stay in groups? No, they do not do that. But mothers and babies do stay together.	9	When the mothers are looking for food, they take their babies with them. They put their babies on their backs.
10	The anteater eats a lot of the time, but it does not eat all of the time. It also has to do other things like resting. How does it do those things?	11	It does them in a funny way. It does not have a nest of its own. It does not make the places where it stays. It just finds the places other animals make and stays in those places. What a funny animal! It looks funny and the way it lives is funny.

12   **Gleaning Meaning**

The anteater is an animal that has no _____. But it does have

a mouth with a long _____. It also has big claws. It uses its

_____ and tongue to get into the _____ of

bugs. Then it _____ the bugs. Anteaters do something funny

about their nests. They don't make their _____ nests. They use

the nests of other _____.

* * *

animals   claws   eats   nests   own   teeth   tongue

Book 24

Theme: People dreaming of and succeeding with trip to moon.

Words taught before reading book: *sky, moon, earth, people, start, our, until, day, than.*

Page	Text	Page	Text
Cover	**Going to the Moon**	1	On our earth, there is water, land, and <u>sky</u>. There are <u>lots</u> of things in the water and there are lots of things on the land. There are also lots of things in the sky.
2	Some of <u>those</u> things look small to us, but one of them looks big. It is the <u>moon</u>. The moon is a long way from <u>earth</u>, but it is nearer to us than any other thing in the sky.	3	Have you looked at the moon a lot? You <u>have</u> to do that to see <u>what</u> the moon does. The moon is kind of <u>funny</u>. It does not look the same all the time. <u>Sometimes</u> you can see all of it.
4	After that, each <u>day</u> it starts to get <u>smaller</u> and smaller. Then it gets to a place where you cannot see it at all. What <u>happens</u> <u>then</u>?	5	Then each <u>day</u>, the moon starts to get <u>bigger</u>. It gets bigger and bigger until you can see <u>all</u> of it again.
6	Looking at the moon is nice, but some people <u>have</u> wanted to do more than that. They have <u>wanted</u> to go to the <u>moon.</u>	7	For a long time, they could not do that <u>because</u> they had no <u>way</u> of getting there.
8	There were things to get to places, but <u>those</u> things <u>weren't</u> good for getting to the moon. There were trucks, but trucks could not get them to the moon. There were <u>planes</u>, but planes could not get them to the moon.	9	Then people <u>started</u> to make rockets. With <u>rockets</u>, there was a <u>way</u> to get to the moon. Some men did that. They used <u>rockets</u> to get to the moon.

(continued)

Page	Text	Page	Text
10	When they got there, they <u>looked</u> at a lot of things. They saw that there were big <u>holes</u> on the moon. They also saw that there were <u>many</u> kinds of rocks on the moon.	11	Did <u>those</u> men stay on the moon? No, they did not stay. They could not stay <u>because</u> people cannot live on the moon. But they did take some of the rocks with them and now those rocks are here on <u>earth</u>.

12   **Gleaning Meaning**

One of the things in the sky is the _____. The moon does not

look the same all the _____. Sometimes, it looks big. Then it

starts to look smaller and _____ until you can't

_____ it at all. For a long time, people have wanted to

_____ to the moon, but they had no way to get there. Then

people started to make _____ and rockets did take some men

to the moon. When they were on the moon, the men saw some

_____. Now some of those rocks are here on our

_____.

* * *

earth   go   moon   rockets   rocks   see   smaller   time

Soaring Program

Book 25

Theme: A homeless dog who finally finds a home.

Words taught before reading book: *home, as, scare, over, hungry, open, yell, luck, went, bad, candy, much, him.*

Page	Text	Page	Text
Cover	**The Bad Times Stop**	1	There was a dog. When people looked at him, they would think he was like any other dog. But he wasn't. Most other dogs have homes. This dog did not. He wanted a home, but no one wanted him.
2	One day it was raining and the dog was getting very wet. He wanted to get out of the rain. To do that, he went near a house. He stayed near the house to get out of the rain.	3	A man who was in the house saw him. He ran out and started yelling. He did not want a dog near his house. The yelling scared the dog and he ran away.
4	Another time, the dog was hungry. He just had to find something to eat. He saw a can near someone's house. He went over to it, thinking there could	5	be some food in it. He wanted to open the can and see if he could find some food. Just as he was opening it, a lady in the house saw him. Then, just like the man, she started to yell at the poor dog.
6	The dog had to run away again. One bad thing after another happened to the dog. He seemed to have only bad luck.	7	He started to walk. He did not want to be near the houses. He did not want to be near places where people would see him and where they would yell at him.

(continued)

Page	Text	Page	Text
8	He did not think he would see anyone, but he saw Candy. Candy was a girl. When the dog saw Candy, he was scared. He was thinking that the girl would yell at him the way all the other people had.	9	But the girl did not do that. The girl liked animals and she liked the dog very, very much.
10	When she saw him, she said, "That dog needs my help." She talked to the dog in a very nice way and the dog could see that the girl was nice. He wasn't scared anymore.	11	Candy wanted to take the dog home with her. And that is what she did. Now the dog had what he needed. His bad luck was over.
12	**Gleaning Meaning**		

There was a dog who did not have a _____. One bad thing

after another happened to that _____. People

_____ at him and he was very hungry. Then when he was

thinking that nothing good could _____, he saw a girl. The

girl was very _____. She wanted the dog to go home with

_____. He did that. The dog was happy because his bad

_____ was over.

* * *

dog   happen   her   home   nice   luck   yelled

Book 26

Theme: A stingray who overcomes her problem.

Words taught before reading book: *fish, so, ray, top, sand, became, float, better, try.*

Page	Text	Page	Text
Cover	**The Fish Who Floated**	1	All animals have to eat. It is a good thing to do and it is something they need to do. But <u>it's</u> not good when they eat too <u>much</u>. There was a <u>fish</u> who did that. Here she is. The fish is Ray.
2	Ray did not <u>start</u> <u>out</u> eating too much. When she was small, she was like the other fish and she would eat only what she needed.	3	But she liked eating <u>better</u> than swimming. She said, "I think I will not <u>swim</u> so much. I like to eat more than I like to <u>swim</u>." So she did that. For a time, it was nice, but then she started to get fat. She became fatter and fatter.
4	When they are in water, fat things <u>float</u>. So when Ray became fatter, she went <u>up</u> in the water. After some time, she could not swim. All she could do was float.	5	That is not the thing for <u>fish</u> to do. Fish need to swim to do the things they have to do. And for this <u>kind</u> of fish, floating was a very, <u>very</u> bad <u>thing</u> to do.
6	Ray and other fish like her have to <u>dig</u> in the <u>sand</u> and stay <u>there</u> much of the time. They swim just	7	on the top of the sand. Ray <u>could</u> not do that <u>because</u> the only thing she could do was to <u>float</u> on the top of the water.

(continued)

Page	Text	Page	Text
8	Ray wanted to get to the <u>sand</u>. She tried to get there but she could not <u>get</u> to it. All she could do was to <u>float</u> on the top of the water.	9	Ray <u>became</u> sad. She <u>tried</u> not to cry, but all she did was to cry. In place of eating, she was crying.
10	When that happened, things started to get better for Ray. <u>After</u> not eating for some time, she was not so fat. She <u>wasn't</u> floating <u>anymore</u>. She could swim again! She could swim to the sand.	11	When she did that, she saw all the other <u>fish</u> of her kind. They were happy to see her and she was happy to see them. After that, Ray did not eat too much. She would eat <u>only</u> what she needed and she did not have to <u>float</u> anymore.

12 **Gleaning Meaning**

There was a _____ who liked to eat and eat. She became very

fat. Then she could not swim. All she could do was to _____.

Floating is not good for fish. They need to swim. The fish became so sad that

she stopped _____. When she did that, she did not stay fat.

Then the fish did not have to stay up in the _____. She did not

have to float. She could _____ again. She went with the other

fish and she was _____. She also did not eat too

_____ anymore.

* * *

eating fish float happy much swim water

Book 27

Theme: A baby bee who is unhappy about her name until reassured by her mother.
Words taught before reading book: *ask, such, bite, your, sure, name, letter, three, know, real, smile, once.*

Page	Text	Page	Text
Cover	**Not a B, But a Bee**	1	Once upon a time, there was a bug. She was like other bugs and did a lot of the things they did. She would fly, she would eat, and she would drink.
2	Sometimes she would do things that people did not like. She would bite. But she would only do that when she was scared.	3	Most of the time, she was a nice, happy bug. Then one day, the bug was not happy anymore. She would not smile. All she would do was cry.
4	Her mother went to her and asked her why she was crying. She said, "You were such a happy bug. Now your face looks so sad. Can I help? I do not want you to be so sad.	5	You are too nice to be so sad." The bug stopped crying. She looked at her mother and said, "I do not want to be this way but I can't help it. I am sad because I do not have a name. I did not know that bugs have names, but now I know that they do.
6	Do you see those bugs over there? The name of that one is ant and the name of the other one is fly. They have names such as those."	7	The mother bee looked at her baby and said, "But you do have such a name. Just like those bugs do."

(continued)

Page	Text	Page	Text
8	Then the bug started to cry again. She said, "No, I don't. That is just what I was trying to say. I don't have a real name. All I have is a letter. My name is just a letter. It is B."	9	The mother bug smiled. "Your name is something like that letter, but that letter is not your name. Your name is bee, not B."
10	The small bee looked up at her mother. "Are you sure?"	11	Then the small bug was so happy. She could not stay still. She jumped and jumped, all the time yelling, "I DO HAVE A NAME! I DO HAVE A REAL NAME!" After that time, the bee was happy once more.

12   **Gleaning Meaning**

There was a bug who used to be _____. Then one day she be-

came very _____ and started to _____. She

said to her _____ that she was crying because other bugs had

names and she did not have _____. She said that her name

was not a _____ name. It was only a _____.

Her mother said to her, "No, that is not true. Your name is not a letter. Your

name is _____." Then the bug was happy

_____.

★ ★ ★

again   bee   cry   happy   letter   mother   one   real   sad

Book 28

Theme: A cat who teaches herself to use the computer to win back her computer-loving owner.

Words taught before reading book: *cliff, ever, daisy, from, change, computer, even, nothing, sleep, got.*

Page	Text	Page	Text
Cover	**A Boy, A Pet and A Computer**	1	Cliff was a boy who liked <u>pets</u>. He had a lot of <u>them</u>, but the one he liked most was <u>Daisy</u>, his cat.
2	Daisy is a <u>funny</u> name for a cat, but this cat liked to eat daisies. So that became her name. Cliff and Daisy did lots of things <u>together</u>. When he would go out to play, he would <u>take</u> Daisy with him and they would play together.	3	When he would go walking, he would take Daisy with him and they would walk together. When Cliff went to eat, Daisy would go after him and they would even eat together.
4	Daisy liked doing <u>all</u> those things with Cliff. She did not want anything to <u>change</u> and it seemed to her that <u>nothing</u> ever would. But one day, things did change. Cliff got a <u>computer</u>.	5	From that <u>day</u> on, Cliff was not with <u>Daisy</u>. He was with his computer.
6	Daisy <u>tried everything</u> she could <u>think</u> of to get Cliff back. She would try to sit on Cliff, but he just pushed her away. She would take food to Cliff that he liked, but he did not even look at it. Nothing seemed to help.	7	By now the only thing that Daisy would do was to sit and <u>ask</u>, "Will things <u>change</u> back to the way they were?" But that did not <u>happen</u>.

(continued)

Page	Text	Page	Text
8	Then one time, Cliff was sleeping. Daisy started to think. She went to the <u>computer</u> and stayed there for a long time. She did not <u>know</u> what to do, but she started to play with the computer. She <u>tried</u>	9	to do anything and everything with it that she could think of. Daisy was <u>still</u> at the <u>computer</u> <u>when</u> Cliff got up. He saw Daisy and asked, "What are you doing here?"
10	Daisy could not <u>talk</u>, but by now she could <u>use</u> the computer. On it, she put the words, "I can use this now. So can we play <u>together</u> again?"	11	Cliff <u>smiled</u>. Then he <u>put</u> some words on the computer too. He put the <u>words</u>, "Yes we can." From that time on, Cliff and Daisy were together again.
12	**Gleaning Meaning**		

A boy and his _____ used to play together all the

_____. Then one day the boy got a _____.

When that happened, he stopped playing with his cat. He would

_____ play with his computer. The cat was

_____ but she started to _____ about what

she could do. One time, when the boy was sleeping, she stayed at the computer

and worked with it a lot. When the boy got up, he _____

when he saw that his cat could use the computer. After that time, the boy and

his cat were _____ again.

* * *

cat   computer   only   sad   smiled   together   think   time

Book 29

Theme: A kite with magical powers that the owner finally recognizes.

Words taught before reading book: *penny, tell, every, kite, hand, idea, high, true, hear, told.*

Page	Text	Page	Text
Cover	**The Kite That Could . . .**	1	Once upon a time, there was a girl named Penny who owned a kite. It looked like any other kite, but it was not like them.
2	Most kites cannot do things on their own. But this kite could. Penny did not know any of this. The kite tried to tell Penny what it could do, but every time it tried, Penny would say, "This can't be true.	3	This can't be for real. I must be hearing things. Kites can't talk." So Penny had no idea that her kite could do anything more than other kites.
4	One day, Penny was taking a walk with her kite. When some other kids saw her, they wanted to take the kite away from her. The kite did not want	5	that to happen. To stop the kids, the kite started to do some of the things it could do. The kite could go any place it wanted. So when one boy tried to get the kite by putting his hands up, the kite just moved away.
6	The boy jumped up but the kite just went higher and higher. It moved up and away from the boy.	7	The boy did not think this could be happening, but it was. There was no way for him to get the kite. So he stopped trying.

(continued)

Page	Text	Page	Text
8	After some time, the kite went back down. Another kid put her hands out. This time, the kite was not looking and the girl got the kite. But just as she put her hands on it, the kite did another thing it could do. It got smaller and smaller. It became so small that no one could even see it.	9	The girl looked at her hand. She asked, "Where is the kite? What happened to it?" But no one could tell her what had happened.
10	Penny was looking at everything the kite was doing. She saw that the kite was doing all the things it had told her it could do. She started to think, "It was for real. The kite was really talking to me. And the things it was saying were true.	11	From now on, the kite can talk as much as it wants. I will hear what the kite says." And that is just what she did.
12	**Gleaning Meaning**		

A girl had a _____ that could do many

_____. The kite tried to tell the _____ what

it could do. But the girl did not hear what the kite tried to

_____ her. Then one day, some kids tried to take the kite

_____. The kite did not _____ that to hap-

pen. It did many of the things it could _____ and it stopped

the kids from doing what they were trying to do. When that happened, the girl

saw what the kite had said was _____. After that, when the

kite talked, the girl did _____ what the kite wanted to tell her.

* * *

away   do   girl   hear   kite   tell   things   true   want

Book 30
Theme: Stubborn baby frog who is changed after a dangerous encounter.
Words taught before reading book: *bull, never, head, slow, -self, tree, down.*

Page	Text	Page	Text
Cover	**The Bullheaded Bullfrog**	1	Rocky was a <u>bullfrog</u>. That is a kind of frog that is very big. But Rocky was <u>still</u> a baby and so he was not as big as he was going to be. Rocky was not only a bullfrog. He was also <u>bullheaded</u>.
2	Bullheaded things do what they want to do and not what they are <u>told</u> to do. That was the way with Rocky. Much of the time, bullfrogs stay near water. His mother would tell Rocky that he had to do that too. But he had other <u>ideas</u>. His idea was to go to many other <u>places</u>.	3	One day, when Rocky was going to some of <u>those</u> <u>places</u>, he saw a tree with many holes. He jumped over to the <u>tree</u> and started to put his head into one of the holes.
4	Just then, something moved. It was a cat. The cat was <u>looking</u> for something to eat. When she saw Rocky, she said, "I <u>sure</u> <u>want</u> that frog."	5	Then it was not Rocky who was jumping. It was the cat. She was trying to get Rocky. The <u>bullfrog</u> pushed himself into the hole and <u>away</u> from the cat. Did that <u>make</u> the cat mad?
6	No, it <u>did</u> not. The cat was very <u>sure</u> of herself. She said, "That frog has to come out <u>sometime</u>. I will just stay here until he does."	7	Rocky was <u>scared.</u> He stayed in the <u>tree</u>, not <u>knowing</u> what to do. Lots of time went by. The cat got sleepy, but Rocky was too scared to sleep. He did not stop looking at the cat.

(continued)

Page	Text	Page	Text
8	The cat's head was down. Was the cat <u>sleeping</u>? It seemed that she was. When Rocky was sure she was asleep, he moved <u>out</u> of the <u>hole</u>. He was very <u>slow</u> and the cat did not hear him. Rocky got away!	9	After some time, the cat got up. She <u>saw</u> that the frog was not <u>there</u>! Was the cat mad <u>now</u>?
10	She sure was. She said <u>over</u> and over <u>again</u>, "Why did I go to sleep?" But it did not <u>help</u>. Those words did not get Rocky back.	11	Rocky <u>never</u> went back to that tree and he never went to places his mother told him not to go. From that time on, Rocky was <u>still</u> a <u>bullfrog</u>, but he was not bullheaded.
12	**Gleaning Meaning**		

There was a baby _____ that was very _____

He liked to go to places on his _____ and he did not stay with

his mother. One day, he saw a tree with _____ in it. He was

going into one of the holes when a _____ jumped near him.

The cat wanted to _____ the bullfrog. The bullfrog stayed in

the tree for a long time. He was too scared to sleep, but the cat did go to

_____. When that happened, the bullfrog went out of the

_____ and he got away. When the cat got up, she was very

mad but she could not get the bullfrog. After that, the baby bullfrog did what

his mother _____ him to do and he _____

went to places on his own.

* * *

bullfrog   bullheaded   cat   get   holes   never   own   sleep   told   tree

Illustrations for the Books

The following pages contain illustrations that you may use for the books. As mentioned earlier, you may also use illustrations that you and your child make or find elsewhere.

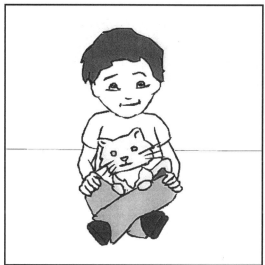

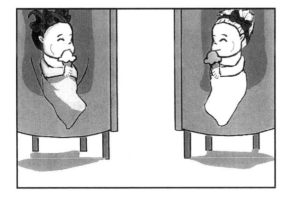

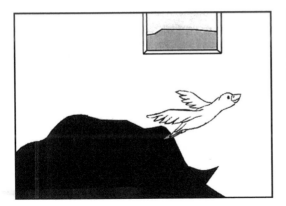

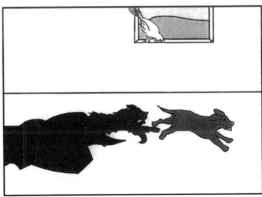

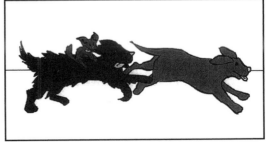

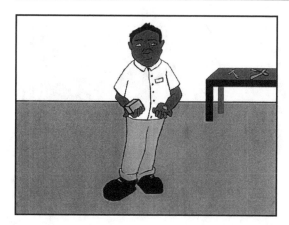

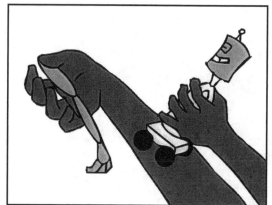

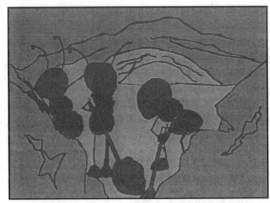

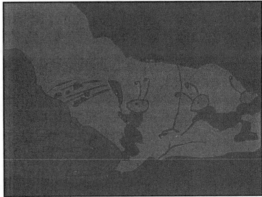

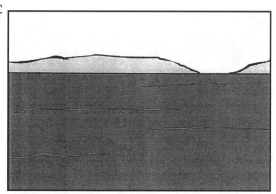

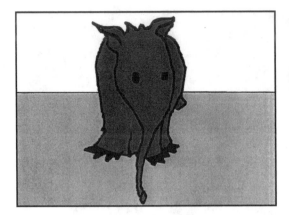

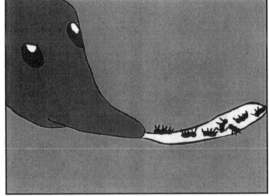

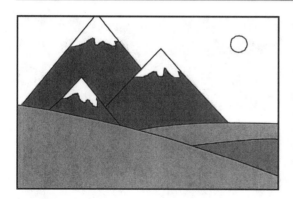 

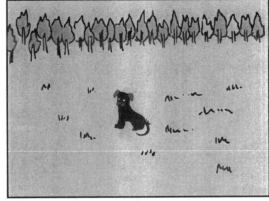

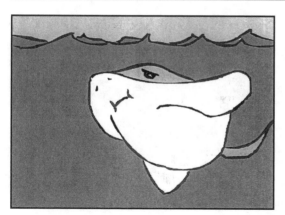 

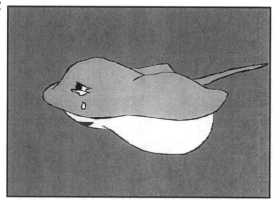 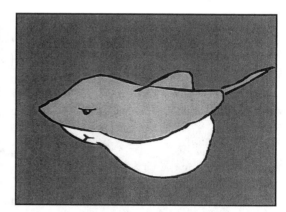

Progress Check and Review

It is important to check how well your child is doing throughout the reading instruction and to provide help if it is needed. The material in this chapter is designed with these goals in mind.

The Progress Check is designed to let you see how well your child is holding onto the material. You use the Progress Check when your child completes the last set of words in each reading program (Boarding, Runway, Liftoff, Airborne, and Soaring). If the results show that your child has done well in a program, you move on to the next program. If the results show that your child's skills are not as firm as they should be, you carry out the review activities described in the second part of this chapter.

Conducting the Progress Check

The Progress Check generally takes less than fifteen minutes. However, it's best to carry it out in a session that is separate from the teaching. Make sure your child is rested, and you are in a quiet area for working. There is a separate Progress Check for each program, but each follows the same pattern of having your child write sentences that you dictate. The sequence is as follows:

Offering the Sentences
Step 1. Provide your child with lined paper and a pencil, and say, "I'd like you to do some writing today. I'll say some sentences and then you'll write them." Use a fresh sheet of lined paper for every sentence.

Step 2. Do not show the sentences to your child. Say the complete first sentence and then say, "Now I'll repeat it one word at a time and you'll write the word after I say it."

Step 3. Do not offer any help or feedback on whether the work is correct or not.

Step 4. Continue in this way until all the sentences have been completed.

Scoring

A word is scored as either *fully correct* (if the spelling and capitalization are totally accurate) or as *not correct* (regardless of the number of errors it may have).

Action to Take

After you have scored the Progress Check for a program, you will see the heading Action to Take. This section offers guidelines for continuing your child's reading instruction.

Content of the Progress Check

Each program has its own Progress Check so make sure to do the one that matches the program your child has just completed. For example, if your child has just finished the Boarding program, then you only do the Progress Check: Boarding Program; if he or she has just finished the Runway program, then you only do the Progress Check: Runway Program. The Progress Check items for each of the programs are as follows:

Progress Check: Boarding Program

Item	Sentence to Dictate*	# Words Correct
1.	The kid is not a girl.	_____
2.	Some rockets are flying.	_____
3.	This robot cannot jump.	_____
4.	Can they walk here?	_____
5.	Some more boys are swimming.	_____
Total		_____

*Circle every word written correctly.

Action to Take

- If your child has written twenty or more words correctly, in the next session have your child read Book 6, and then begin the Runway program.

- If your child has written nineteen or fewer words correctly, he or she needs to review some of the work in the Boarding program. Follow the steps outlined later in this chapter under Materials for Review. The review may take from one to four weeks. Once the review is completed, in the next session have your child read Book 6, and then begin the Runway program.

Progress Check: Runway Program

Item	Sentence to Dictate*	# Words Correct
1.	Do both boys want to rest?	_____
2.	What are the ways to use this thing?	_____
3.	One of the their pets is a bird.	_____
4.	Frogs use their legs for moving in water.	_____
Total		_____

*Circle every word written correctly.

Action to Take

- If your child has written twenty-four or more words correctly, in the next session have your child read Book 12, and then begin the Liftoff program.

- If your child has written twenty-three or fewer words correctly, he or she needs to review some of the work in the Runway program. Follow the steps outlined in this chapter under Materials for Review. The review may take from one to four weeks. Once the review is completed, in the next session have your child read Book 12, and then begin the Liftoff program.

Progress Check: Liftoff Program

Item	Sentence to Dictate*	# Words Correct
1.	That is the only kid who wants to clean this place.	_____
2.	The mice would not move out of the hole.	_____
3.	Which of the two kids pushed the rocks out here?	_____
Total		_____

*Circle every word written correctly.

Action to Take

- If your child has written twenty-four or more words correctly, in the next session have your child read Book 18, and then begin the Airborne program.

- If your child has written twenty-three or fewer words correctly, he or she needs to review some of the work in the Liftoff program. Follow the steps outlined in this chapter under Materials for Review. The review may take from one to four weeks. Once the review is completed, in the next session have your child read Book 18, and then begin the Airborne program.

Progress Check: Airborne Program

Item	Sentence to Dictate*	# Words Correct
1.	How do some animals use their claws?	_____
2.	Until a short time ago, people could not get to the moon.	_____
3.	Because the boys were together, they both could see the rainbow.	_____
Total		_____

*Circle every word written correctly.

Action to Take

- If your child has written twenty-four or more words correctly, in the next session have your child read Book 24, and then begin the Soaring program.

• If your child has written twenty-three or fewer words correctly, he or she needs to review some of the work in the Airborne program. Follow the steps outlined in this chapter under Materials for Review. The review may take from one to four weeks. Once the review is completed, in the next session have your child read Book 24, and then begin the Soaring program.

Progress Check: Soaring Program

Item	Sentence to Dictate*	# Words Correct
1.	The girl was never scared to go out by herself.	_____
2.	Do most of the kids know how to read their names?	_____
3.	When the computer went down, the girl really started to yell.	_____
Total		_____

*Circle every word written correctly.

Action to Take

• If your child has written twenty-six or more words correctly, then congratulations! Your child has completed all the programs of the Phonics Plus Five system.

• If your child has written twenty-five or fewer words correctly, he or she needs to review some of the work in the Soaring program. Follow the steps outlined in this chapter under Materials for Review. The review may take from one to four weeks. Once the review is completed, in the next session have your child read Book 30. Then congratulations! Your child has completed all the programs of the Phonics Plus Five system.

Materials for Review

If the Progress Check on a particular program indicates that your child needs some review, it is important to take the time to go over the program material. The review is designed to help your child build the memory base that is critical to smooth reading and writing. It may take a few weeks for this to happen, but when it does, you will find the rewards to be enormous. With memory skills in place, your child has the power to become an independent reader. It is at that point that you will see him or her start to decode and spell words never seen before. Memory is the key to effective reading!

The review involves a two-step process:

1. Identifying the words that your child has not solidly grasped
2. Reviewing those words

Identifying the Words

To find the words your child needs to review, do the following:

Step 1: Go to the Appropriate Program. In the last half of this chapter, there are two charts for each program. Go to the charts for the program your child has been working in and find the one titled Identifying the Words. For example, if your child has been working in the Boarding program, find the Identifying the Words chart for that program and use the list of words you find there; if your child has been working in the Runway program, use the list of words you find for that program, and so on.

Step 2: Write the Words. Start with the first word listed on the chart. In the case of the Boarding program, that word is *kids*. (a) Say to your child, "I would like you to do some writing." (b) Give your child a pencil and some clean lined paper. Then, without letting your child see the word, say, "Write _____." (b) If your child writes the word accurately, enter a ✓ in the appropriate column and say, "Fine, let's do another word." Continue down the list until your child comes to a word that he or she fails to write correctly. (c) If your child writes the word inaccurately, enter an X in the appropriate column. You have identified a word that needs review, and at that point you move on to Reviewing the Words, discussed next.

Reviewing the Words

The review activity is set up so that your child reads and writes the word in sentences containing other words he or she has learned. For example, if your child failed to write *kids* correctly, the sentences you would ask him or her to read and write are

- Kids cannot fly.
- Can kids talk?

For each sentence, go through the following activities with your child.

Step 1: You Write the Sentence. The sentences you will be using are provided next to each word in the Reviewing the Words charts that follow. First, you write each of the sentences on a separate sheet of lined paper, so that the first sheet your child sees looks like this:

Kids cannot fly.

Show the first sheet to your child and have him or her read the sentence on it. If there are any errors, supply the correct word and have your child reread the sentence.

Step 2: Your Child Copies the Sentence, One Word at a Time. Provide clean lined paper and a pencil. Point to the first word you have written, and say, "Tell me what this word is." (If your child cannot read the word, say the word and have your child repeat it.) Then cover the word and say, "Now write that word." Continue in this manner until all the words and punctuation of the sentence have been written correctly.

Step 3: Respond to Any Error in Step 2. If there is an error in writing, immediately stop your child. Say, "No, that is not right." Remove the paper, provide a new clean sheet, and say, "Let's start again." Then repeat the writing from the first word. In other words, in correcting any error your child always starts anew with the first word of the sentence. Do not point out the error because it is valuable for your child to learn how to independently analyze and correct sets of words.

Step 4: Your Child Reproduces the Complete Sentence from Dictation. When your child completes step 2 (writing the sentence correctly by looking at and then writing one word at a time), once again show the complete sentence you have written and ask your child to read it. Then cover the sentence and dictate the words one at a time, until your child reproduces the entire sentence. At this point your child is writing the complete sentence without having a chance to see the words.

Step 5: Respond to Any Error in Step 4. If there is an error, immediately stop your child. Say, "No, that is not right." Then remove the paper that he or she has been writing on and provide a clean sheet of paper. Say, "Let's start again." Show the sentence as you did in step 4, and have your child read it again. Say, "Look at all the words carefully because you have to write them again." Then starting from the first word, dictate the sentence again, one word at time, and have your child write the sentence without seeing it.

Boarding Program

Identifying the Words

	✓	X		✓	X		✓	X
1. kids			6. rest			11. walk		
2. some			7. are			12. plane		
3. boys			8. here			13. this		
4. more			9. swim			14. they		
5. bird			10. jump			15. rocket		

Reviewing the Words

Remember: Your child writes only the sentences for the words he or she has not written correctly.

kids	Kids cannot fly.	Can kids talk?
some	Some boys are eating.	Can some dolls walk?
boys	The boys are not here.	Can some boys swim?
more	Some more kids are jumping.	More robots are here.
bird	Some more birds are flying.	Is this bird resting?
rest	Can the birds rest here?	The boys are not resting.
are	The rockets are flying.	Some kids are sitting.

here	Some girls are here.	The boys are not here.
swim	Swim some more!	Can a robot swim?
jump	Can the bugs jump?	They are not jumping.
walk	A robot is walking.	Some kids walk here.
plane	Is the plane here?	The planes are not flying.
this	This is a robot, but it is not a toy.	Can this kid swim?
they	The kids can sit. They are sitting.	The planes can fly, but they are not flying.
rocket	Can the rocket fly?	Here are more rockets.

Runway Program

Identifying the Words

	✓ X		✓ X		✓ X
1. thing		6. what		11. truck	
2. baby		7. other		12. you	
3. who		8. want		13. stop	
4. that		9. there		14. water	
5. does		10. puppy		15. move	

Reviewing the Words

Remember: Your child writes only the sentences for the words he or she has not written correctly.

thing	What things does the girl like?	Those things in there are not frogs.
baby	Are some babies big?	The baby cannot walk and the baby cannot run.
who	Who is sitting here? She is a baby. She is resting here.	Who are they? They are some baby birds.
that	That big kid is in the water.	Does the kid also want to pet that cat?

(continued)

does	The baby is not big, but she does talk.	Does that kid have some toys we can use?
what	What does the girl want to do now?	Those birds are eating what they like to eat. They are eating bugs.
other	Some kids want to swim, but some other ones do not want to do that.	That bug can jump. What other things can it do?
want	The girls want to sit in the truck now.	Who wants to jump in the water?
there	"We want to swim. We want to run. Can we do both those things there?"	There are many frogs in the water. They like to swim there.
puppy	Those are puppies. They are like babies.	What other things does that puppy like to do?
truck	Which of the trucks has some kids sitting in it?	Some of the trucks are not here now.
you	"Which one is jumping? I do not want you doing that!"	You are a kid. I am not a kid.
stop	You have to stop using those things.	The man is stopping all the trucks.
water	Does the man want more water?	Yes, that thing does look something like water.
move	Those robots are moving many things.	You can move the truck away.

Liftoff Program

Identifying the Words

	✓	X		✓	X		✓	X
1. was			6. happy			11. still		
2. could			7. them			12. dirty		
3. where			8. push			13. two		
4. think			9. mice			14. clean		
5. play			10. place			15. would		

Reviewing the Words

Remember: Your child writes only the sentences for the words he or she has not written correctly.

was	That frog was not swimming. It was jumping and it was hopping, but it was not swimming.	Was someone moving this truck? No, no one was doing that.
could	Only some of the kids could hop. They all wanted to hop, but only some of the kids could do that.	Could both babies walk? Yes, they could and they did that all the time.
where	That kid has some pets. Where are the kid's pets? They are not here.	The bug could not hop where it wanted. Something was in its way.
think	He thinks the rocks in the water hurt his puppy.	They still look very sad. What are they thinking now?
play	The girl was crying. She would not play that time.	Who played very near to those trucks?
happy	He was happy but his face did not look that way.	All the kids are happy to see their pets.
them	The boy likes all his pets. He likes to pet them all the time.	Those are planes but you cannot fly in them.
push	"Do not push the dirt near here! We do not want it here."	Was someone pushing the big rock out of the way?
mice	The mice stayed in the hole all that time.	Yes, there are some mice there but they do not hurt anyone.
place	We think this place is not very clean for the pets.	The girls are placing some rocks in the bag.
still	Was the cat still near the bird? Yes, it was and the bird did not like it.	The baby could walk then but he still could not run.
dirty	Did you find any dirty things in that place?	Most of us do not like anything dirty to be near us.
two	That boy wanted two pets, but he could not have that many.	All of us have two arms and two legs.

(continued)

clean	He likes to clean, but most kids do not.	They cleaned all the dirty things and put them away.
would	The girl would say to us that she would be on time but we did not think that she would be.	Would you both like to go to swim in the pool now?

Airborne Program

Identifying the Words

	✓ X		✓ X		✓ X
1. animal		6. rainbow		11. drink	
2. another		7. about		12. mother	
3. happen		8. work		13. teeth	
4. each		9. together		14. people	
5. again		10. group		15. until	

Reviewing the Words

Remember: Your child writes only the sentences for the words he or she has not written correctly.

animal	There were no animals facing any of the kids.	Which of the two big animals did you say needs help?
another	Why did all the kids want to go to another place?	The girl liked planting things in the earth and she said she wanted to do it many more times.
happen	What happened to the boys who were in the park again?	Those kids are not sad. They just happen to look that way.
each	Each one of the girls wants to go on those swings.	Each of the toys can fly but no one is here to get them to do that.
again	No one wants to go again to a place that is not nice.	The boy jumped and hurt his leg. He does not want to jump again.
rainbow	When the kids saw the rainbow, they were very happy.	Rainbows are very nice things to see. Don't you think that they are?

about	About now, the mother bird pushes the babies out of the nest.	Look at her face! That kid is about to cry.
work	Each one of the kids is a good worker and a good helper.	Who worked to fix these swings? They are good to play on now.
together	Did the boys walk together because it was safer that way?	The man said to the kids, "You have to work together to get the truck moving."
group	Which group of kids still wants to go to the pool?	He put all the things into two groups because he thinks it is the way to do it.
drink	Do not drink any water when it is dirty!	The boy is drinking all that because he needs the water.
mother	That puppy isn't near his mother. She is looking for her baby.	The girl's mother was saying that all the kids were cold.
teeth	That small baby doesn't have any teeth. She can't eat that food.	Can you think of an animal that has no teeth?
people	The people who were here did not want to stay and they didn't.	We saw lots of people there and all of them were men.
until	Until we see you coming with the trucks, we will not move.	The kids had to stay in the house until it stopped raining.

Soaring Program

Identifying the Words

	✓	X		✓	X		✓	X
1. scare			6. such			11. change		
2. hungry			7. your			12. sleep		
3. went			8. letter			13. every		
4. much			9. once			14. slow		
5. float			10. cliff			15. never		

Reviewing the Words

Remember: Your child writes only the sentences for the words he or she has not written correctly.

scare	It was scary to see that big animal starting to run.	Nothing scares that dog as much as people who yell.
hungry	Why did all the hungry kids want to go to another place?	The cat looked very hungry but she wasn't. She just had some food.
went	Whoever went with the group to the waterfall was lucky.	The kids became scared when they went to that place.
much	The man did not say how much time it would take to fix the truck.	For now, we have as much food as we need. We will tell you if we need more.
float	That animal floats when it wants to stop swimming.	What is it like to float in the sea? Is it nice?
such	The kids wanted to see a rainbow but they had no such luck.	Those are such nice puppies to play with. We try to do that whenever we can.
your	The mother asked, "Where did you put your things this time?"	The man said, "I have fixed your rocket and now it will go."
letter	There are sure a lot of letters in the house but not even one is for me.	Can you name three animals that have three letters in their names?
once	Once the baby got some food, she started smiling.	Some animals eat three times a day, but some eat only once a day.
cliff	The cliffs are very big and it is not good to run on them.	The boy thinks it's safe to go up that cliff.
change	The group of people had to change from one plane to another. They were not happy about that.	He changed his computer because the one he had was not working.
sleep	Those people are still sleeping because they have worked so much.	It is much too cold to sleep now. Can we make it hotter in here?

every	Every one of the men had to stop working at that time.	Every day a group of frogs jumps near here. It is funny to see them do that.
slow	The man said, "Once the trucks slow down, the people can get on them."	One of the kids said to the others, "It is too slow to go to the park this way. We have to change and go another way."
never	The girl never did anything by herself. All the time, she wanted someone to help her.	"I was never as scared as when I saw the bull running near me."

REFERENCES

American Heritage Dictionary of the English Language, Fourth Edition. (2000). Boston: Houghton Mifflin.

Batten, M. (1998). *Baby wolf.* New York: Grosset & Dunlap.

Bissex, G. L. (1980). *Gyns at wrk.* Cambridge, MA: Harvard University Press.

Blank, M. (1978). Review of *Toward an understanding of dyslexia: Psychological factors in specific reading disability.* In A. L. Benton & D. Pearl (Eds.), *Dyslexia: An appraisal of current knowledge.* New York: Oxford University Press.

Blank, M. (2002). Classroom discourse: A key to literacy. In K. G. Butler & E. R. Silliman (Eds.), *Speaking, reading, and writing in children with language learning disabilities.* Mahwah, NJ: Erlbaum.

Blank, M., & Bruskin, C. (1982). Sentences and noncontent words: Missing ingredients in reading instruction. *Annals of Dyslexia, 32,* 103–121.

Bokoske, S., & Davidson, M. (1993). *Dolphins.* New York: Random House.

Brown, R. (1973). *A first language.* Cambridge, MA: Harvard University Press.

Brownstein, S. C., Weiner, M., & Green, S. W. (1994). *Barron's SAT I.* Hauppauge, NY: Barron's.

Bruner, J. S., Goodnow, J. J., & Austin, G. A. (1956). *A study of thinking.* Hoboken, NJ: Wiley.

Carroll, J. B., Davies, P., & Richman, B. (1971). *Word frequency book.* Boston: Houghton Mifflin.

Chall, J. (1967). *Learning to read: The great debate.* New York: McGraw-Hill.

Cunningham, P. M. (1980). Teaching *were, with, what,* and other "four-letter words." *Reading Teacher, 34,* 163–169.

Dehaene, S. (1999). *The number sense.* New York: Oxford University Press.

Dr. Seuss. (1976). *The cat in the hat.* New York: Random House.

Ehri, L. C. (1992). Review and commentary: Stages of spelling development. In S. Templeton & D. R. Bear (Eds.), *Development of orthographic knowledge and the foundations of literacy: A memorial festschrift for Edmund H. Henderson.* Mahwah, NJ: Erlbaum.

Elkind, D. (1987). *The hurried child.* Reading, MA: Addison-Wesley.

Flesch, R. (1955). *Why Johnny can't read: And what you can do about it.* New York: Harper Collins.

Fritz, J. (1987). *Shh! We're writing the Constitution.* New York: Putnam.

Gough, P. (1972). One second of reading. In J. F. Kavanagh & I. G. Mattingly (Eds.), *Language by eye and by ear.* Cambridge, MA: MIT Press.

Gough, P. B., & Hillinger, M. L. (1980). Learning to read: An unnatural act. *Bulletin of the Orton Society, 30,* 179–196.

Halliday, M.A.K., & Hasan, R. (1980). Text and context: Aspects of language in a social-semiotic perspective. *Sophia Linguistica, 6* (entire issue).

Hautzig, D. (1989). *The pied piper of Hamelin.* New York: Random House.

Krieger, V. K. (1981). A hierarchy of "confusable" high frequency words in isolation and in context. *Learning Disability Quarterly, 4,* 131–138.

Kunhardt, E. (1987). *Pompeii . . . buried alive.* New York: Random House.

Milton, J. (1998). *Bears are curious.* New York: Random House.

Moore, N. V. (2003). *Getting the word out.* St. Paul, MN: Pioneer Press.

Newburger, R. C., & Curry, A. (2000). *Educational attainment in the United States.* Washington, DC: U.S. Census Bureau.

Orton, S. T. (1928). Specific reading disability: Strephosymbolia. *Journal of the American Medical Association, 90,* 1095–1999.

President's Commission on Excellence in Special Education. (2002). *A new era: Revitalizing special education.* Washington, DC: Author.

Rhodes, R. (1986). *The making of the atomic bomb.* New York: Simon & Schuster.

Rowland, P. T. (1995). *Beginning to read, write and listen.* New York: Macmillan/McGraw-Hill School Division.

Snow, C. E., Burns, M. S., & Griffin, P. (Eds.). (1998). *Preventing reading difficulties in young children.* Washington, DC: National Academies Press.

Templeton, S., & Bear, D. R. (Eds.). (1992). *Development of orthographic knowledge and the foundations of literacy: A memorial festschrift for Edmund H. Henderson.* Mahwah, NJ: Erlbaum.

Tunmer, W. E., & Hoover, W. A. (1992). Cognitive and linguistic factors in learning to read. In P. B. Gough, L. C. Ehri, & R. Treiman (Eds.), *Reading acquisition.* Mahwah, NJ: Erlbaum.

U.S. Department of Education, Office of Educational Research and Improvement, National Center for Educational Statistics. (2001). *The nation's report card: Fourth-grade reading 2000* (NCES 2001-499). Washington, DC: Author.

INDEX

A

Accommodation: in joining phonics and whole language, 12

Accurate spelling, 104, 124; *See also* Spelling

Airborne program, 4–5, 35, 50, 85, 110, 120, 144, 149, 181, 188, 313, 317; *All Water Is Not the Same,* 263–264; *Anteater, The,* 265–266; *Birds and Flying,* 258–259; *Going to the Moon,* 267–268; materials, 258–268; materials for review, 324–325; progress check, 316–317; *In the Rain,* 259–261; *Some Animal Workers,* 261–262; words and books of, 183–184

All Water Is Not the Same (Airborne program), 263–264; illustrations, 303

Alphabet, current approach to teaching, disadvantage of, 78

"Alphabet Song, The," 79

Anteater, The (Airborne program), 265–266; illustrations, 304

B

Babies, The (Runway program), 246; illustrations, 288

Bad Times Stop, The (Soaring program), 269–270; illustrations, 306

Balanced teaching rubric, 12

Birds and Flying (Airborne program), 140–142, 147–148, 258–259; illustrations, 300

Bit blends, 91–92

Blending of sounds, 104

Boarding program, 4–5, 35, 50, 85, 120, 131, 144, 149, 181, 188, 313; *Bugs, the Kids, The,* 244, 245; materials, 243–245; materials for review, 320–321; *Pets, The Kids, The,* 244; progress check, 314–315; *Some Kids,* 243; *Some Pets,* 244; *Toys, The,* 245; words and books of, 182

Books: Airborne program materials, 258–268; anticipation of what is to come, 135–136; beginner texts, 135; Boarding program materials, 243–245; comprehension required by, 137–148; connecting sentences, 138–140; constructing, 239–240; creating, 239–311; decoding, ensuring success in, 129–131; to enact, 144; evaluating your child's progress, 126–129; gleaning meaning, 147–148; Gleaning Meaning activity, 242; illustrations, adding, 240, 281; length of, 129–131; Liftoff program materials, 250–257; main idea, 146–147; materials for, 243; moving to the next program, 242;